IMAGES
of America

MARITIME WILMINGTON

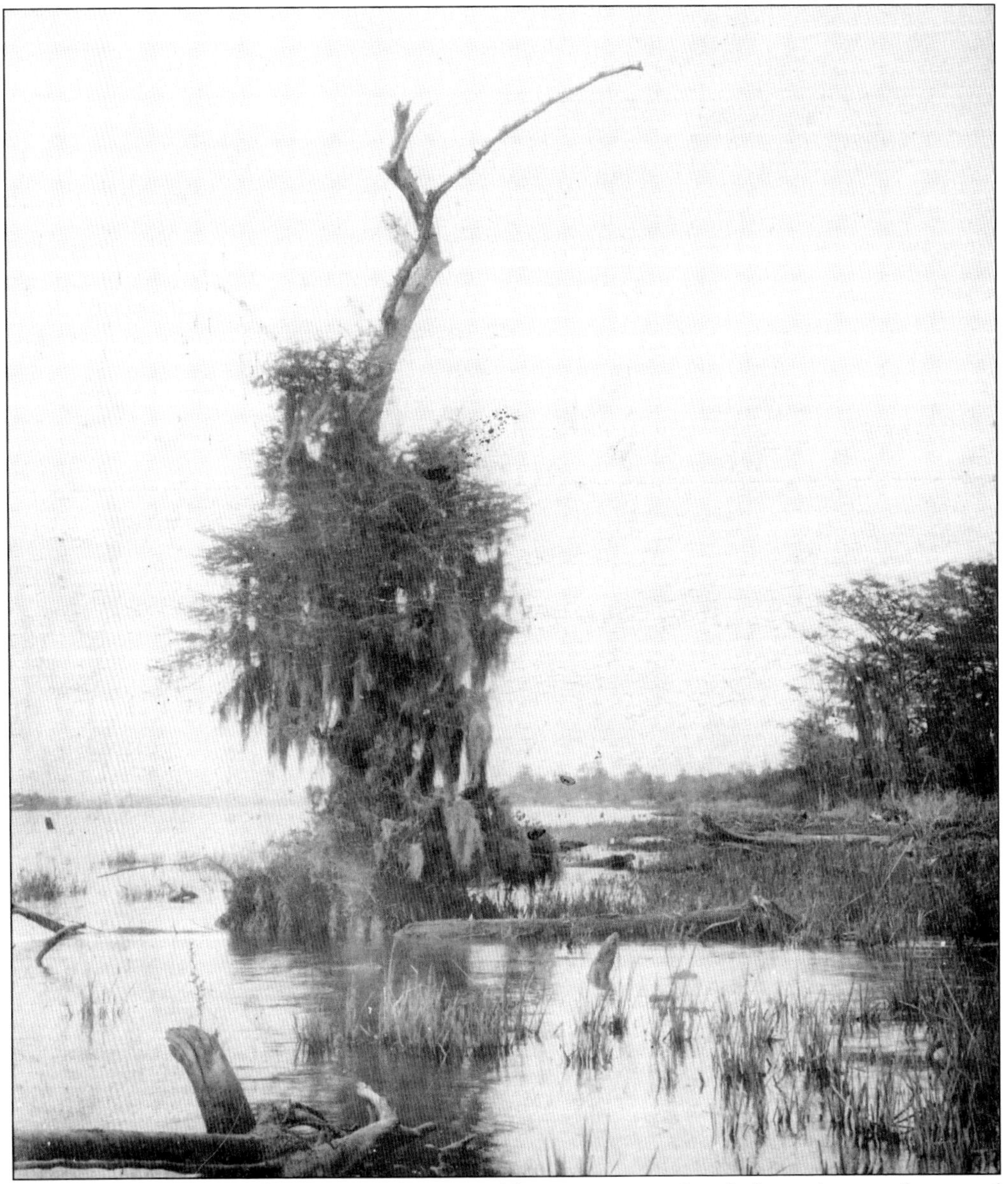

A landmark for sailors, the Dram Tree was an old cypress covered with Spanish moss that stood on the east bank of the Cape Fear River at the entrance to the Wilmington harbor. Upon passing it, sailors were given a dram of rum with which they toasted to their safe passage. When leaving port, they drank again while passing the old landmark, this time in hopes of arriving safely at their new destination. The famous Dram Tree was accidentally destroyed when the area was cleared for an enlarged shipyard during World War II. This photograph was taken in 1918. (Courtesy of the North Carolina Collection, New Hanover County Public Library.)

On the Cover: The US Coast Guard Cutter (USCGC) *Modoc* is docked at the government wharf in front of the US Custom House. The *Modoc* was stationed in Wilmington from 1922 to 1941. Louis T. Moore took this photograph in the 1930s. (Courtesy of the Louis T. Moore Collection, New Hanover County Public Library.)

IMAGES
of America

MARITIME WILMINGTON

Beverly Tetterton

ARCADIA
PUBLISHING

ISBN 978-1-4671-2176-7

Published by Arcadia Publishing
Charleston, South Carolina

Printed in the United States of America

Library of Congress Control Number: 2013952366

For all general information, please contact Arcadia Publishing:
Telephone 843-853-2070
Fax 843-853-0044
E-mail sales@arcadiapublishing.com
For customer service and orders:
Toll-Free 1-888-313-2665

Visit us on the Internet at www.arcadiapublishing.com

This book is dedicated to the amazing photographers who made it possible.

Contents

ACKNOWLEDGMENTS

The majority of the photographs in this book came from the North Carolina Collection at the New Hanover County Public Library (NHCPL). With over 25,000 images, the selection was an embarrassment of riches. It was hard to choose from so many photographs. Unless otherwise noted, all photographs are courtesy of the NHCPL. Library staff members Joseph Sheppard, Jennifer Daugherty, and Jimi Rider and volunteer Michael Whaley were especially helpful in sharing photographs and answering many questions. I thank Henry Mintz and Harry Warren for teaching me about the naval stores business and its historical importance in southeastern North Carolina. I am grateful to Dr. Alan Watson for his important historical writings on the economic history of the port of Wilmington, and to Dr. Chris Fonvielle for his histories of Wilmington during the Civil War. Walter Turner provided an in-depth modern history of the North Carolina State Port at Wilmington. Dr. James Burke's histories of the Wilmington railroads were especially helpful. I also want to thank Dr. Burke's 2013 humanities students at Cape Fear Community College for helping with the maps. Sandy Jackson and my friends at North Carolina Underwater Archaeology, as well as the US Army Corps of Engineers, provided the most inclusive historical information about the Wilmington harbor. Dan Camacho, Capt. Doug Springer, and Capt. Carl Marshburn shared their knowledge and love of the Cape Fear River. Ann Hewlett Hutteman and Elaine Henson shared their experience of working with Arcadia, giving me advice throughout the project. Sharad Shah, the first to encourage me to do this project, helped me choose the photographs and locate the documentation. Keith Longiotti of the University of North Carolina at Chapel Hill was helpful in locating photographs for me. The Wilmington Fire Department answered questions about fireboats. I thank Dylan Lee of the City of Wilmington, who took the 2013 photographs. Abigail Beck, Leslie Lee, Ariel Tetterton, and Speedy Tetterton provided encouragement along the way. I am most grateful to Glenn Tetterton, who kept my life on track while writing this book. He is also a great editor.

Introduction

Incorporated in 1739, Wilmington, North Carolina, was laid out in a grid pattern on seven hills or bluffs located on the east side of the Cape Fear River, about 28 nautical miles from the Atlantic Ocean. The town was named in honor of Spencer Compton, Earl of Wilmington, an Englishman and patron of Gabriel Johnston, North Carolina's governor at the time.

The town was settled by the English, as well as by New Englanders, Virginians, and South Carolinians, many of whom were maritime businessmen looking for investments in a newly opened area of the Atlantic Coast. Thousands of Highland Scots entered North Carolina through the port of Wilmington and settled in the counties upstream. In general, these founding families built their homes on landholdings located along the Cape Fear River and frequented Wilmington to take care of commercial and legal business at the port. Wilmington's long association with the Coast Guard began in 1792, when the *Diligence* sailed into the harbor. She was one of the 10 original cutters built for the nation's new US Revenue Cutter Service (USRC).

From the Revolutionary War through the first few decades of the 19th century, Wilmington evolved into a backwater town. Antebellum growth was hampered by the lack of good roads on which to bring produce to the port. Bogs and swamps surrounded the town, and local officials did a poor job of building and maintaining bridges and causeways. The port was 30 miles from the bar, ensuring all kinds of navigational problems. The crews of sailing vessels were reluctant to dock in Wilmington, where disease was rampant without medical facilities. Fires were common and often devastating. By 1840, the town had fewer than 5,000 inhabitants, although it was still the largest town in North Carolina at that time.

With a series of navigational improvements, including the invention of steam-powered vessels and the advent of rail services, Wilmington began to grow. In the two decades after 1840, it doubled in size, becoming a magnet for entrepreneurs and businessmen. The port enjoyed steady growth, with exports far exceeding imports. Rice, peanuts, flax, cotton, and naval stores left the banks of the Cape Fear River for destinations all over the world. The naval stores industry was by far the leading exporter. During this time, Wilmington also became the terminus of several large railroads.

At the outbreak of the Civil War, the port suffered the loss of its export trade, but, within a short time, it more than made up for it by becoming a home port for the lucrative profiteering business. Blockade runners brought military armaments and supplies into Wilmington, where they were then sent by train to fuel the Confederate army. Outgoing ships carried cotton to foreign ports, especially Nassau and Bermuda. The port of Wilmington was ideally situated for this trade. There were two entrances to the Cape Fear River, and in between was Fort Fisher, a formidable earthwork bastion. Union ships had the impossible task of creating a blockade, which stretched 50 miles to cover the two entrances and maintain their distance from the fort. By late 1864, Wilmington was the only Confederate port not captured by Union forces, which turned their full attention to taking it. Fort Fisher fell after two major battles, in December 1864 and January 1865, and, within two weeks, Wilmington was occupied. With no incoming supplies, the Confederates crumbled in a short time.

Occupation meant liberation to the area's large number of slaves, who realized the benefits of the Emancipation Proclamation on the day that Union troops marched into the city. During Reconstruction, Wilmington became home to large numbers of former slaves and free persons of color seeking employment in lumber mills, cotton compresses, and the naval stores industry.

Wilmington's official status changed from town to city in 1866. The river- and railroad-related businesses continued to grow throughout the rest of the 19th century. Prosperity was apparent in street and wharf improvements as well as the construction of fine houses and public buildings.

About 1910, Wilmington's standing as the state's largest city came to an end when the tobacco and textile towns of the Piedmont began to grow. Cotton exports reached their highest levels just before World War I. During the war, Wilmington had two shipyards, which brought work and prosperity to the city. The Roaring Twenties were enjoyed in flamboyant and risqué roadhouses and speakeasies, and with celebrations such as the festival called the Feast of Pirates, which disappeared with the crash of the stock market.

In the 1930s, federal relief work provided jobs for the unemployed populace, but, by the end of the decade, the Great Depression had left the city a shabby reminder of its former self. The 1940s and World War II brought an influx of newcomers and a renewed energy to the city. The North Carolina Shipbuilding Company employed thousands of workers, who delivered 243 new ships for the cause. In 1952, the North Carolina State Port at Wilmington opened at the former World War II shipyard.

From 1840 through 1960, Wilmington was a railroad town. Early railroad enterprises eventually merged into what became the Atlantic Coast Line Railroad, a national company. The city went into shock in 1955 when the company announced that it was moving its headquarters to Jacksonville, Florida. In the 1960s, as many as 300 families left town with the railroad. In response, a group of prominent businessmen formed the Committee of 100 to bring a new and more diversified industry to the area. They succeeded during the next two decades, and Wilmington began, once again, to grow and prosper. In 1966, Wilmington was named an All-America City.

In 1961, the battleship *North Carolina*, with 15 battle stars from service in the Pacific during World War II, was berthed on the west side of the Cape Fear River. A strong preservation movement, begun in the 1970s, brought the old town back to its former elegance, and tourism began to flourish. In 1990, Interstate 40 was completed, linking Wilmington and the port to the rest of the state and the nation. In the 1990s, Wilmington became one of the fastest-growing cities in the nation. It is also a haven for retirees from all over the United States, who enjoy the warm weather, nearby beaches, and southern living in the old port city.

The maritime history of Wilmington is also about the many vessels that have sailed in and out of the port. All types of boats—from wooden ships to pleasure craft, and blockade runners to cruise ships—have docked here. The North Carolina State Port is a thriving center of international trade. Now the banks of the Cape Fear River, with the Riverfront Park and the Riverwalk, provide a scenic location for tourists and Wilmingtonians alike to enjoy. Restaurants, hotels, marinas, and the Wilmington Convention Center line the waterfront in downtown Wilmington.

One

1739–1880

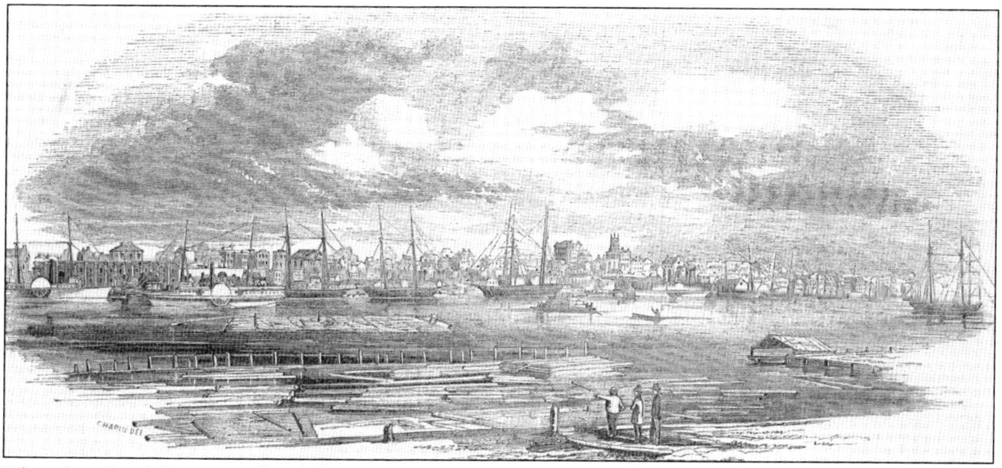

This sketch of the east side of the Wilmington harbor was published in *Ballou's Pictorial Drawing-Room Companion* on July 16, 1853. At the time, the port city had a population of 7,264, the largest in North Carolina. The townspeople lived within a few blocks of the river and worked along its banks.

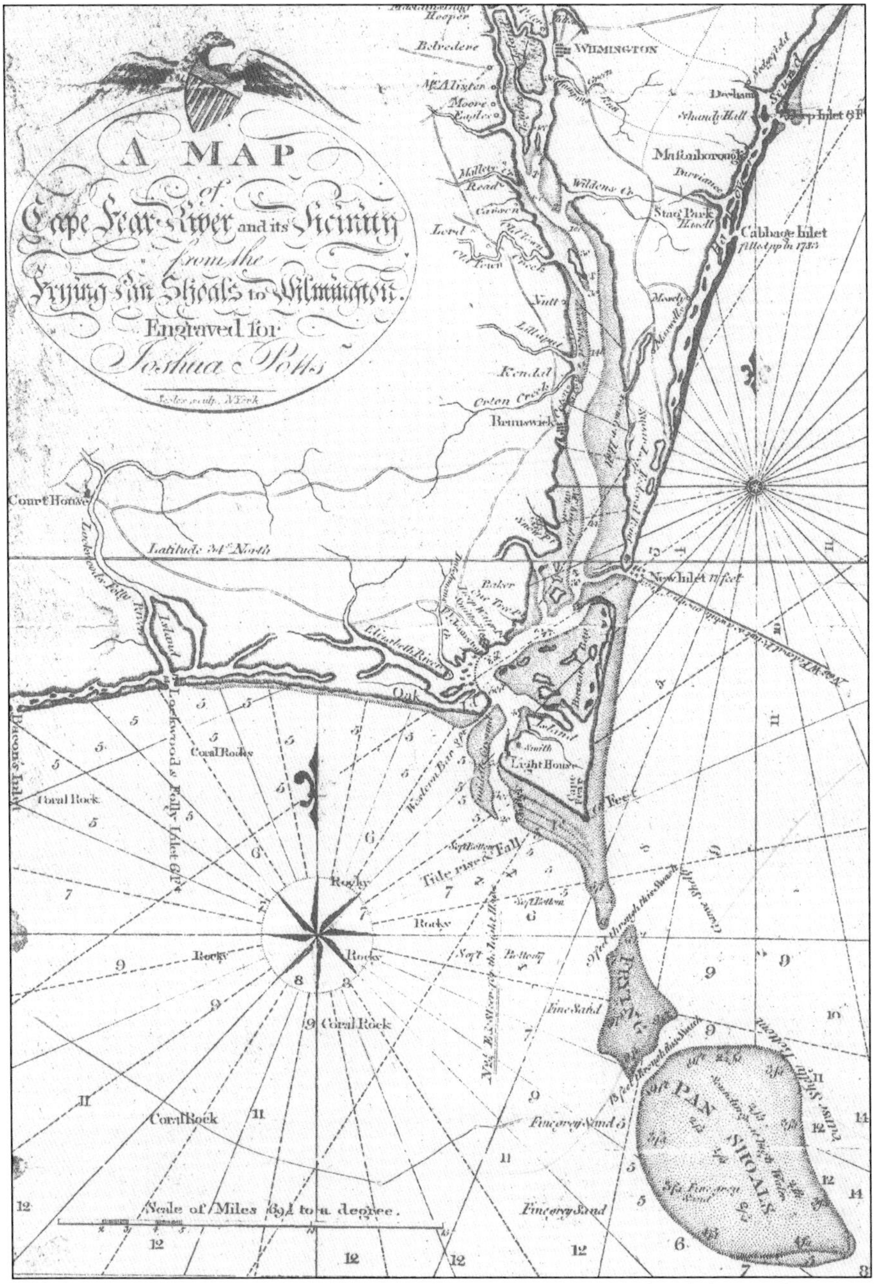

The Cape Fear River was named for the cape where it empties into the Atlantic Ocean. Miles of treacherous shoals and shifting sandbars made early mariners afraid of sailing near the Cape of Fear. In 1662, William Hilton became the first European to extensively explore the river. European settlement occurred along the river in the early part of the 18th century, and the river became a key transportation route for pioneers traveling into the North Carolina backcountry. Located between the mouth of the river and the interior settlements, Wilmington became the region's chief port. A large tributary, the Northeast Branch of the Cape Fear River joins the Cape Fear at Point Peter, just north of the city center. This map, titled *Cape Fear and its Vicinity from the Frying Pan Shoals to Wilmington: Engraved for Joshua Potts*, was created in 1797.

Wilmington was incorporated in 1739. The town was laid out in a grid pattern on high bluffs—actually, high sand dunes—on the east bank of the Cape Fear River, about 30 miles from the bar at the Atlantic Ocean. This 1769 C.J. Sauthier map is the only contemporary source that shows an 18th-century glimpse of the town.

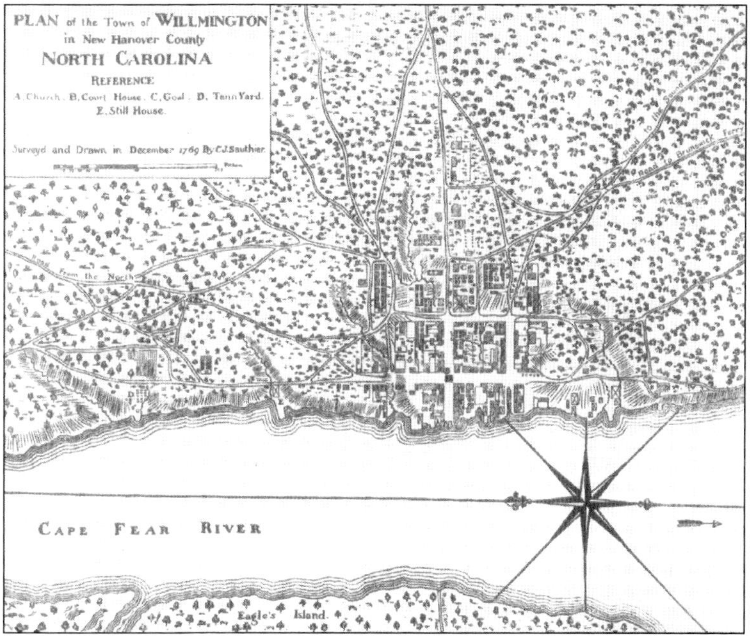

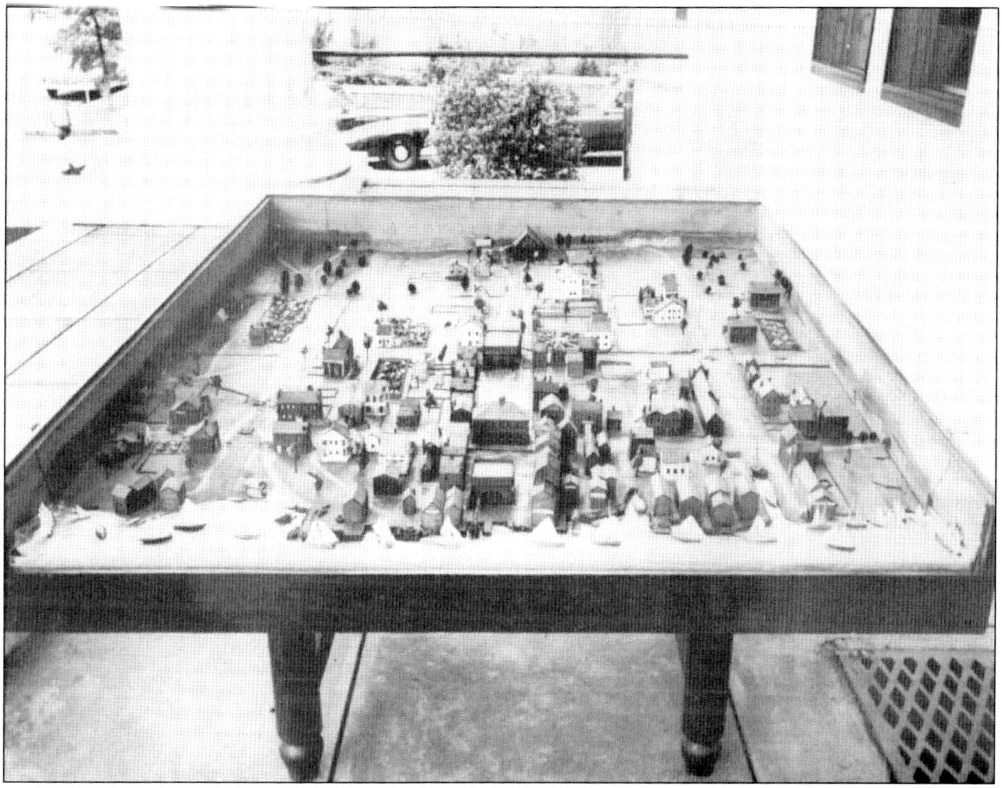

Elizabeth McKoy created this model of how Wilmington looked in 1771. In the center is Market Street, named for the town market, which is the building in the middle of the street, closest to the water. Looking east from the market are the courthouse and, beyond that, the town hall. The Colonial port was located in the area surrounding the foot of Market Street.

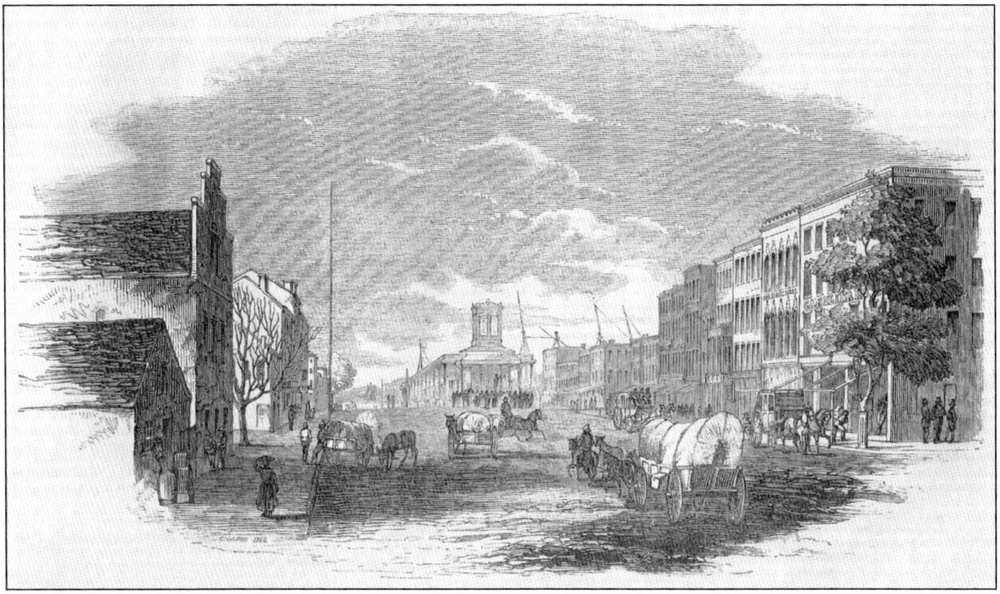

In 1855, a sketch artist for *Ballou's Pictorial Drawing-Room Companion* captured Market Street, looking from Second Street to the river. A market house, built in 1848, is in the center of the street. Masts of several sailing ships can be seen along the waterfront. The large pole on the southeast corner of Market and Water Streets provided telegraph connections to the city.

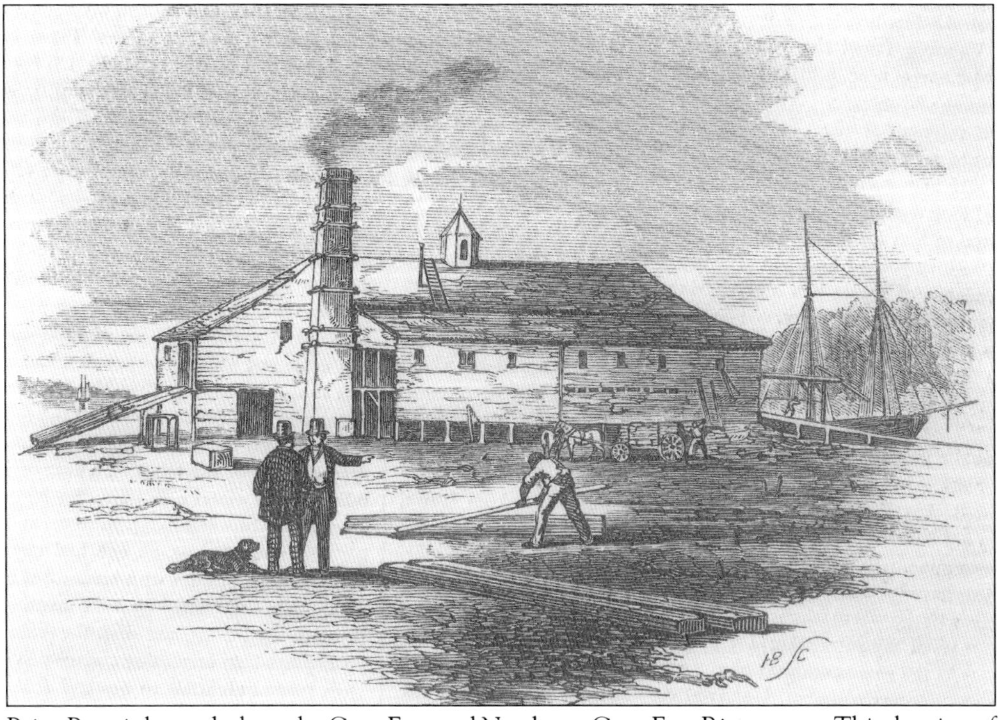

Point Peter is located where the Cape Fear and Northeast Cape Fear Rivers meet. This drawing of the Point Peter sawmill was published in *Ballou's Pictorial Drawing-Room Companion* on February 24, 1855. Due to its location, the mill had a double waterfront. Logs that were taken in on one side of the mill exited as lumber on the other side, where it was loaded directly onto coasting vessels.

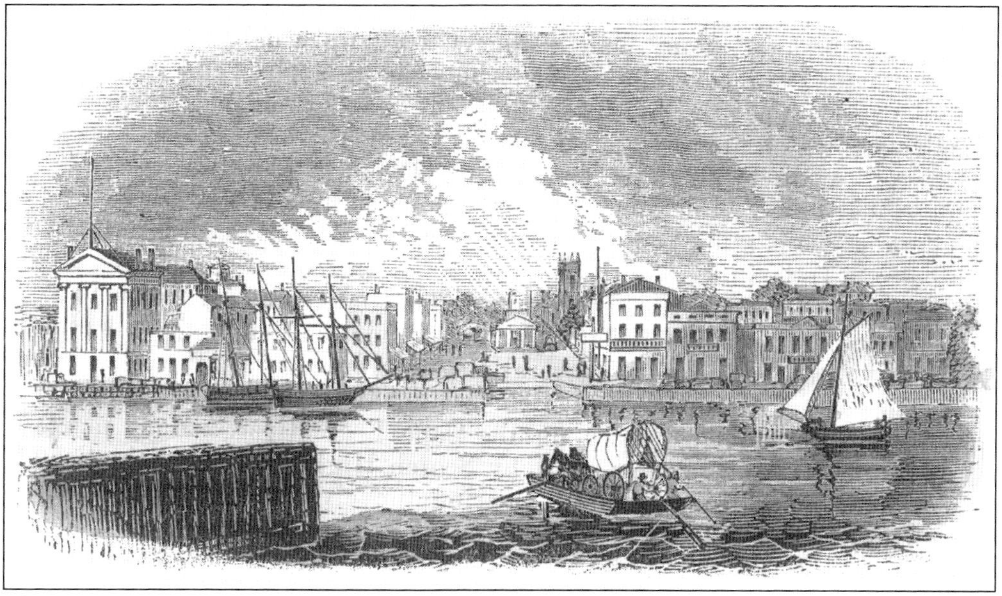

This line drawing made in 1863 depicts a ferry crossing the Cape Fear River toward the foot of Market Street. The three-story building on the far left is the US Custom House, which was completed in 1844. The population of Wilmington in 1860 was 9,552, but, by 1863, the town had swelled with Confederate soldiers and sailors as well as blockade runners and their crews.

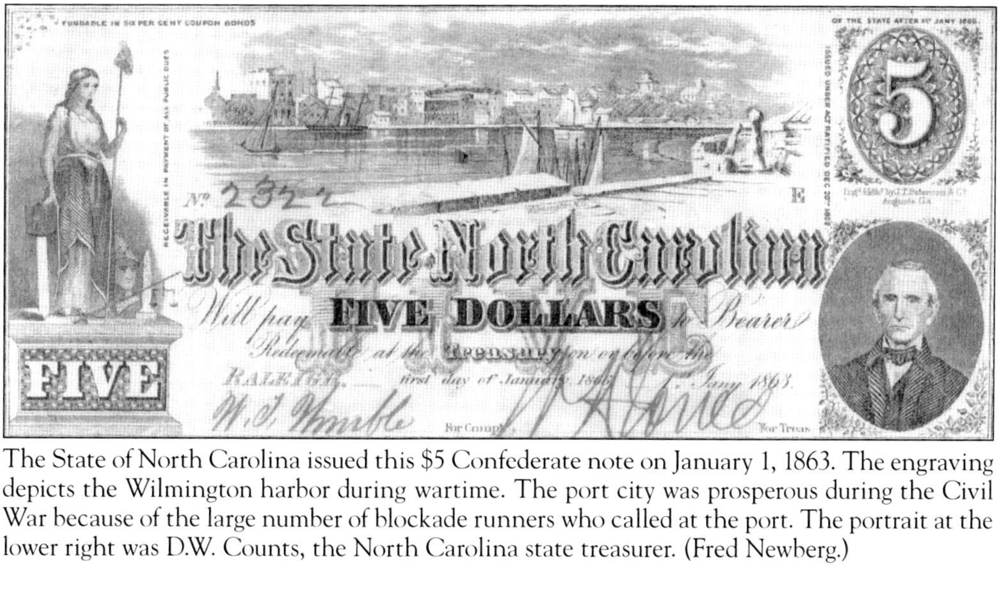

The State of North Carolina issued this $5 Confederate note on January 1, 1863. The engraving depicts the Wilmington harbor during wartime. The port city was prosperous during the Civil War because of the large number of blockade runners who called at the port. The portrait at the lower right was D.W. Counts, the North Carolina state treasurer. (Fred Newberg.)

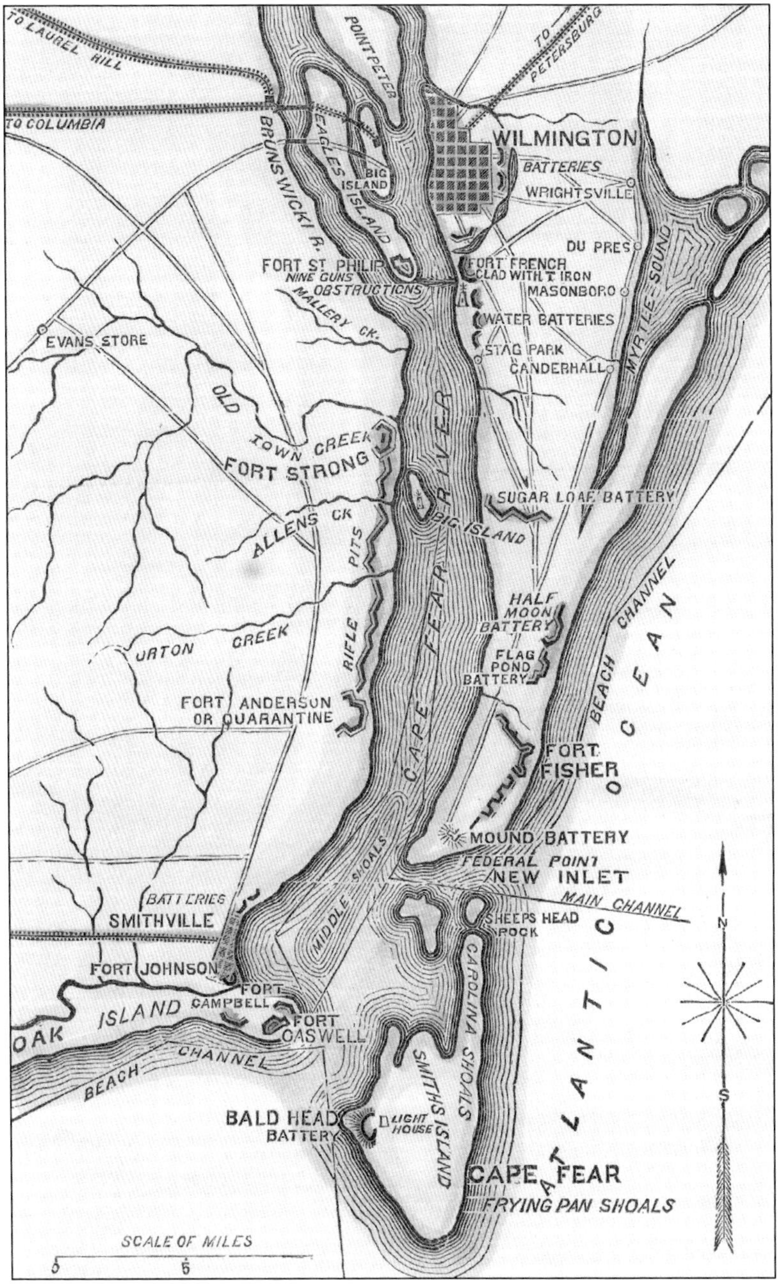

The Cape Fear River was difficult for the Union navy to blockade. There were two entrances into the river: the Old Inlet and New Inlet. Guarding both required a 50-mile arc of blockaders, a luxury that the navy did not have during most of the war. The blockade runners brought military equipment and ammunition into the port, where it was loaded onto trains and shipped to the Army of Northern Virginia. Forts Fisher, Caswell, Johnson, Campbell, Anderson, Strong, St. Philip, and French were well fortified and stretched from river entrances to the city. Several camps and batteries also surrounded and protected the town. A line of range lights or light beacons provided safe passage for vessels to avoid shallow areas along the river. To keep in constant contact, telegraph lines were strung from the port to Fort Fisher, the largest of the fortifications.

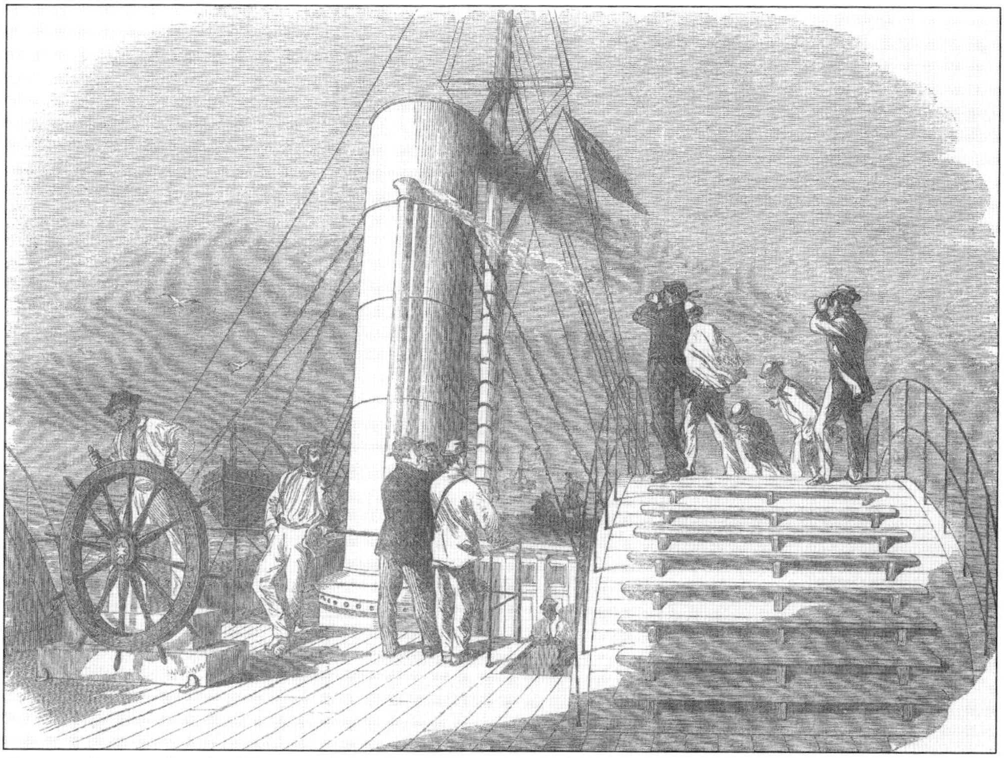

A special artist for the *Illustrated London News* was on board the *Lillian* when it ran the blockade into Wilmington. This sketch appeared in the September 16, 1864, edition of the newspaper. English-built blockade runners were swift and silent. Made more for speed than carrying cargo, they were painted a lead-gray color to make them hard to detect in dark or misty surroundings.

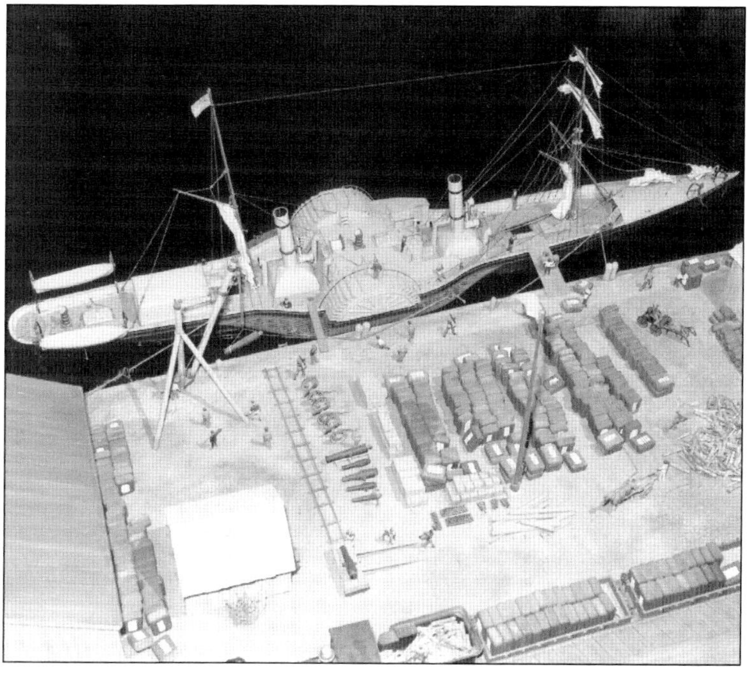

This model of a blockade runner docked in Wilmington during the Civil War was part of the former maritime museum at Chandler's Wharf. It shows weaponry and munitions for the Confederate army being off-loaded, while bales of cotton are being loaded. The cotton, which sold at very high prices, was shipped to England to supply European cotton mills. (*StarNews* Collection, NHCPL.)

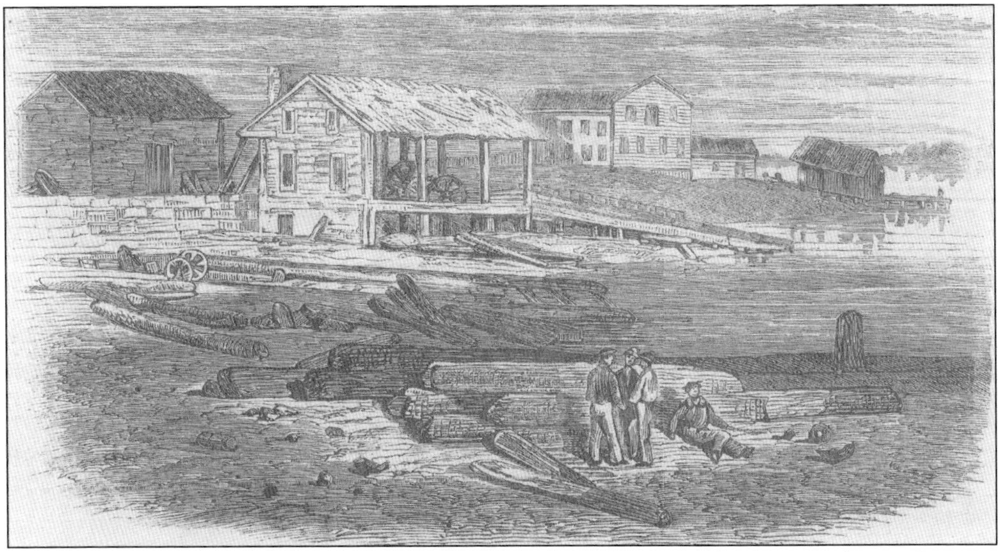

On a second attempt, the Union navy and army succeeded in overtaking Fort Fisher on January 15, 1865. Union troops marched into Wilmington on February 22, 1865, occupying the city. This postwar drawing titled *Rebel Navy Yard* was published in the April 15, 1865, edition of *Frank Leslie's Illustrated Newspaper*. Wilmington had two shipyards during the war.

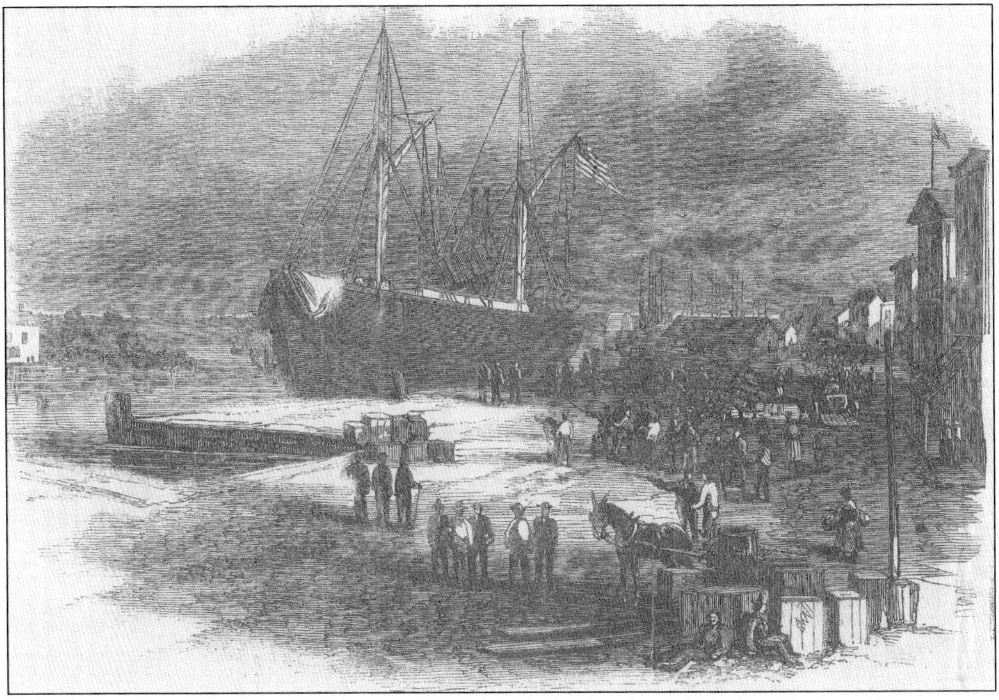

This sketch, which appeared in the April 15, 1865, edition of *Frank Leslie's Illustrated Newspaper*, depicts a Union transport unloading ambulances. Thousands of refugees, prisoners, and freedmen flooded into Wilmington seeking medical attention. Medical supplies were scarce, and many died. The ship was docked at the foot of Market Street, near the US Custom House. The Union army occupied Wilmington for six months.

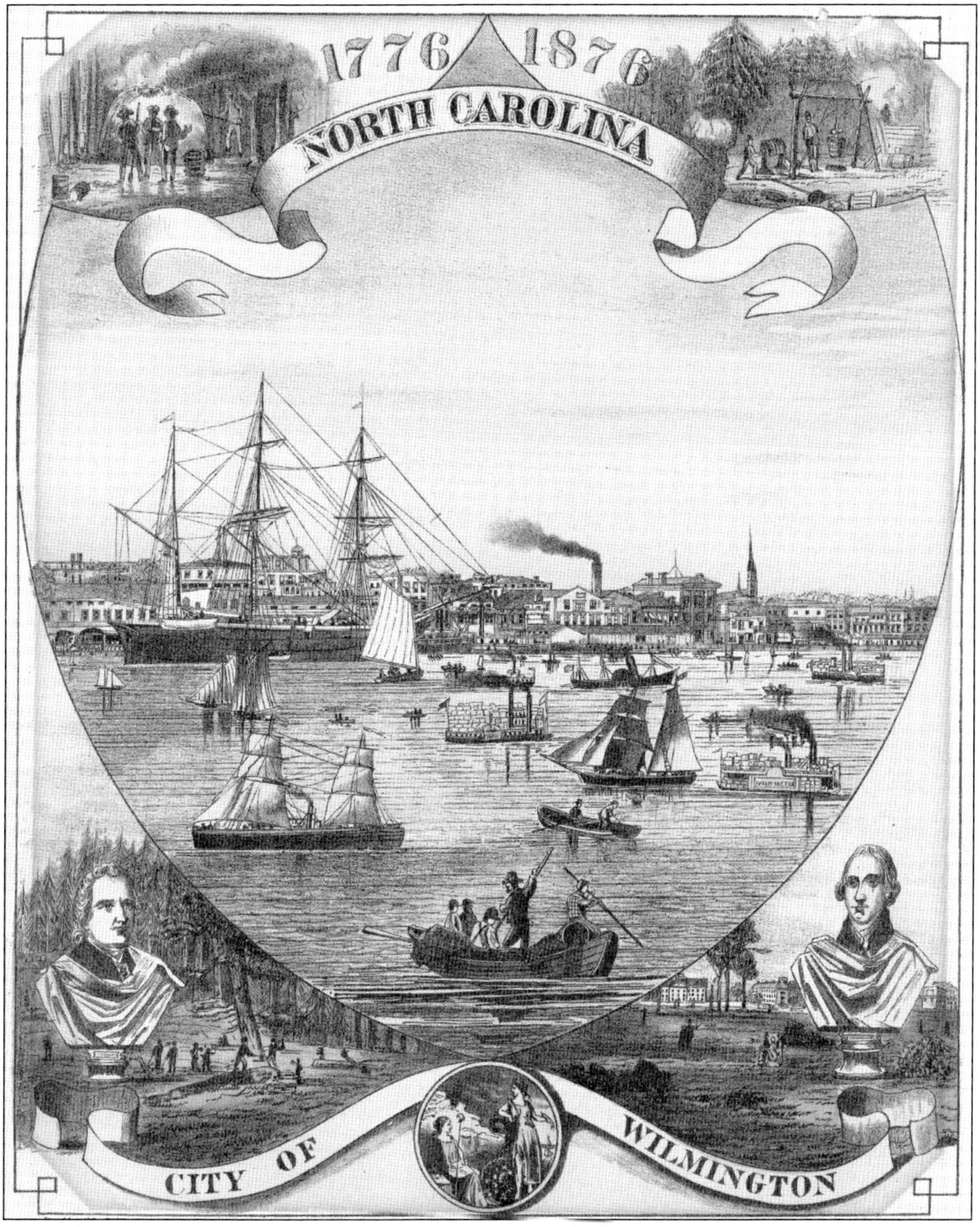

By 1876, the centennial of the United States, the port of Wilmington was back in business as usual and looking forward to the next century. This engraving, which celebrates the centennial, shows North Carolina's largest city as busy and prosperous. Wooden ships, steamers, sailboats, lighters, rowboats, and canoes fill the harbor. The line drawing shows the east bank of the harbor lined warehouses and wharves. The engraving also features the longleaf pine tree. According to the 1860 Wilmington city directory, the abundance of this natural resource made the port of Wilmington the largest exporter of naval stores in the world. Naval stores consisted of tar, pitch, rosin, and turpentine, all of which were used in shipbuilding. The native longleaf pine provided billions of board feet of lumber, used in both civil and naval architecture. The air in the port city was redolent with the aromatic odor of pine products.

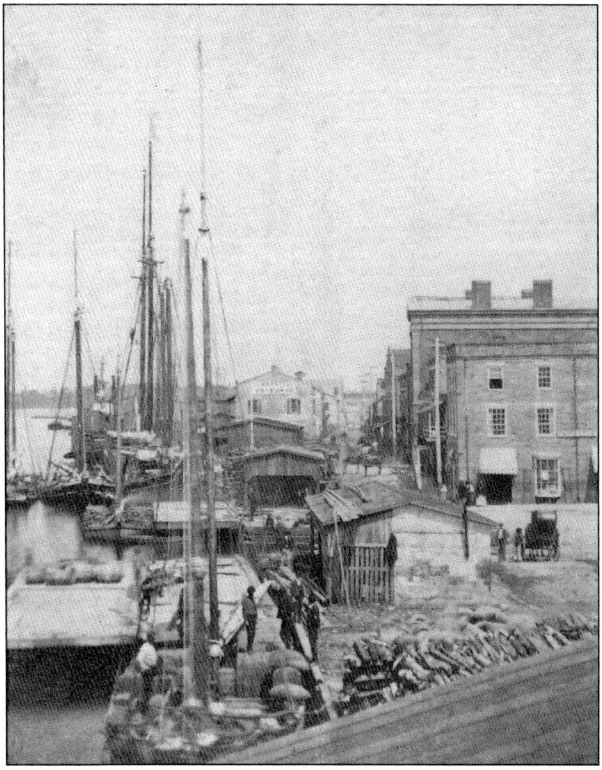

Stereographic photographer Rufus Morgan traveled around North Carolina in the 1870s. He took this photograph of the foot of Market Street, looking north, in 1873. The ferry landing had been located here since the Colonial era. The two-story brick building on the west (left) side of Water Street was the Commercial Exchange, a place where businesses could exchange goods and services. It was operated by the Wilmington Chamber of Commerce, which had its offices on the second floor. The three-story building on the right with the two visible chimneys was the US Custom House. It was good business to have a store as close as possible to the Custom House and the waterfront. Jacob Lyons, a German Jewish immigrant, owned the successful dry goods store on the far right, on the northeast corner of Water and Market Streets.

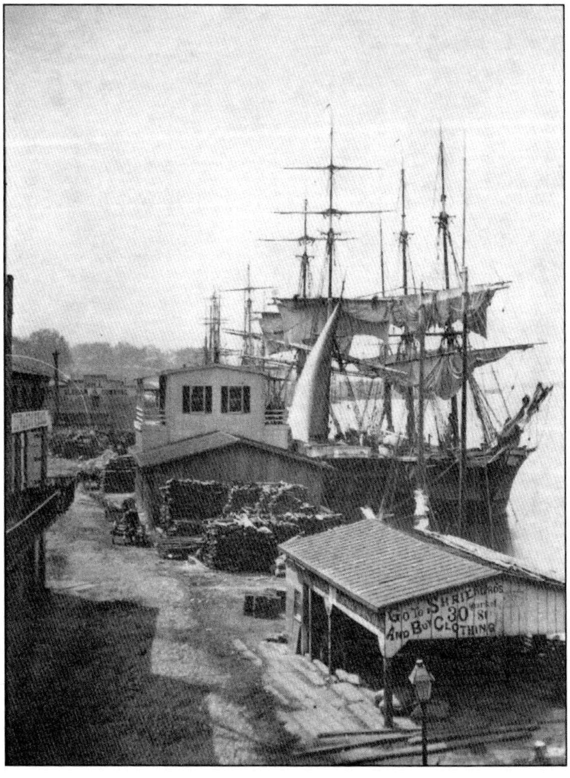

In 1873, Rufus Morgan took this photograph, looking south at the foot of Market Street. Two- and three-masted schooners can be seen docked on Water Street. In 1795, the town began filling in the inlets and wetlands along the waterfront, creating Water Street. Sheds like the one in the foreground were built of wood and easily erected. Even with tin roofs, they often caught on fire, and they had to be replaced frequently. The wharf was also constructed using longleaf pine. Wood yards lined the waterfront, providing fuel for vessels as well as townspeople. Fires along the waterfront were a constant concern. The building in the distance, located at 14 South Water Street, was the Oldham and Cumming Mill, a steam-powered sawmill. Oldham and Cumming were also commission merchants who took exports and imports on consignment and tried to find markets for them. At any given time, there were 30 to 40 commission merchants operating on Water Street.

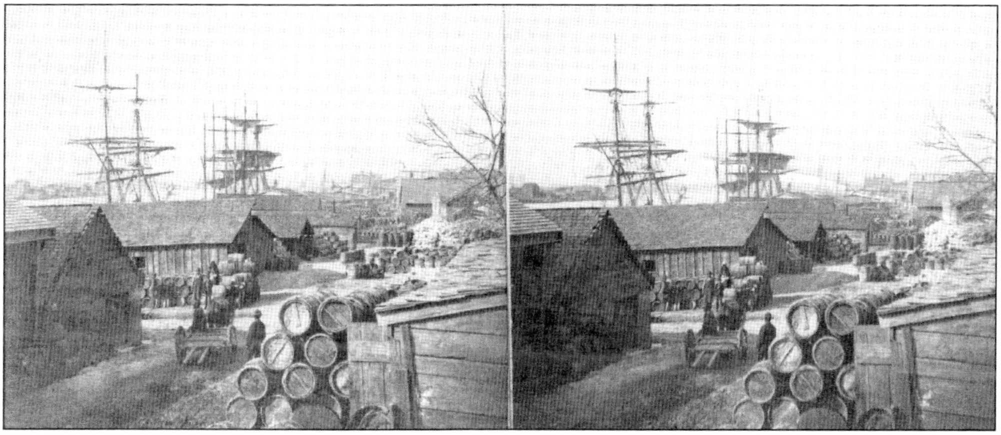

Rufus Morgan took this photograph titled *View from Sunset Hill* in 1873. Located at the foot of Nun Street, Sunset Hill is a high bluff overlooking the Cape Fear River that had, and still has, beautiful sunsets. Barrels of naval stores products line both sides of Water Street in the photograph, looking north. (Historical Society of the Lower Cape Fear.)

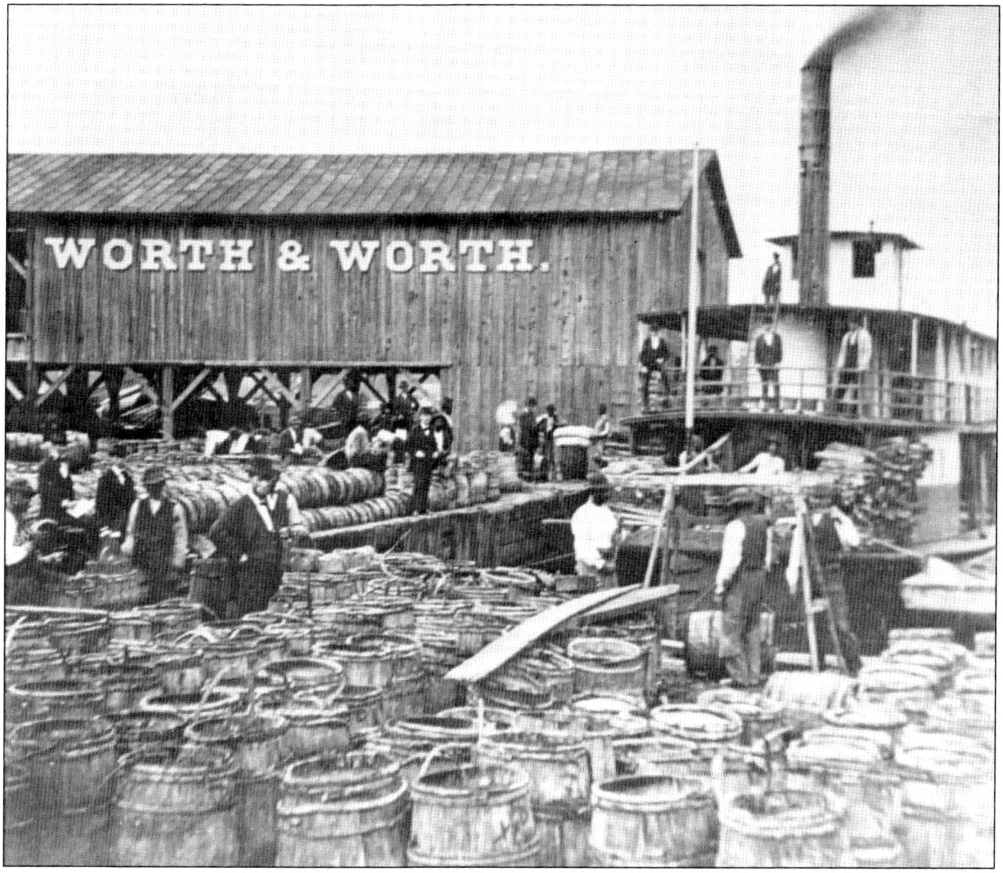

Brothers B.G. and D.G. Worth were large commission merchants. They owned wharves and warehouses at the foot of Mulberry (now Grace) Street. They also owned the Cape Fear Steamboat Company. One of their steamers is unloading rosin at their wharf in this 1873 photograph taken by Rufus Morgan.

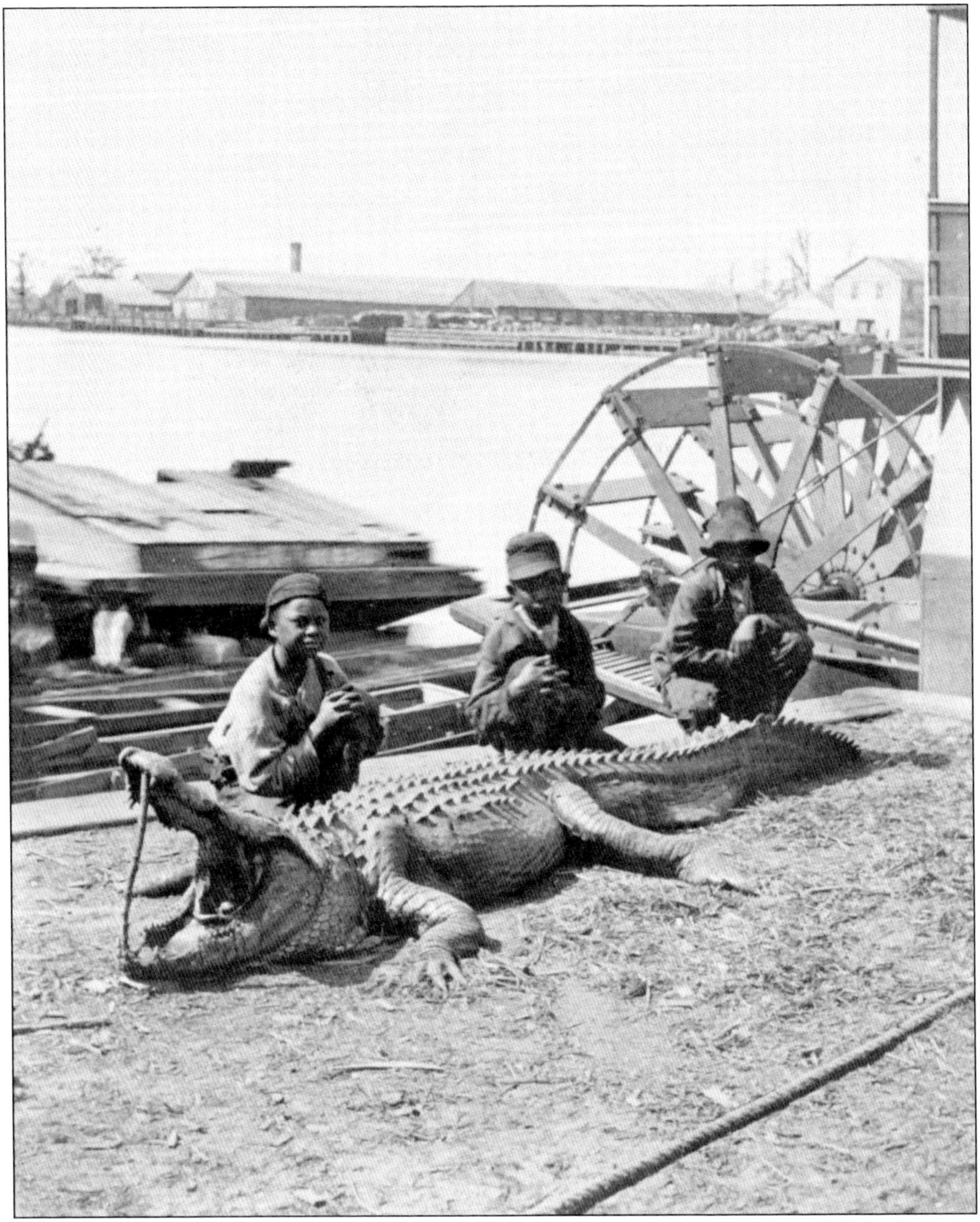

Alexander J. Orr and Charles W. Yates were partners in a photography business from 1879 to 1883. They took stereographs of places and events in Wilmington and the surrounding area. They would advertise their photographs for sale by hanging them in their store window. This one, the viewing of the 10.5-foot-long alligator, was a good seller. Alligators live in eastern North Carolina, the most northern area of their habitat. Yates and Orr took several shots of the alligator, this one on the east bank of the Cape Fear River. A paddle wheel and a flatboat frame the little boys. Newspaper accounts of the time reveal that boys were frequent visitors to the waterfront; however, girls were rarely seen there. Warehouses on Eagles Island can be seen on the other side of the river. Eagles Island, or the west bank of the Wilmington harbor, was named for the Eagles family, the first Europeans to own the island.

Two

1880–1920

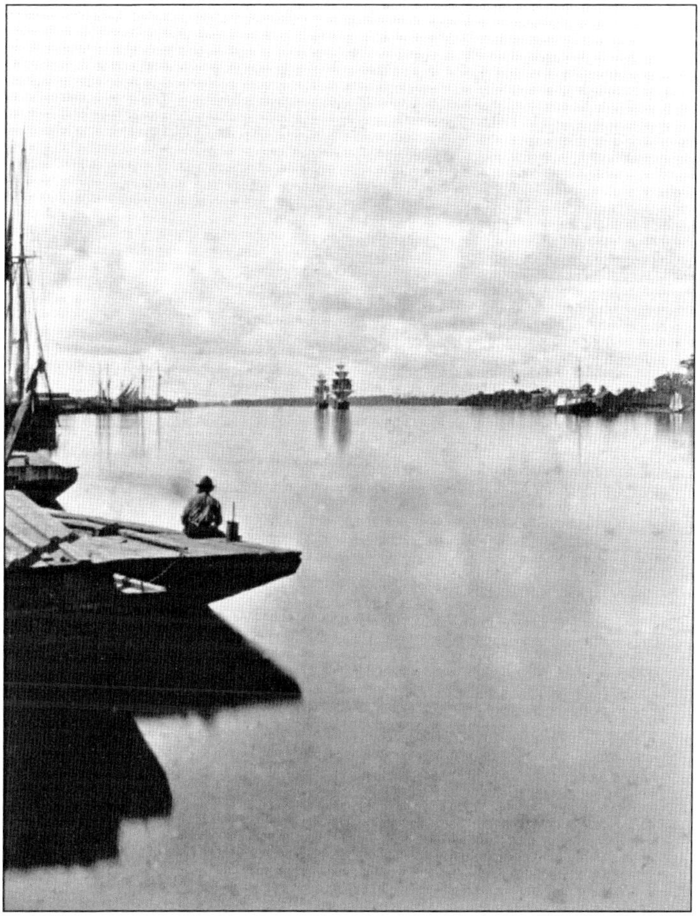

Photographers C.W. Yates and Alexander J. Orr took this contemplative photograph of the Wilmington harbor about 1880. The tide is going out, and the waterfront is quiet. At a distance, two schooners are seen leaving the port.

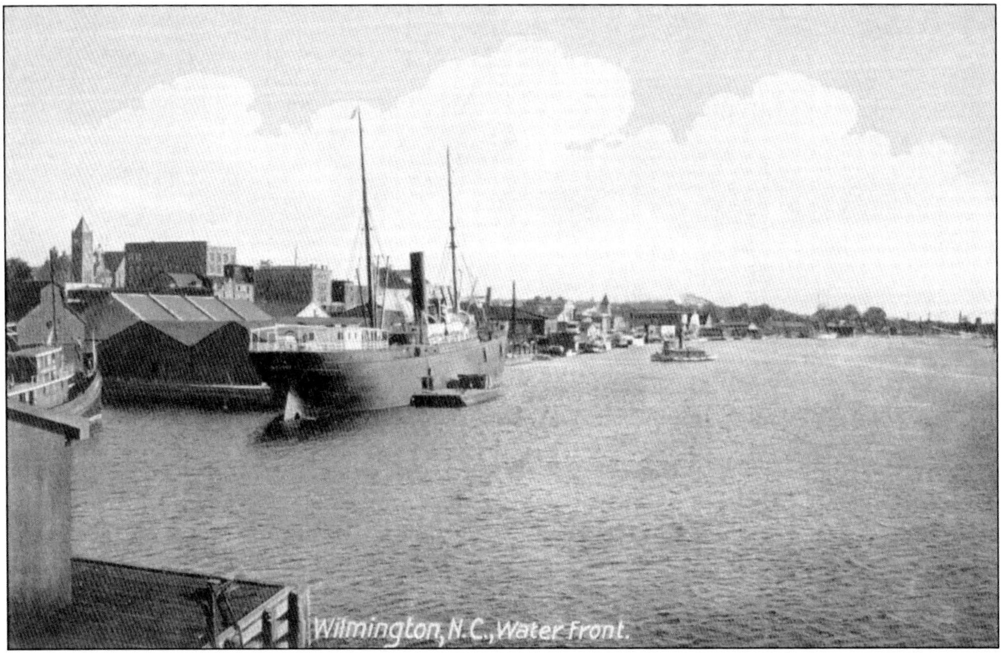

This 1910 postcard shows the east bank of the Wilmington harbor. A New York freighter is docked at the Champion Compress & Warehouse Co. wharf, located between Walnut and Red Cross Streets. Owned by Alexander Sprunt & Sons, they were cotton brokers who sold most of their product to European markets.

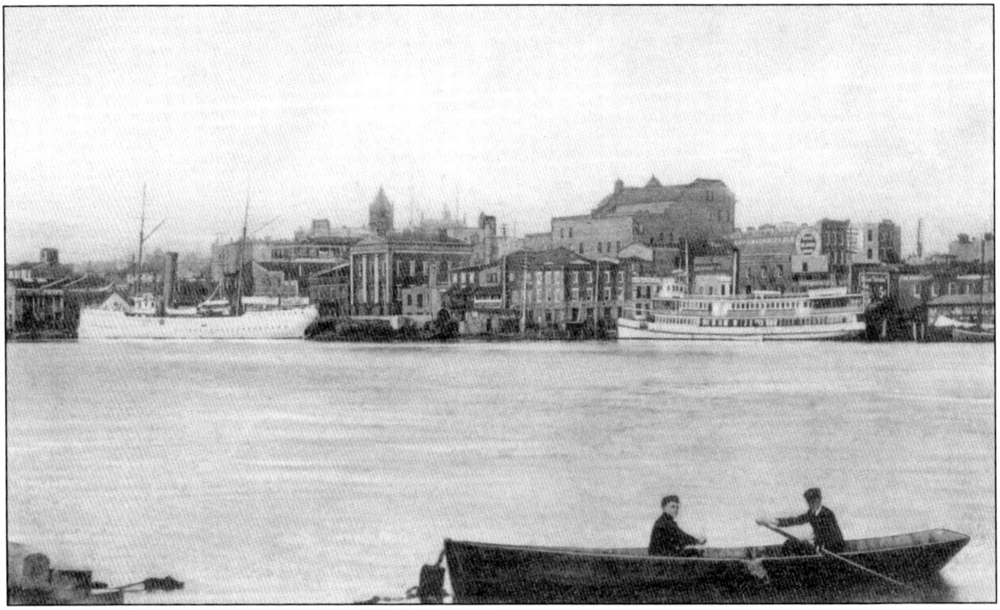

This photograph was taken from the west bank of the Cape Fear River, looking toward Water Street, between Market and Princess Streets. The USRC *Seminole* (left) is docked at the government wharf, which was located in front of the US Custom House. The steamer *Wilmington* (right) is docked at the foot of Market Street.

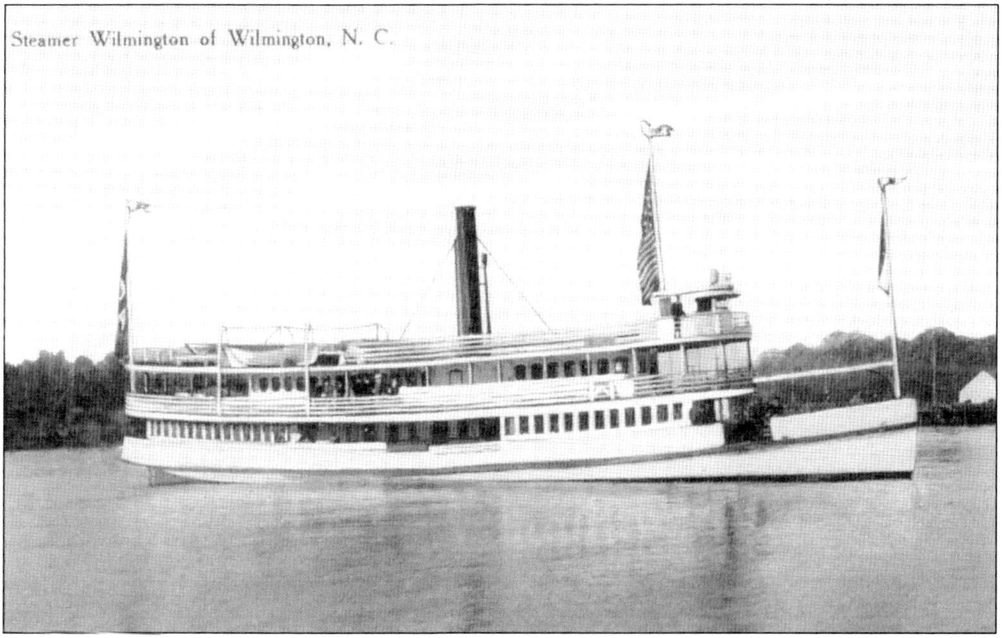

The legendary steamer *Wilmington* was built in 1881 in Wilmington, Delaware. There was no need to change her name when Capt. John W. Harper brought her to Wilmington, North Carolina. She was popular from the time of her arrival on April 28, 1891. An iron-hull steamer, she was 130 feet long, had a beam of 23 feet, drew 6 feet of water, and had three decks.

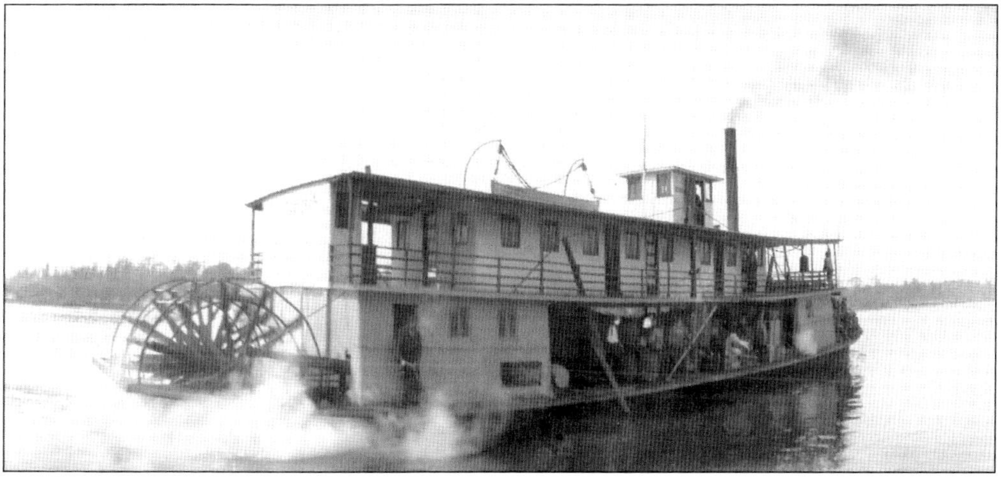

The stern-wheeler *Thelma* was built for wholesale grocer John W. Brooks in 1914. She was purchased by Henry Hunt in 1922, about the time this photograph was taken. He ran the *Thelma* between Wilmington and Fayetteville. The last passenger-freight boat on the river, it sank near the bridge at Elizabethtown in 1940. (Louis T. Moore Collection, NHCPL.)

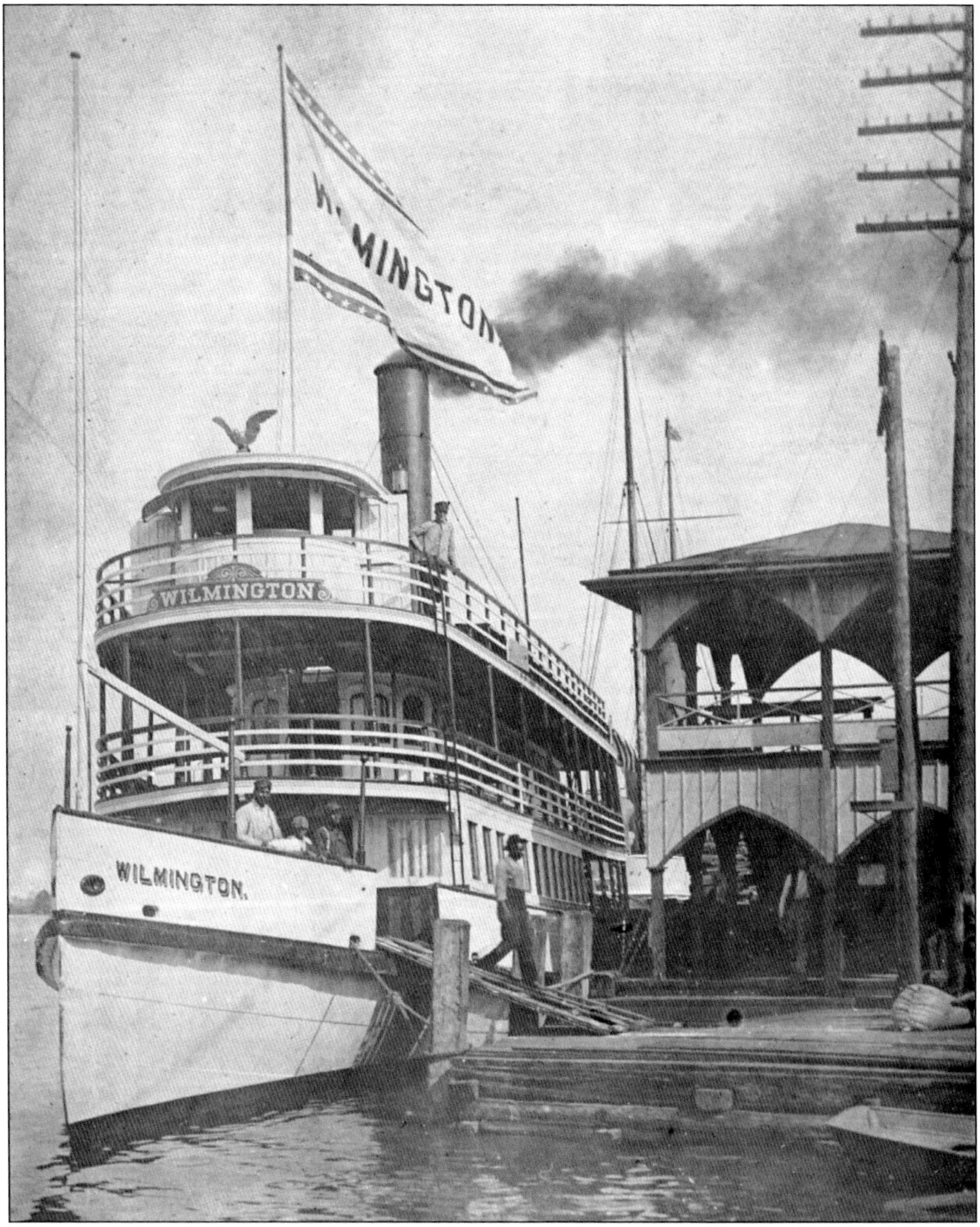

The *Wilmington* made two daily runs to Southport, where Captain Harper had the contract to deliver the US mail. He also contracted with the US Army to furnish transportation for the soldiers stationed at Fort Caswell during World War I. In peak tourist season, the *Wilmington* carried as many as 2,000 passengers a day. Within an hour, she delivered pleasure-seekers from downtown Wilmington to Carolina Beach. Captain Harper specialized in offering excursion rates. Institutions, professional organizations, Sunday school classes, and other groups from all over southeastern North Carolina rented the boat to take them to the ocean for the day. At one time or another, a large percentage of the population took a trip on the *Wilmington*, making her one of the most beloved vessels in town history. This photograph was taken about 1915. (Thalian Hall Center for the Performing Arts.)

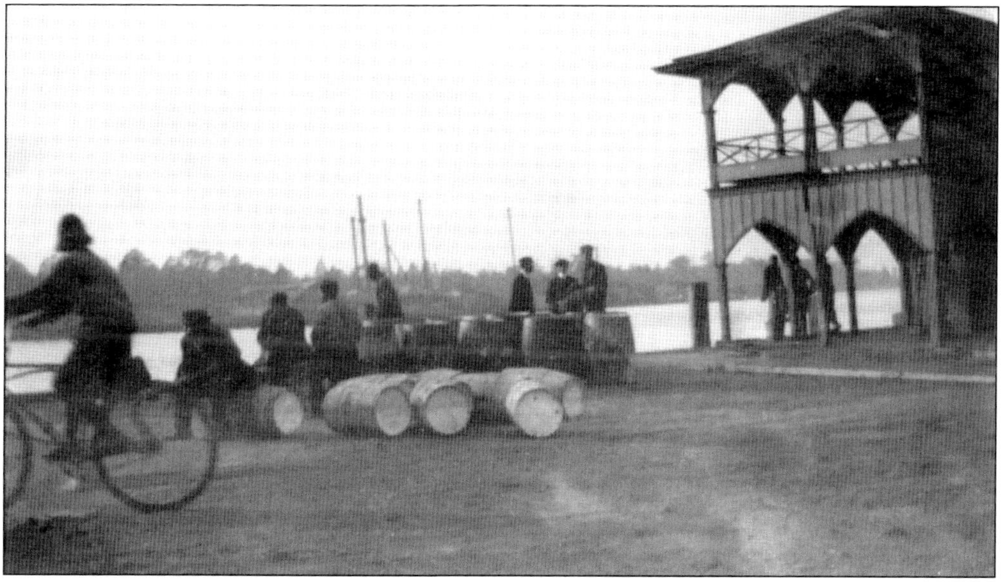

This photograph of the foot of Market Street was taken in 1915. Passengers waited for the steamer *Wilmington* in the building at right. Families did not usually frequent the waterfront, especially the working dock areas; however, they would wait here, out of the elements. Children would climb to the second floor as lookouts for the approach of the popular passenger boat.

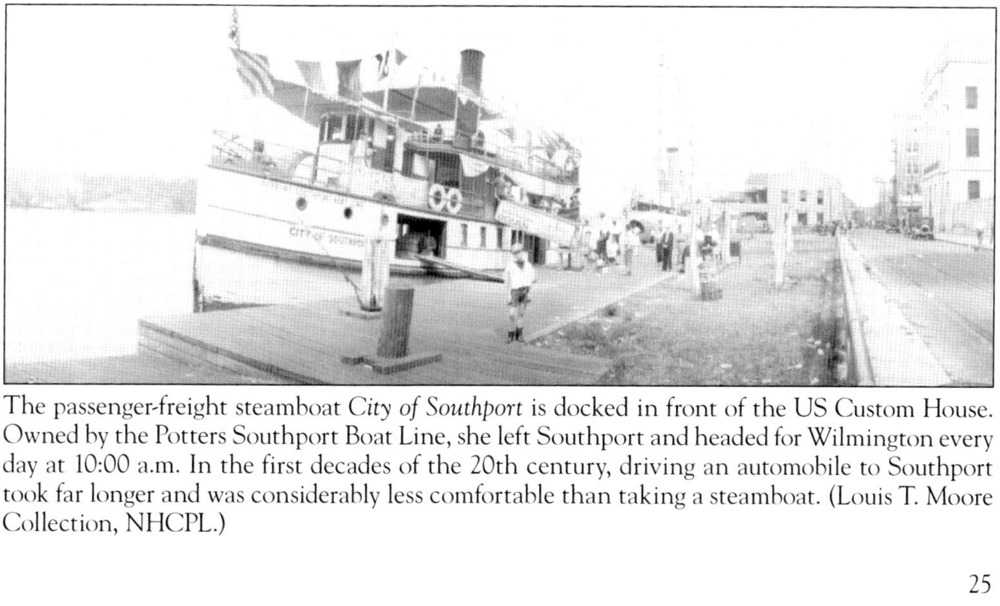

The passenger-freight steamboat *City of Southport* is docked in front of the US Custom House. Owned by the Potters Southport Boat Line, she left Southport and headed for Wilmington every day at 10:00 a.m. In the first decades of the 20th century, driving an automobile to Southport took far longer and was considerably less comfortable than taking a steamboat. (Louis T. Moore Collection, NHCPL.)

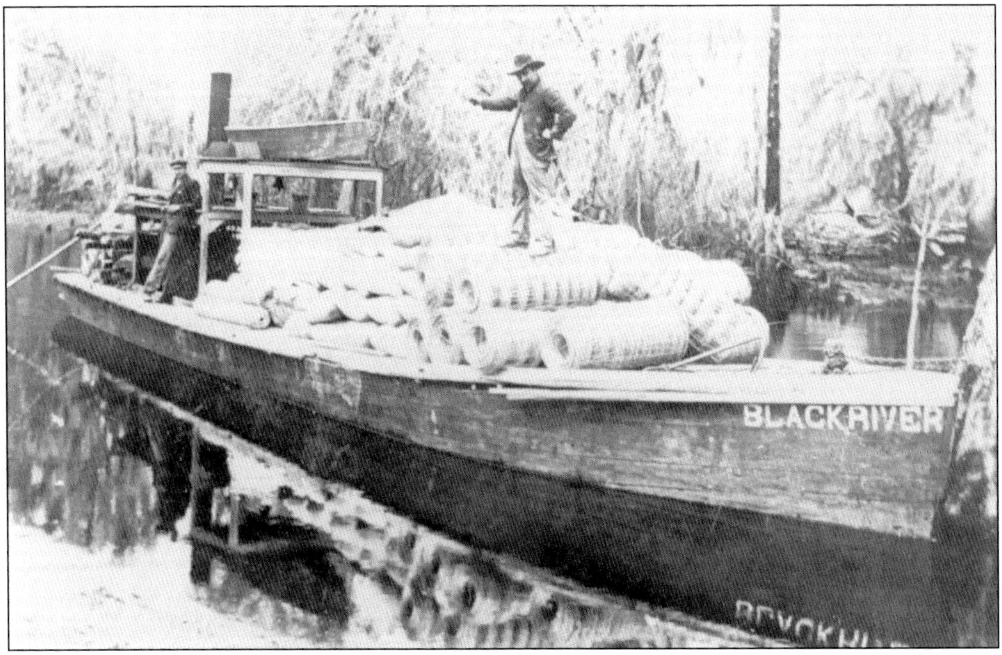

This photograph of the *Black River II* was taken about 1915. She was a steam flat built about 1907. Her master, seen on top of the bales of wire, was Willis Johnson. The boat operated on the Black and Cape Fear Rivers until 1918. During the last decade of operation, naval stores had ceased to be as lucrative as they had previously been, so Johnson began hauling virtually anything farmers wanted.

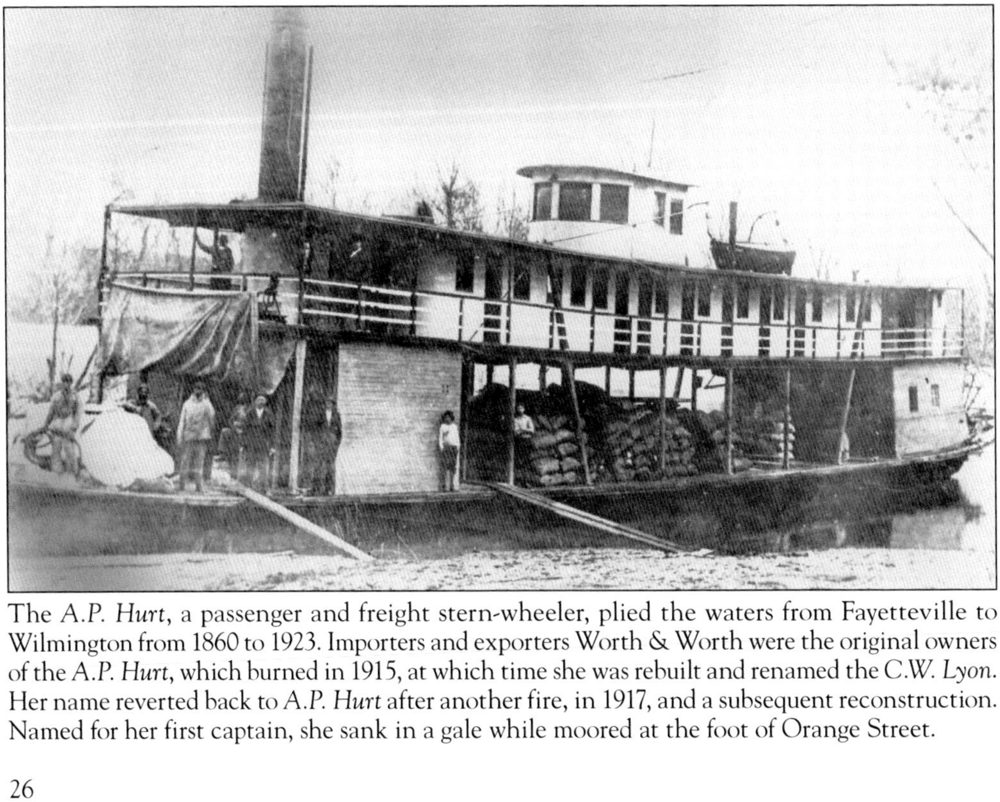

The *A.P. Hurt*, a passenger and freight stern-wheeler, plied the waters from Fayetteville to Wilmington from 1860 to 1923. Importers and exporters Worth & Worth were the original owners of the *A.P. Hurt*, which burned in 1915, at which time she was rebuilt and renamed the *C.W. Lyon*. Her name reverted back to *A.P. Hurt* after another fire, in 1917, and a subsequent reconstruction. Named for her first captain, she sank in a gale while moored at the foot of Orange Street.

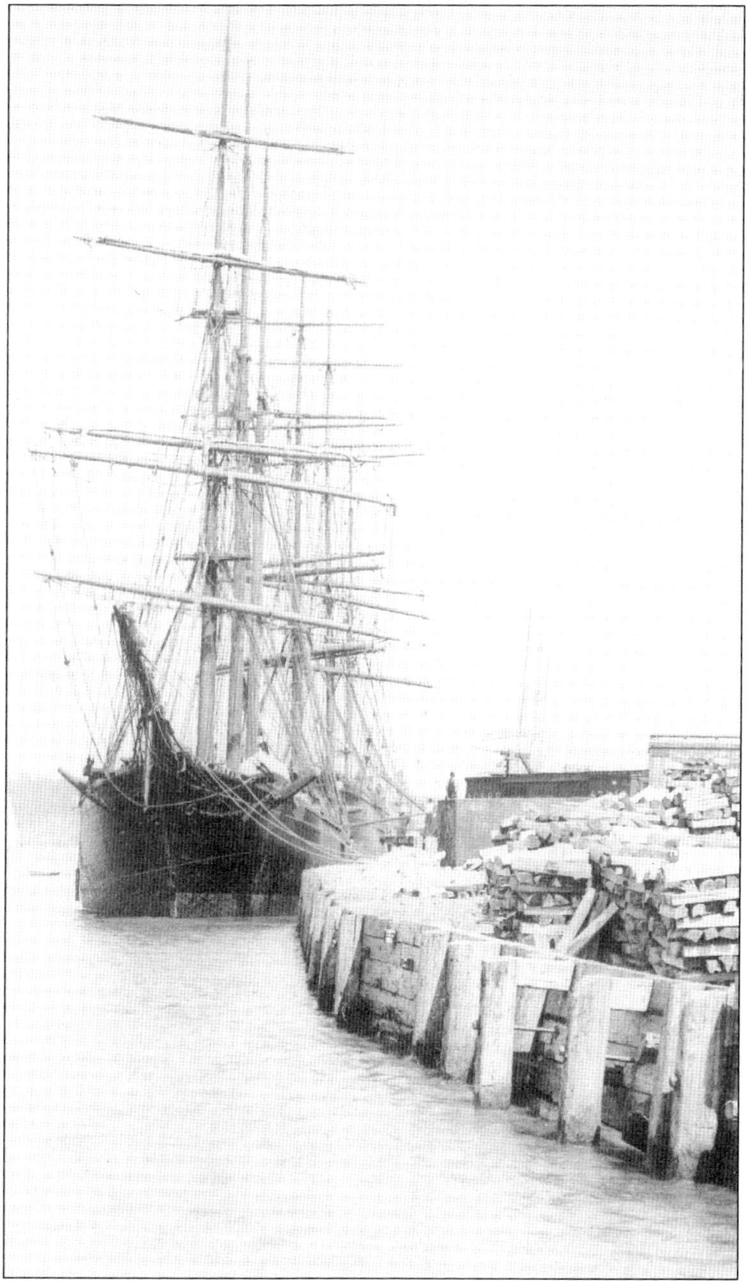

Schooners wait in line to load lumber products at the Atlantic Coast Line Railroad dock. Everything in the photograph, including the boxcar, is made of wood. The wooden schooners unloaded imports for rail transport throughout the south, but the main reason they called at the port was to pick up the following lumber products: sawn lumber (boards, plank, and scantling), shingles, staves, heading, hoops, hogsheads, posts, oars, masts, spars, yards, and house frames, all of which were produced in and around Wilmington. The most profitable exports were lumber and shingles. In 1895, when this photograph was taken, the chamber of commerce heralded the "City by the Sea" as the lead trade center of the state. The waterfront was truly the crossroads of that trade. By 1900, the population of the port city had grown to 20,976.

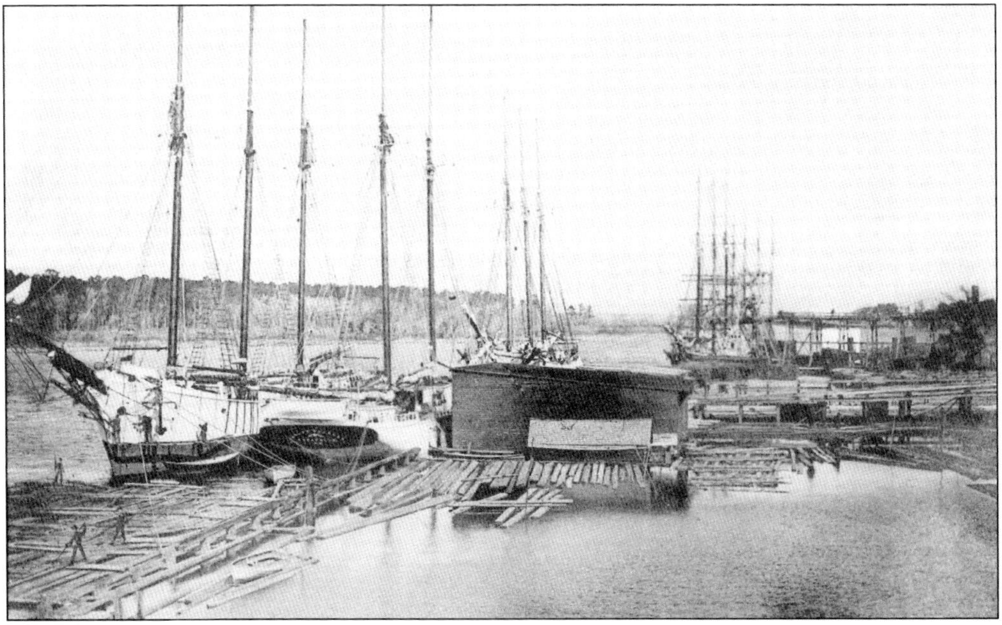

Here, two- and three-masted schooners load longleaf pine logs. The trees were cut upriver and then floated to Wilmington. At the lower left of this 1903 photograph, men balance on the logs while steering them into the timber pen, which can be seen in the foreground. Numerous timber pens were located on the northern banks of the Wilmington harbor.

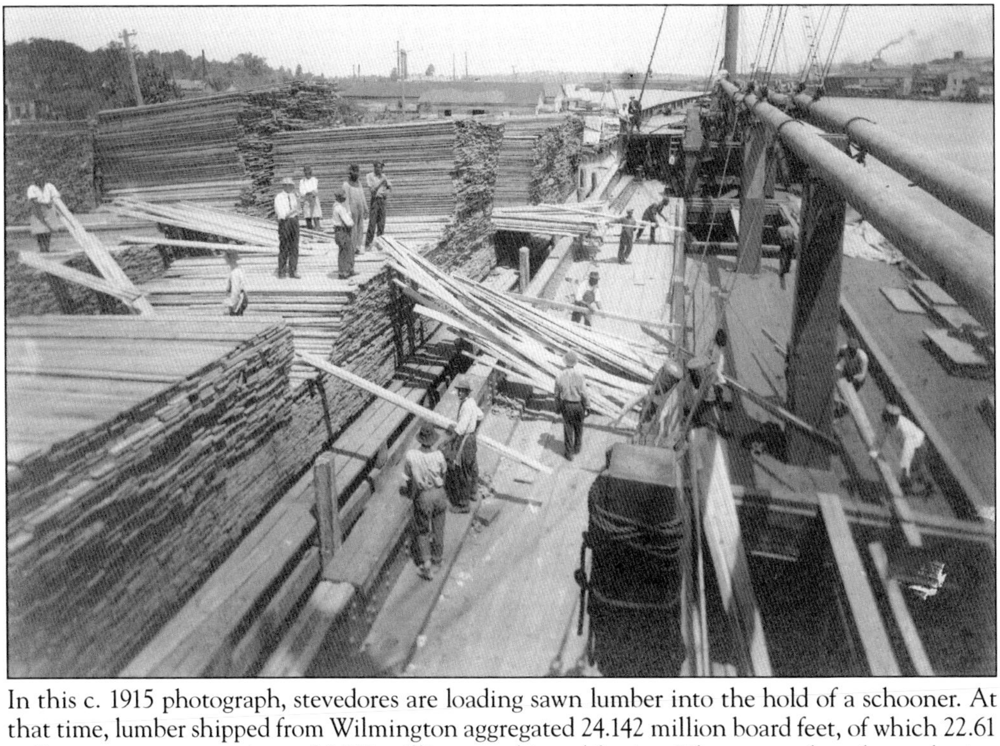

In this c. 1915 photograph, stevedores are loading sawn lumber into the hold of a schooner. At that time, lumber shipped from Wilmington aggregated 24.142 million board feet, of which 22.61 million was sent coastwise and 1.797 million was shipped foreign. There were three large planing mills and sawmills that employed from 75 to 125 men, depending on the order.

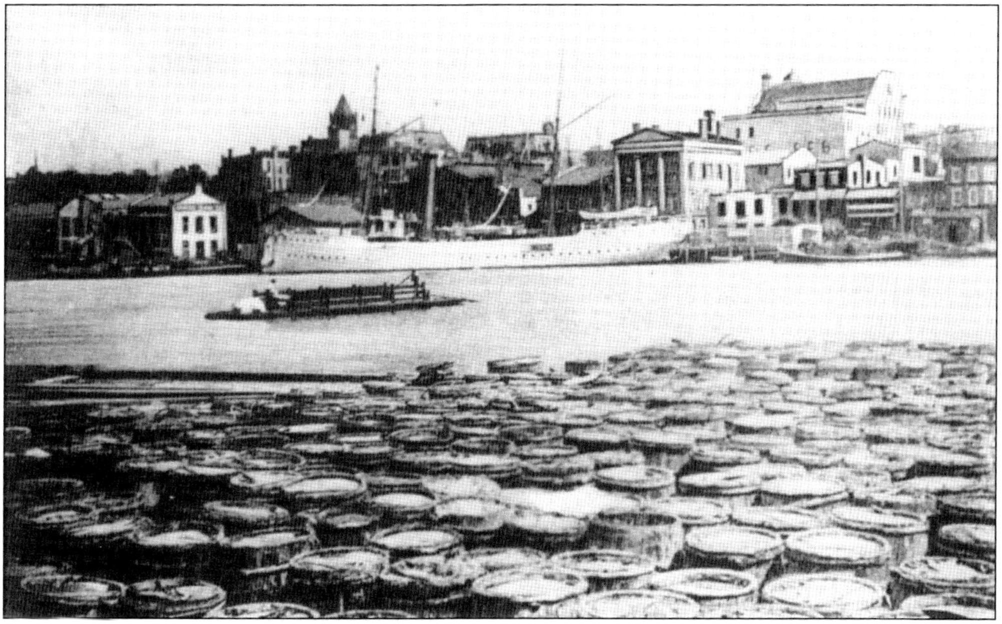

Taken from Eagles Island, looking toward the US Custom House, this photograph of the Wilmington harbor was featured in a 1908 publication written by the Wilmington Chamber of Commerce. According to the chamber, "Wilmington has one of the finest harbors on the Atlantic coast. It has ample room for enlargement of dockage facilities and has a depth at low water of 22 feet."

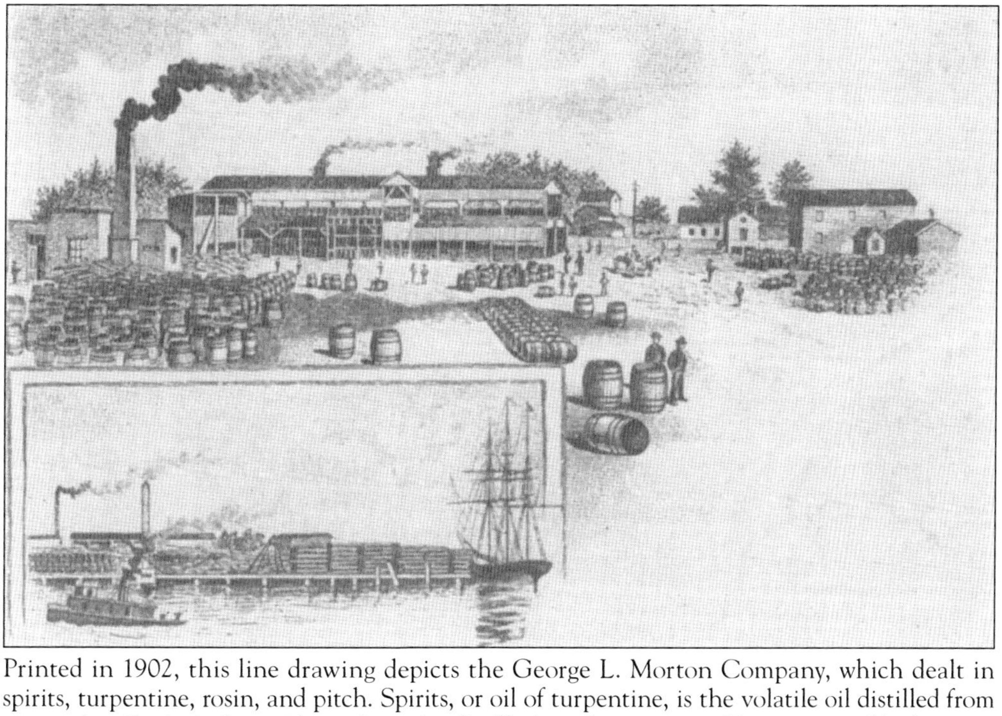

Printed in 1902, this line drawing depicts the George L. Morton Company, which dealt in spirits, turpentine, rosin, and pitch. Spirits, or oil of turpentine, is the volatile oil distilled from turpentine. Rosin is the residuum from the distillation of turpentine. Tar is procured by burning pine in kilns. Pitch remains after the oil has been extracted from the tar. Morton's distillery and wharf were located on Eagles Island.

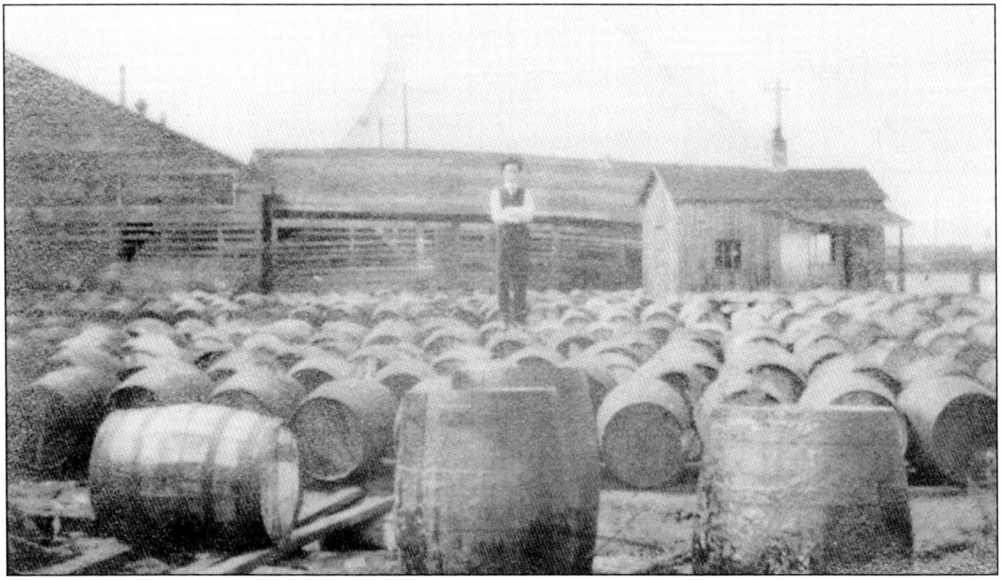

The Columbia Naval Stores Company tar yard is seen in this undated photograph. As an 1884 description explains, "The term naval stores is an exceedingly comprehensive one, but as it is commercially used it includes only those products of turpentine known as spirits, rosin, tar, pitch and crude turpentine. They are obtained from longleaf pines which are abundant on the coast of the Carolinas, Georgia, upper Florida and lower Alabama and Mississippi." (C.E. Fonvielle.)

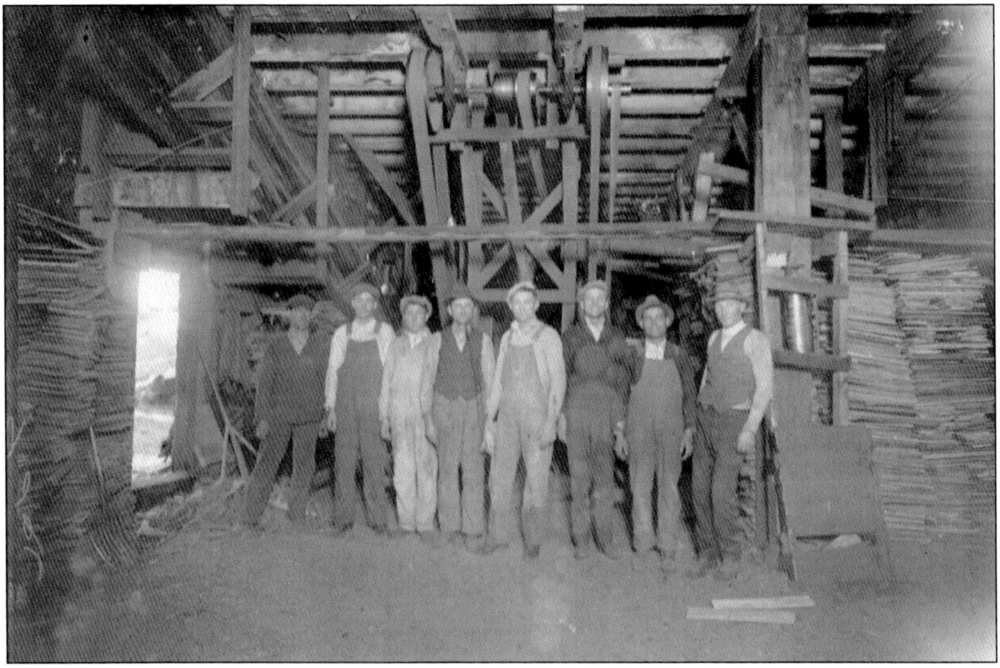

Shown in this photograph, taken about 1918, are the workers at the Wilmington Cooperage Company, located at the foot of Wright Street. Hundreds of coopers were employed to make the thousands and thousands of barrels needed for the naval stores business. Clynn Simmons Korney Jr. is the cooper at the far left. Second from right is his cousin Jackson Carney. (Amy Korney Hotz.)

As early as 1819, the US Custom House was on the east side of Water Street, between Market and Princess Streets. After the building burned in 1843, it was replaced by a handsome three-story, pedimented Greek Revival structure, designed by architect John Norris of New York. At the time this photograph was taken, the structure was 60 years old.

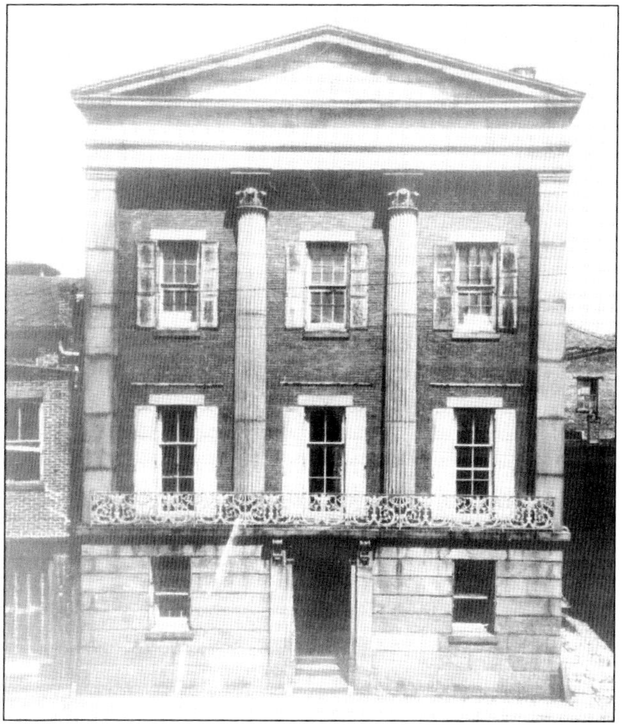

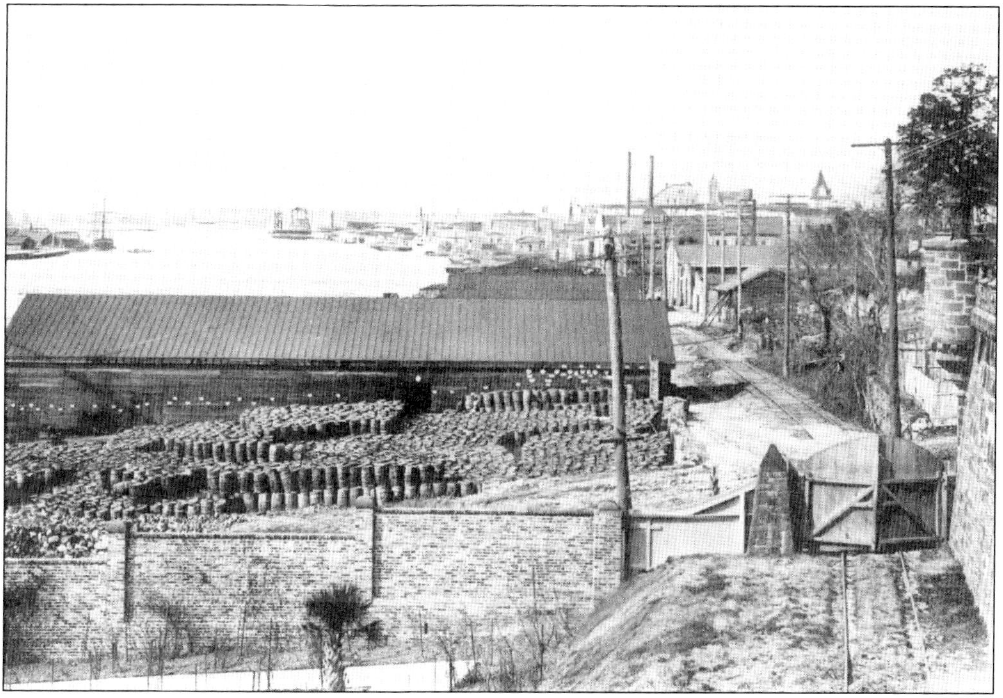

Pictured in this c. 1905 postcard is a view of Water Street, looking north from Nun Street. The ballast stone and brick walls surrounded the home of James Sprunt, a cotton broker. The turpentine barrels and warehouses along the river occupied the same location as modern-day Chandler's Wharf.

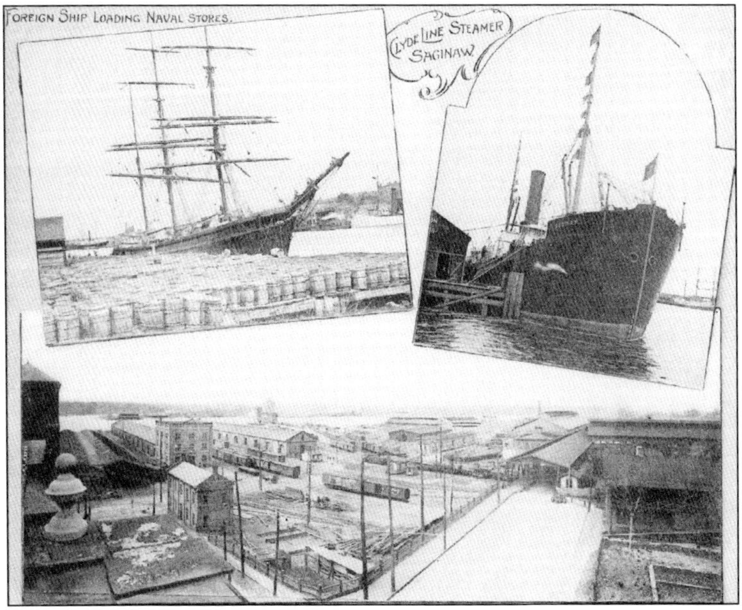

This collage was taken from the 1902 booklet *Souvenir of Wilmington*. All three photographs show port activity. Ships provided trade and transportation, while the railroad also offered both. In the lower image of the montage, the Atlantic Coast Line Railroad passenger station is seen at right. A railroad had been headquartered in Wilmington since 1840.

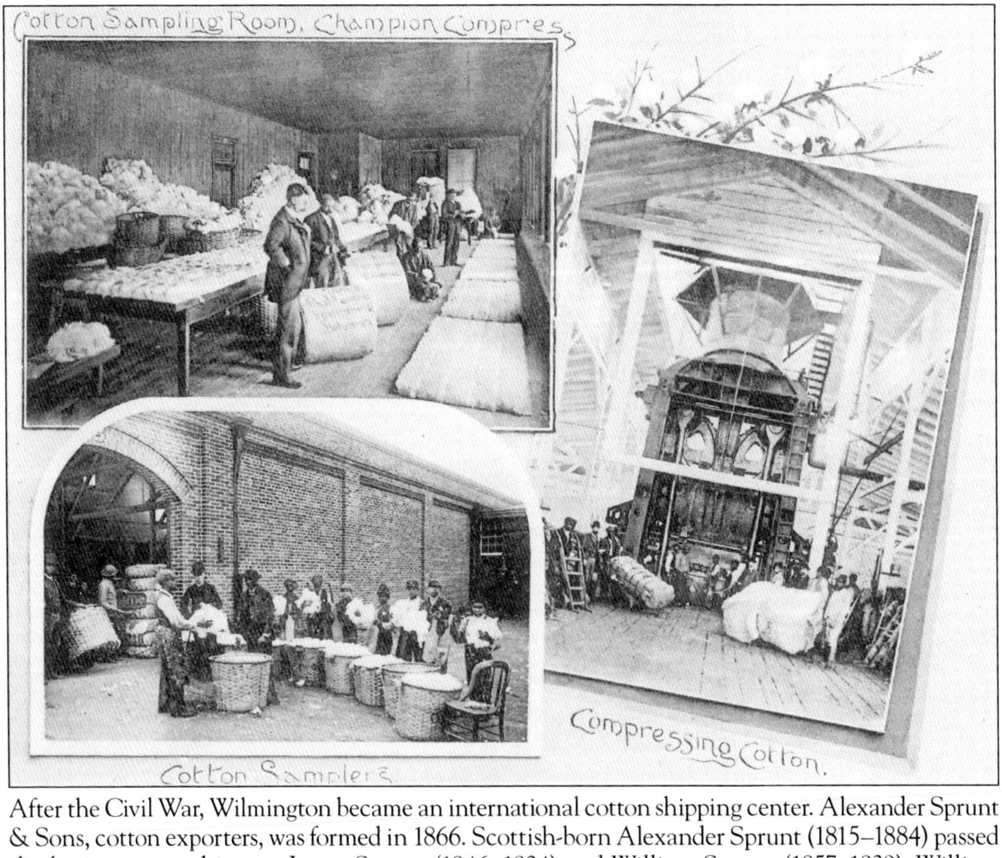

After the Civil War, Wilmington became an international cotton shipping center. Alexander Sprunt & Sons, cotton exporters, was formed in 1866. Scottish-born Alexander Sprunt (1815–1884) passed the business on to his sons James Sprunt (1846–1924) and William Sprunt (1857–1939). William Sprunt was responsible for purchasing the cotton, and James Sprunt handled the overseas sales.

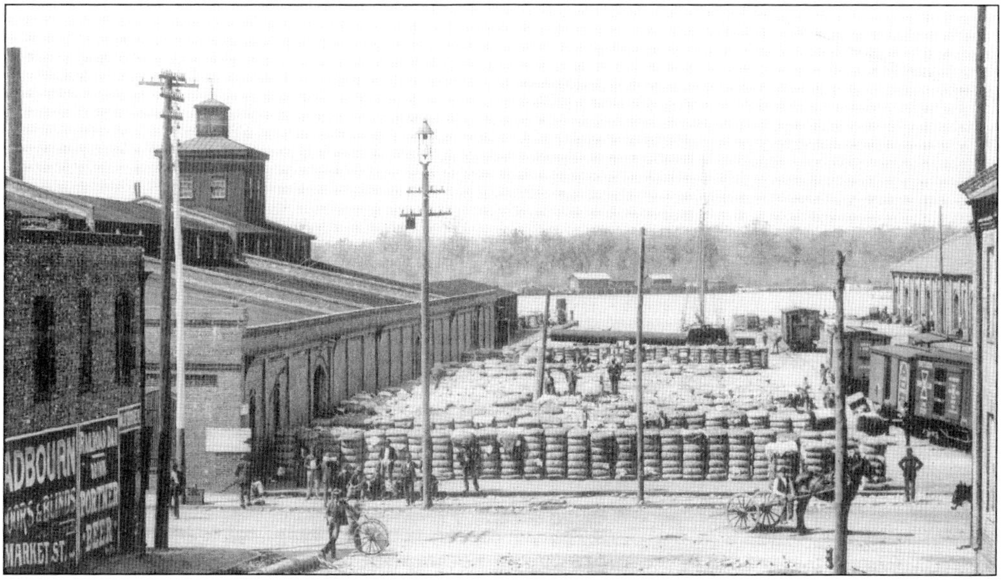

Alexander Sprunt & Sons prospered by getting rid of the middleman. They shipped straight from farms all over the South to European import houses. This 1895 photograph shows their waterfront warehouses, located at Red Cross and Water Streets. The company also had warehouses in Liverpool, Bremen, Le Havre, Barcelona, and Rotterdam.

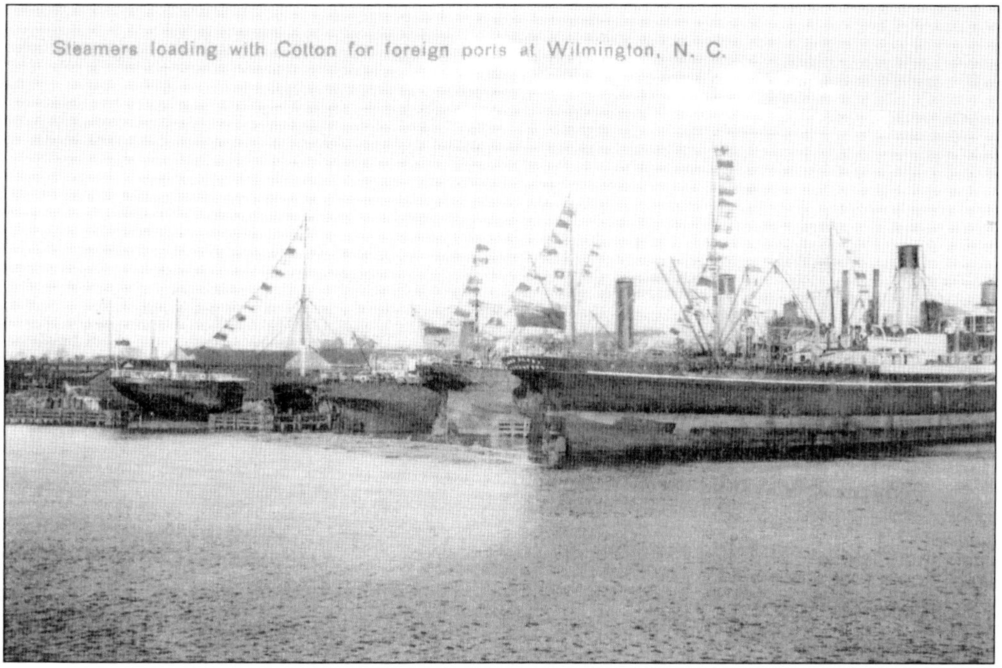

At the time of this 1912 postcard, Alexander Sprunt & Sons exported 500,000 bales of cotton annually. Three ships could load simultaneously at the docks of the Champion Compress & Warehouse Co. The compress, warehouses, and docks were conveniently located at the terminus of the Atlantic Coast Line Railroad, providing a link to cotton markets all over the South.

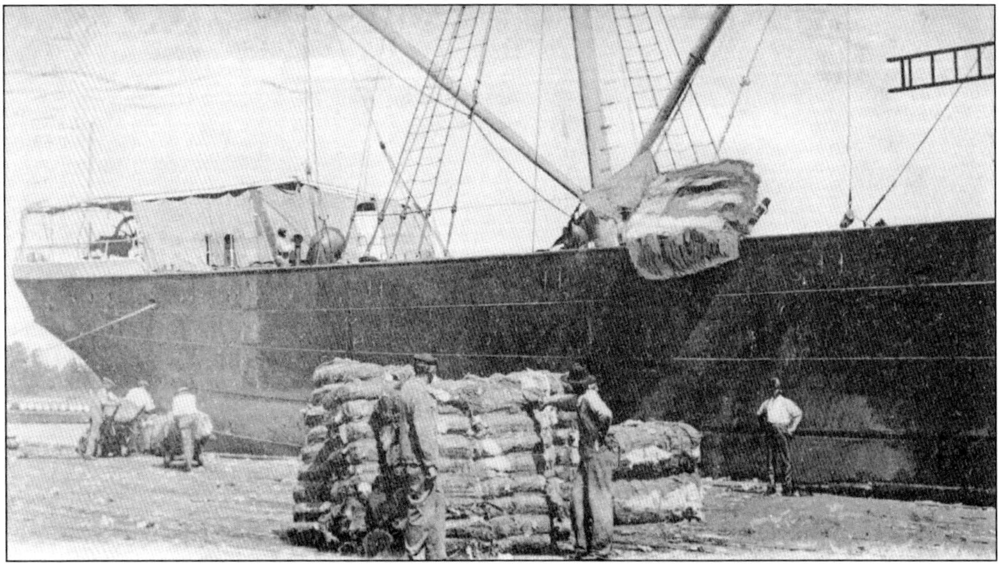

Aside from the railroad, Alexander Sprunt & Sons was the largest employer in Wilmington. In the 1880s, they did $2 million worth of business. Their fortunes continued to climb until the start of World War I, when shipments to Europe were halted. Hundreds of stevedores loaded the compressed cotton on board freighters that called from all over Europe. In this 1912 postcard, they are loading an English vessel.

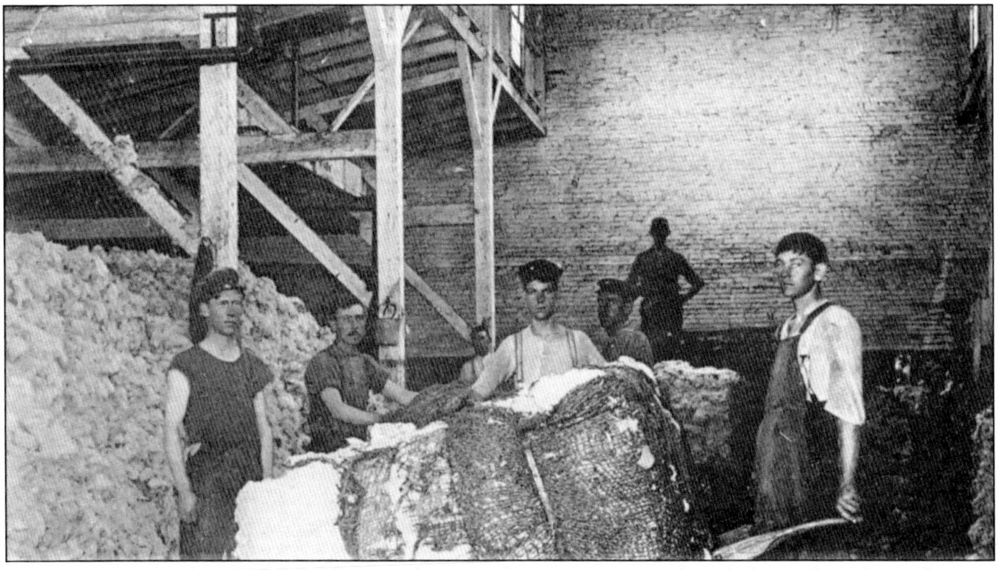

Loose cotton was brought into the warehouse, where it was sorted and cleaned in the pickery. It was then sent to the compress. However, if a quality-control employee found damaged cotton, it was cleaned and re-baled. It was hot work in the humid Wilmington summer months.

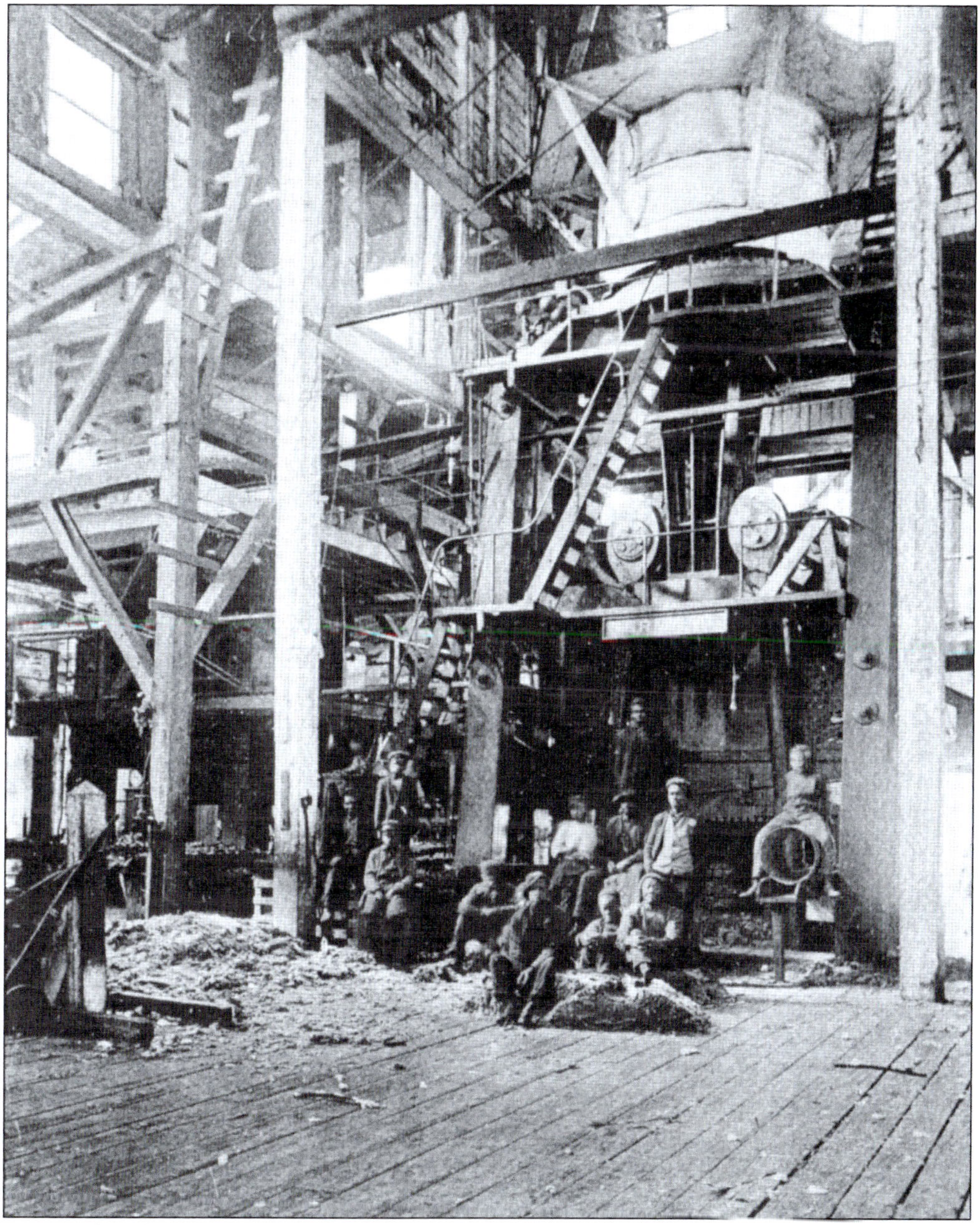

Eventually, Alexander Sprunt & Sons operated five compresses, which produced 5,000 bales of cotton per day. Pressing cotton reduced shipping costs by significantly reducing the size of a bale. The compress exerted a pressure of 1,800 tons, with a 90-inch cylinder and a compressing capacity of 800 bales of cotton in 10 hours. This 1912 postcard shows African American workers of all ages posing for the photographer in the compress room. Champion Compress employees worked long hours and, often, double shifts. The majority of them lived close by and could walk to and from work. The work was dangerous, but there are few accounts of workplace accidents. Once the cotton had been compressed, it was moved to warehouses, where it was stored until stevedores loaded it onto outgoing European freighters. Along the cotton wharf, it was common to hear Cockney, Norwegian, German, French, and Spanish. (Elaine Henson.)

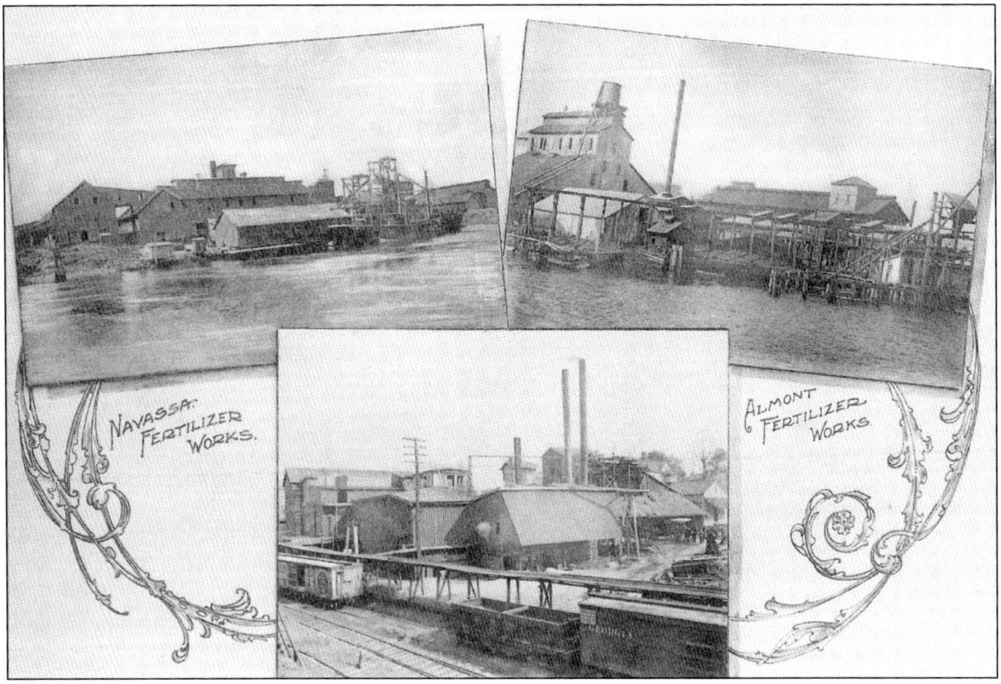

While cotton exports were waning, fertilizer became the mainstay of Wilmington shipping. The industry began after the Civil War, when companies began importing guano, or seabird droppings, that was procured from island rookeries and South America. Ships entered the port with guano and left with lumber, cotton, and naval stores. Inland farmers needed the fertilizer, and the railroad provided the means to get the commodity to market.

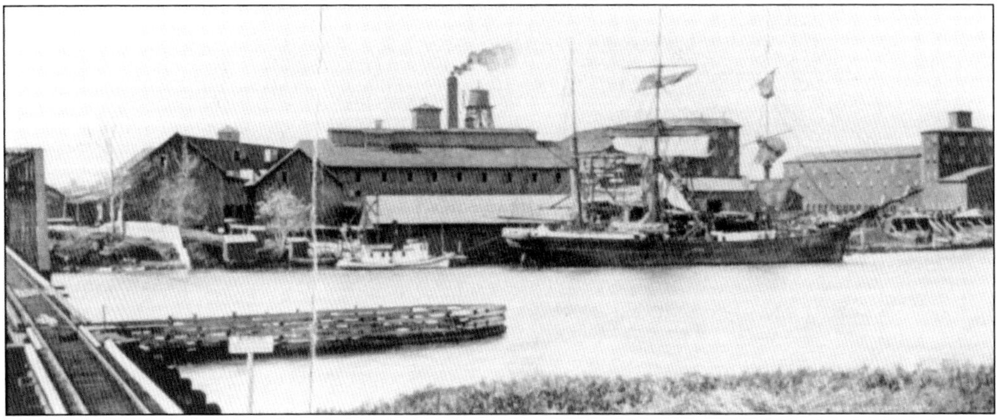

In 1910, there were 11 fertilizer factories operating in the Wilmington harbor. One of the largest was the Navassa Guano Factory, pictured here. The noisome factory was constructed in 1869 on the west side of the Cape Fear River, where it intersects with the Brunswick River. The term *guano* became synonymous with any manure, which could also include nitrate of soda, fish, potash, blood, bone, phosphate rock, and cottonseed.

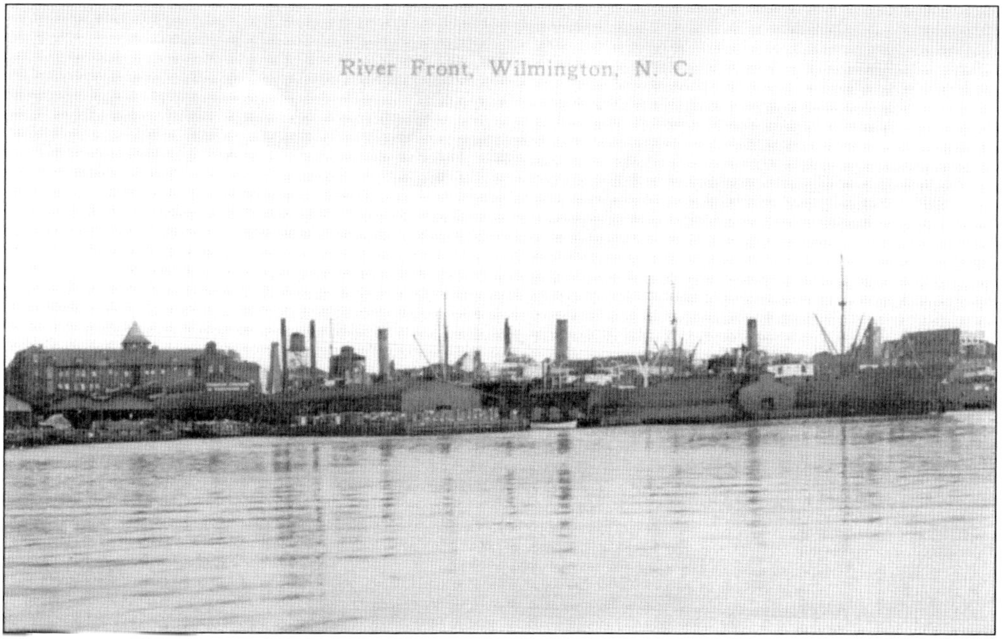

This postcard shows the Champion Compress & Warehouse Co. dock in 1911. The three-story brick building at left housed the general offices of the Atlantic Coast Line Railroad, located on the southwest corner of Front and Red Cross Streets. The railroad employed hundreds of workers, and the town grew exponentially around it.

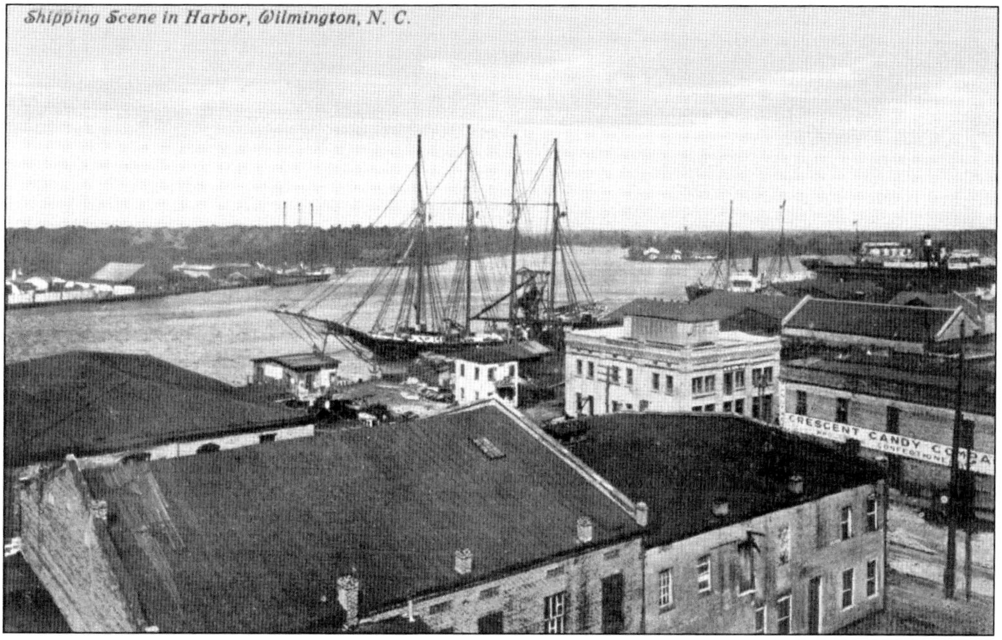

A four-masted schooner is docked at the foot of Grace Street in this bird's-eye view from 1911. The two-story building in the center was the fireboat station. Wilmington suffered devastating fires that started on the wharves and spread throughout the town. For this reason, the Wilmington Fire Department was one of the first in the country to train firefighters in the operation of these water-spraying boats.

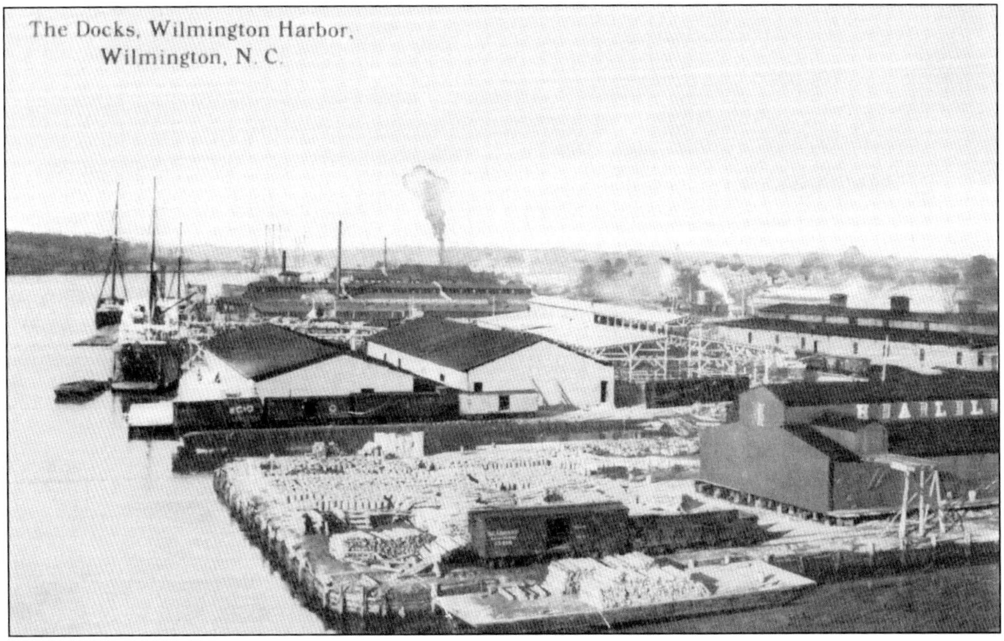

Boxcars are lined up at the Seaboard Air Line Docks in 1912. Tracks were laid right up to the riverfront for easy loading and unloading at the large warehouses, the far right of which belonged to Hall and Pearsall, wholesale grocers. At the time of this photograph, the building had large bins where grocery staples were stored until they were bagged for the market.

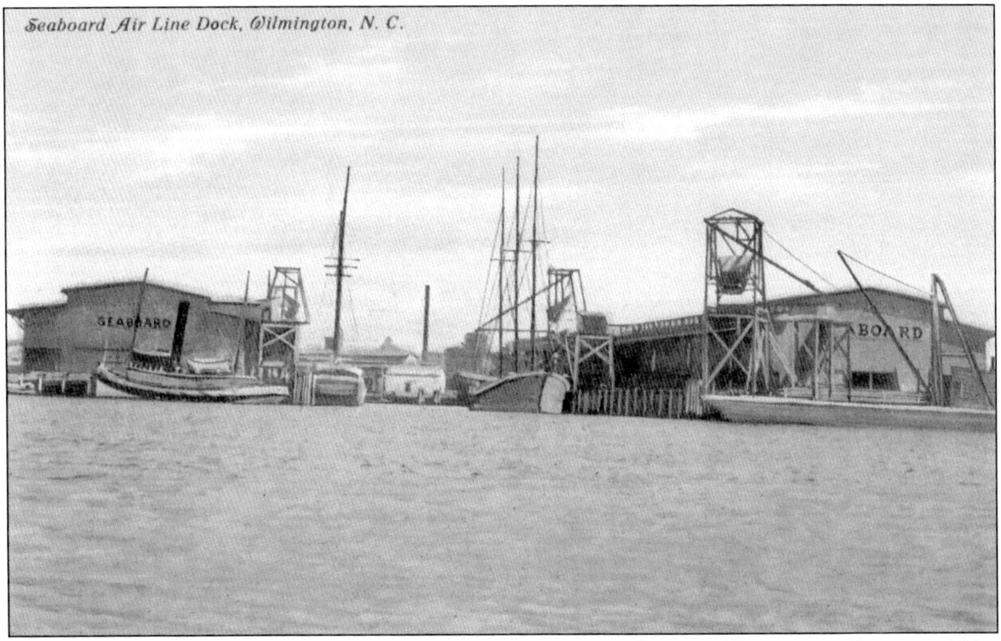

Ships would unload directly into the Seaboard Air Line warehouses. The commodities could be stored there if need be, but they often went through the building, directly to the boxcar loading site. Postcards like this one, dated 1918, were popular. Some of the senders worked for the railroad or in one of the warehouses.

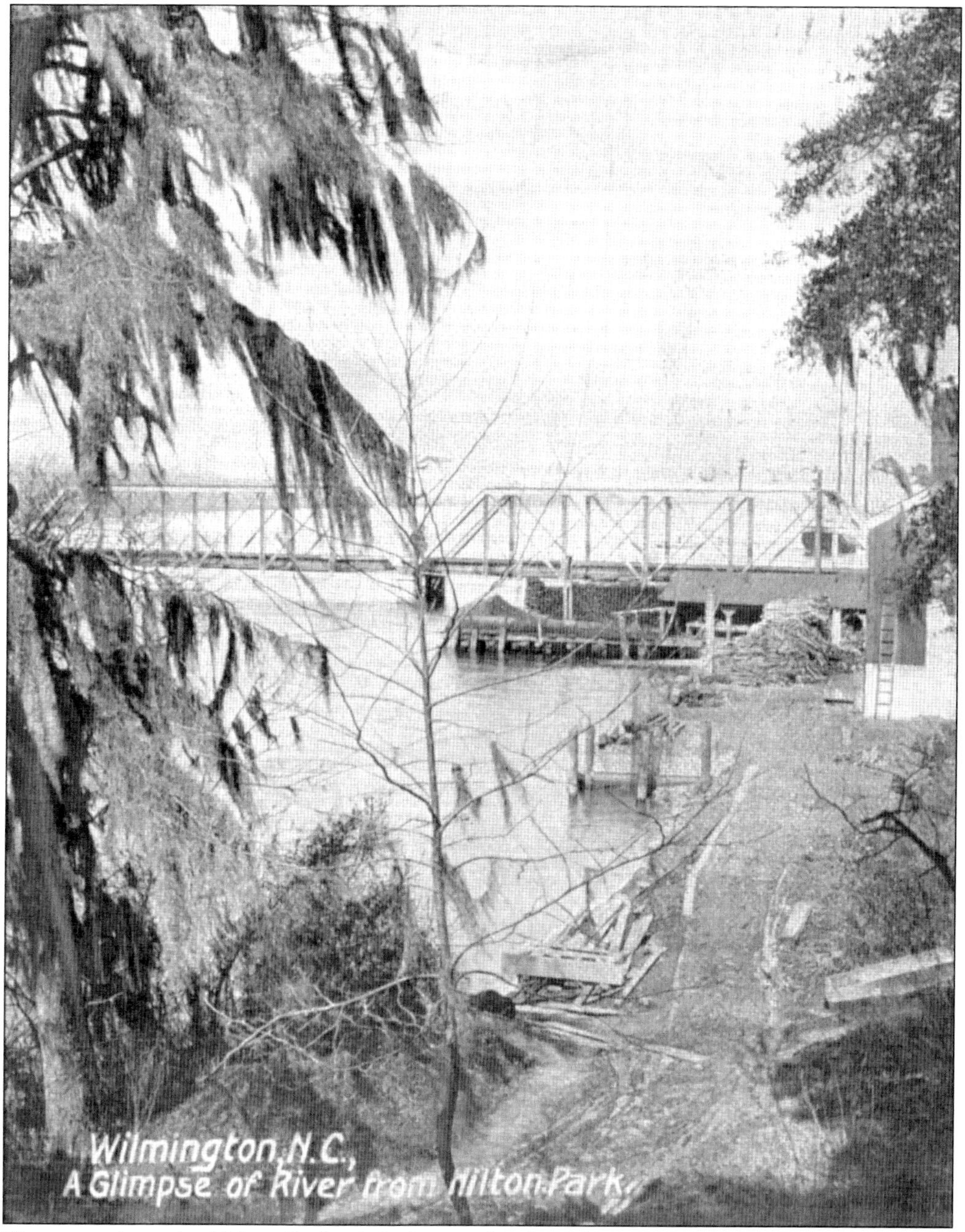

The area where the Hilton Bridge left the east bank of the Cape Fear River was named for a plantation house that once stood there. Revolutionary statesman Cornelius Harnett built it in 1750. In 1784, it was sold to John Hill, who named it Hilton. Hill was a lawyer, legislator, congressman, and planter, and was involved in the founding of the University of North Carolina. The house was torn down in 1892, and the area became Hilton Park, a popular venue for political rallies, picnics, and other social occasions. It was also the first place that Wilmingtonians played organized football, baseball, and golf. Families often arrived by boat and spent the day in the park, where enormous live oaks draped in Spanish moss were abundant. It was a popular place to see and be seen. This postcard view is dated 1908. In modern times, the Sweeney Water Plant was built there.

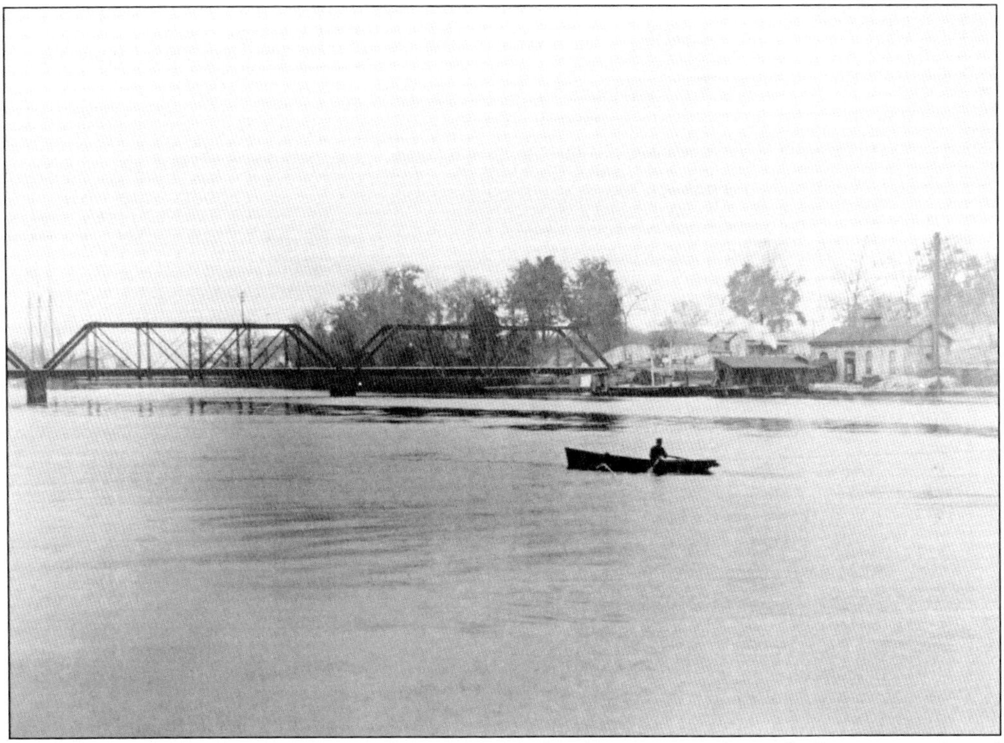

The Hilton Bridge, with a Bollman truss, was completed in 1867. In the early days, it was shared by two railroads; therefore, it had a standard gauge for the Wilmington, Charlotte & Rutherford Railroad and a five-foot gauge for the Wilmington & Manchester Railroad. In the 1895 photograph above, a rowboat quietly approaches the bridge. On the right side of the photograph, the bridge tender's building is visible. Beside it is a small dock where locals could tie up their craft. The image below shows a train noisily passing over the bridge in 1915. After being struck by river-going vessels, the bridge was repaired and rebuilt several times. The latest bridge at Hilton was built in 1971. (Both, Robert M. Fales Collection, NHPCL.)

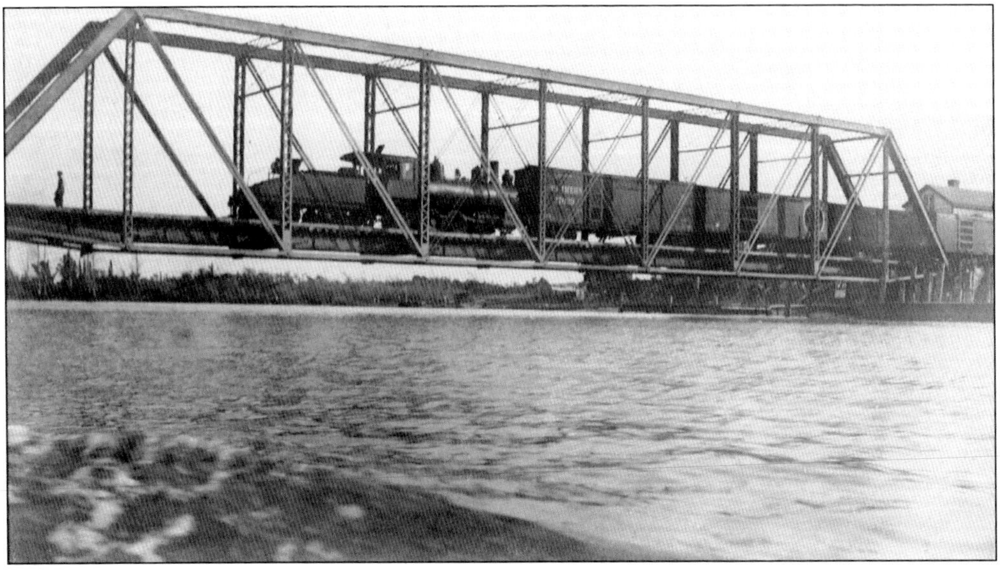

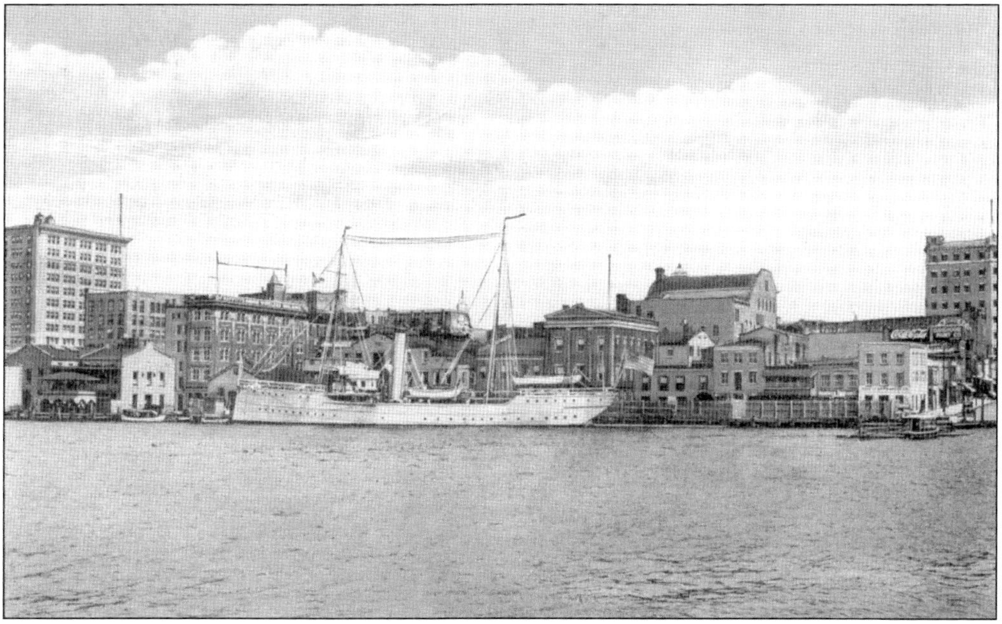

Wilmington's long association with the US Coast Guard began in 1792, when the *Diligence* sailed into the harbor. She was one of the 10 original cutters built for the nation's new US Revenue Cutter Service. The USRC *Seminole* can be seen docked at the government wharf in the postcard above, dated 1911. She was the 11th cutter to be stationed in Wilmington. The postcard below shows her mid-stream, sailing downriver. The *Seminole* was in service in Wilmington from 1904 to 1923. Congress established the modern US Coast Guard by uniting the US Revenue Cutter Service and the US Lifesaving Service in 1915.

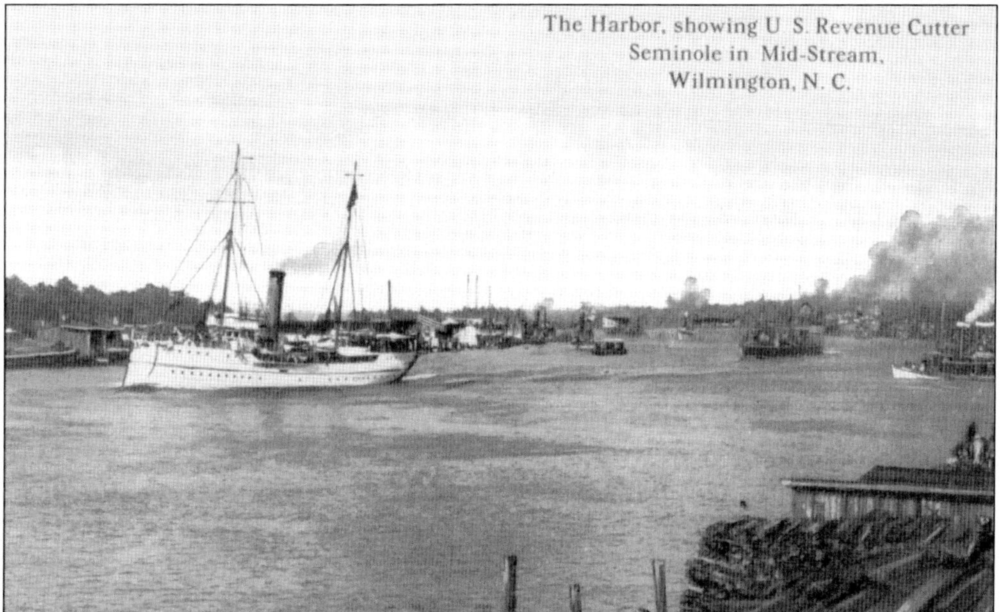

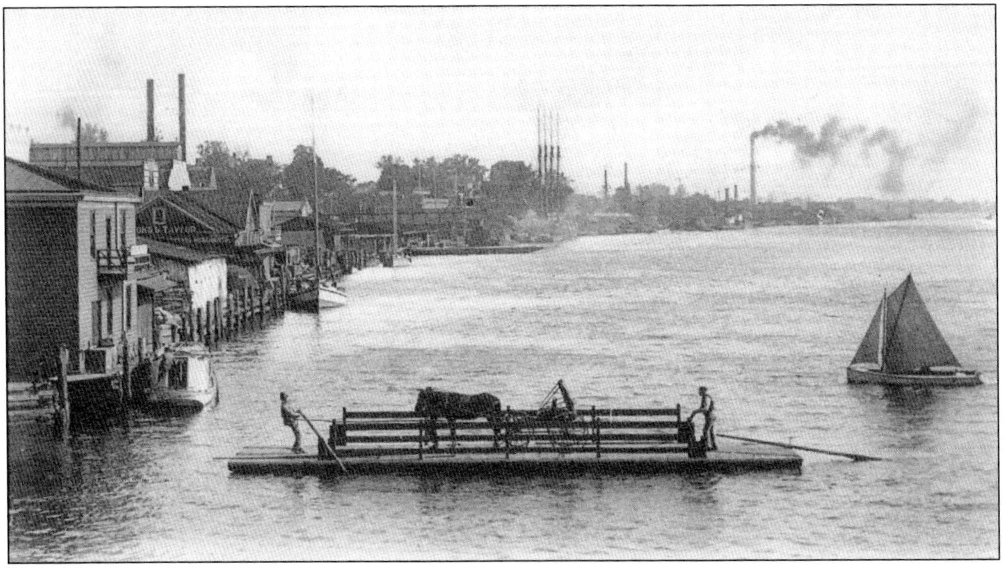

For 175 years, ferries crossed the Cape Fear River, from the foot of Market Street to the Brunswick County side of the river. Early ferries were flatboats, towed by rowboats. There was a bar at the head of the flatboat to keep the horses from tumbling into the river, and another bar to keep the wagon or coach on board. The postcard above, looking south on Water Street, shows a flatboat ferry approaching the landing at the foot of Market Street in 1905. The drawing below, made in 1896, shows a flatboat ferry heading in the opposite direction, toward the landing on Eagles Island. At the time, the cost was 3¢ per wheel for a vehicle and 3¢ per head for man or animal. (Both, Robert M. Fales Collection, NHPCL.)

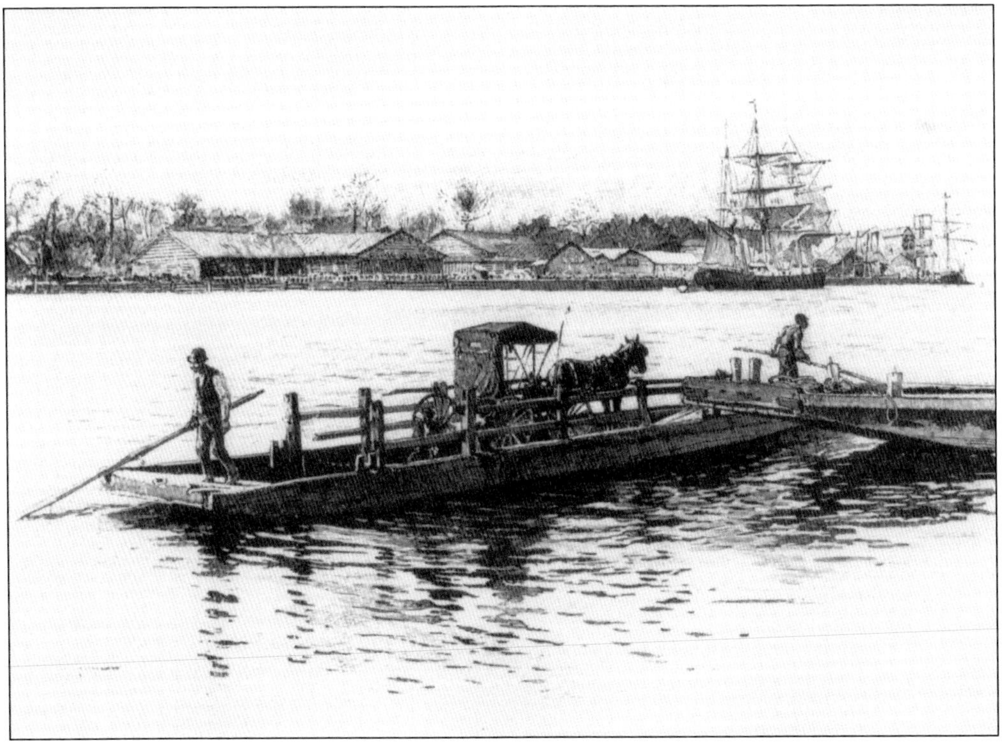

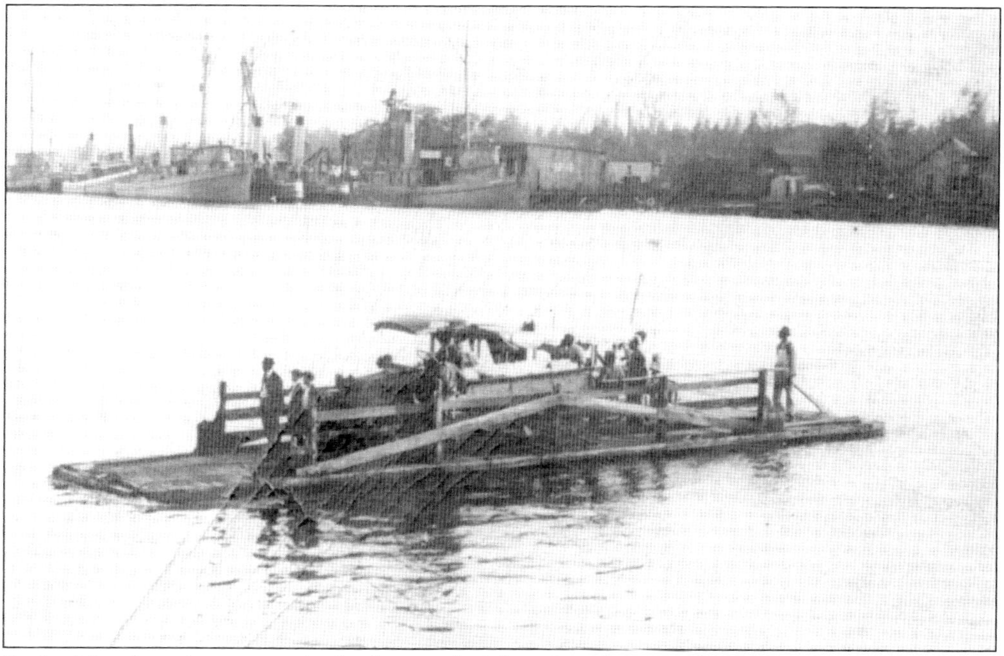

Eagles Island can be seen in the background of this 1912 photograph of a ferry crossing the river. Named for the Eagles family, the "island" is actually a grouping of large, swampy landmasses located between the Cape Fear and Brunswick Rivers, opposite Wilmington. Over time, several shipyards, boatyards, and marine railways were developed on the island, which is seven miles long and two miles wide. (Louis T. Moore Collection, NHCPL.)

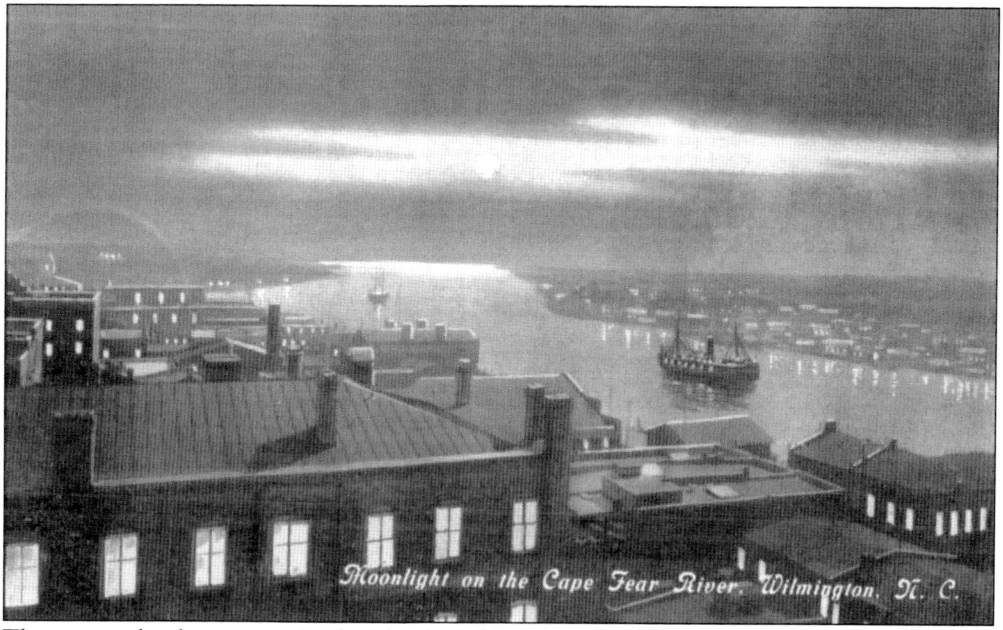

The intense development on Eagles Island can be seen in this 1911 postcard. A 1946 fire destroyed many of the wharves and businesses. The last boatyard closed in the 1960s. Today, the Eagles Island Coalition, a multiagency partnership between municipal and nongovernmental organizations, protects the natural habitat, historic sites, and cultural artifacts that remain on the island.

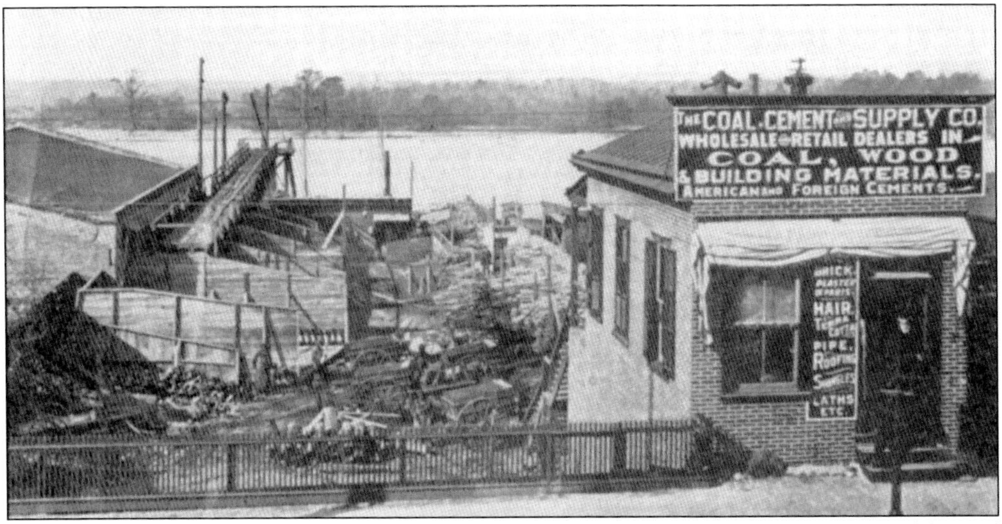

In 1902, the Coal, Cement and Supply Co. was located at 214 South Front Street. They delivered building supplies and coal around town. Their drays can be seen at the Front Street side of the business. On the left side of the photograph is a shoot that went directly from the waterfront to their storage bins.

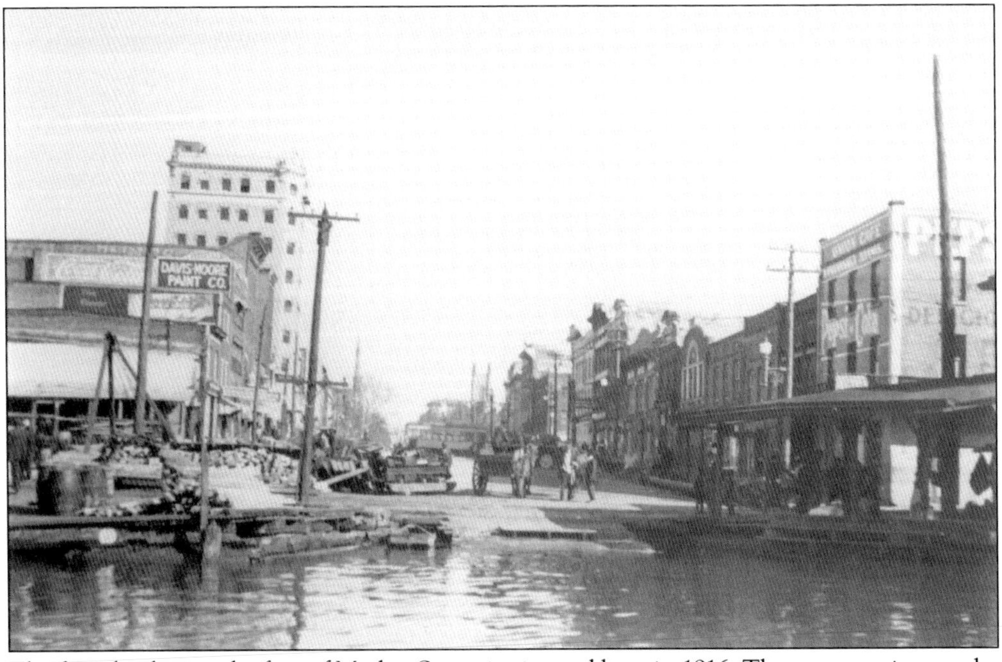

The ferry landing at the foot of Market Street is pictured here in 1916. The construction on the left side of the photograph is related to the building of the new customhouse. Tickets for the ferry were purchased at the building at right, on the waterfront. (Bill Creasy.)

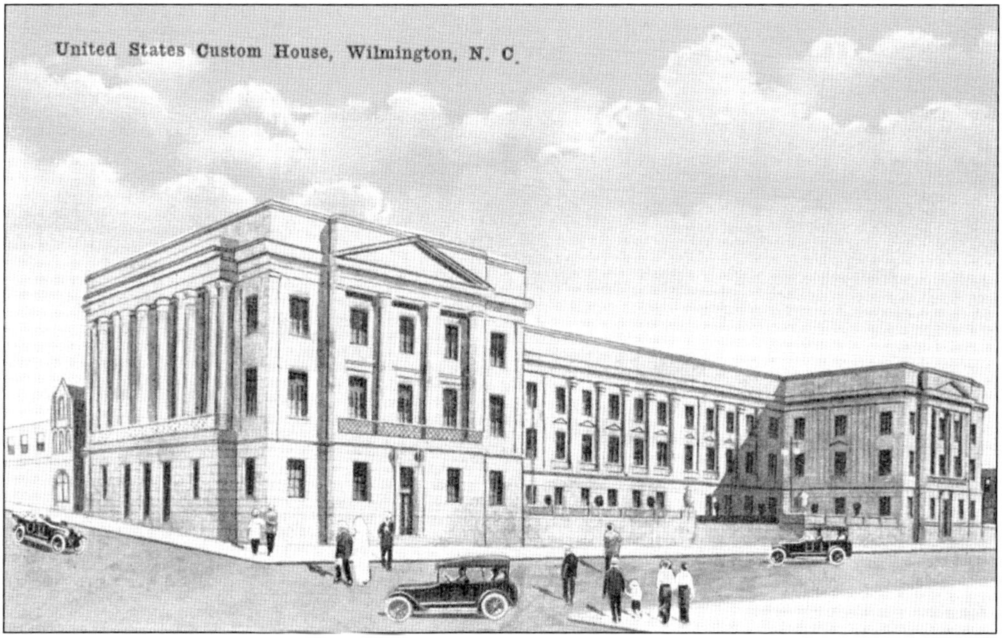

The port of Wilmington had outgrown the 1844 US Custom House by the second decade of the 20th century. James A. Wetmore, supervising architect of the US Treasury, designed this new classical Beaux Arts building, which was constructed from 1916 to 1918. The wings of the three-story building retain the temple-form design of the old customhouse, designed by John Norris. In 1965, the US Customs Appraisers moved to a building at the North Carolina State Port. The downtown building continues to house federal offices and courtrooms, but the exciting hubbub that surrounded the old customhouses is a thing of the past. Gone are the days when contraband or unusual cargo could produce crowds of onlookers at a moment's notice.

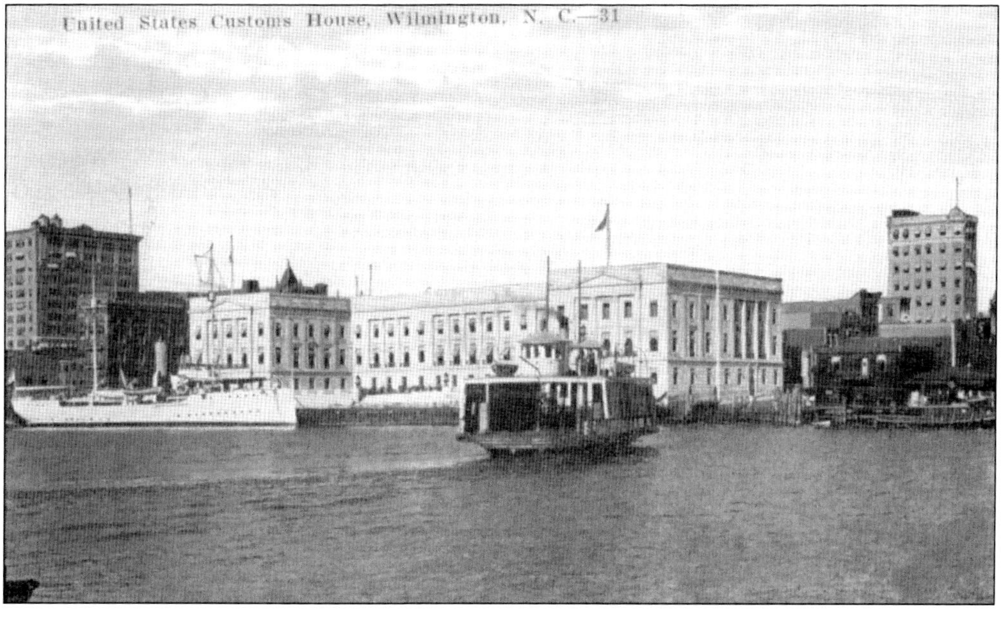

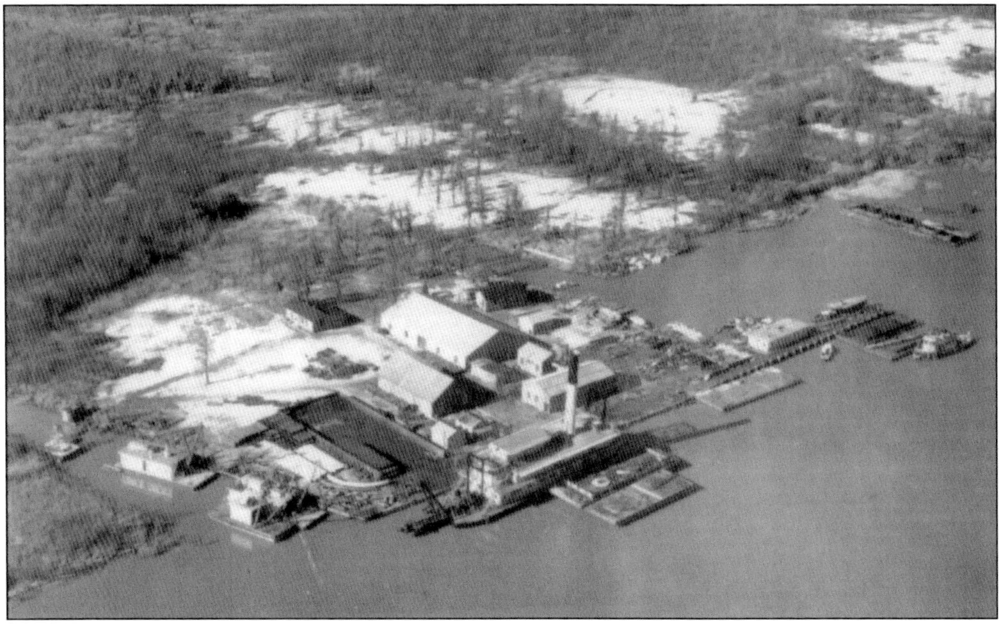

The US Corps of Engineers' long history with the Wilmington harbor began in the 1820s. During peacetime, the corps has surveyed and dredged the river numerous times. This aerial photograph titled *US Engineers Base* was taken about 1920. Dredges surround the base headquarters, the largest of which was the *Henry Bacon*, in the front. (Jim Pleasants Collection, NHCPL.)

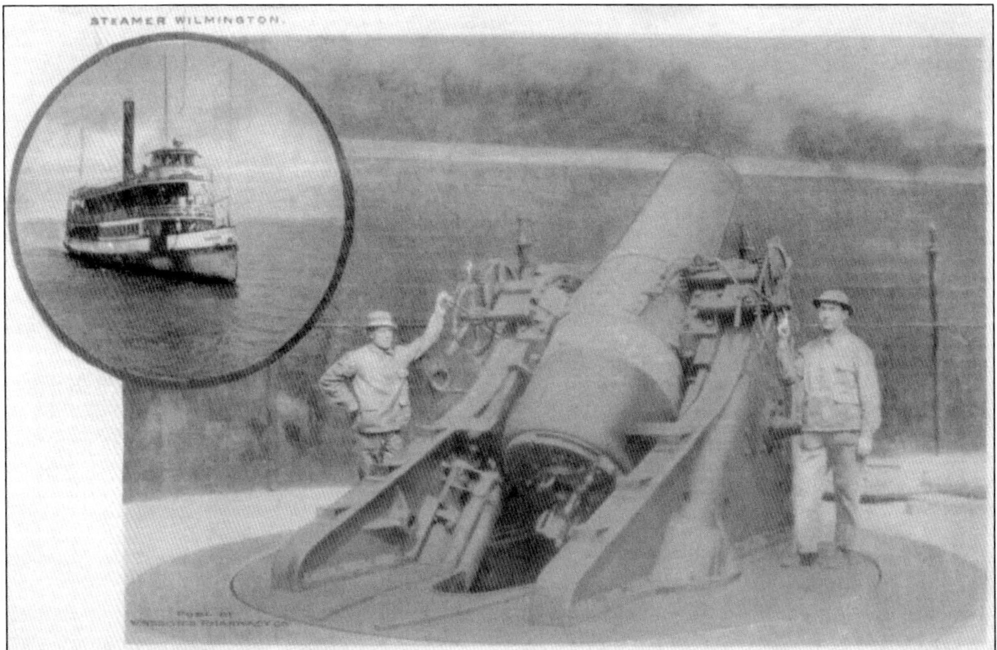

This World War I postcard shows soldiers posing with artillery at Fort Caswell, located at the mouth of the Cape Fear River. The inset shows the steamer *Wilmington*, which contracted with the government to ferry soldiers from Southport to the Wilmington. A message written on the back of the postcard reads, "We had a swell time in Wilmington."

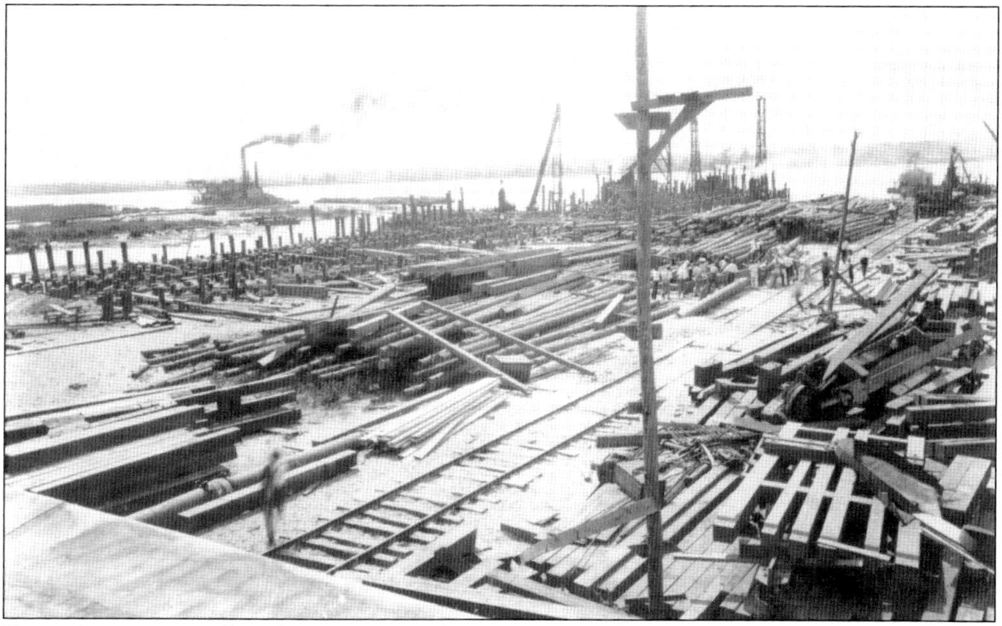

From 1918 to 1920, the Liberty Shipbuilding Company was located at the foot of Greenfield Street, where they built concrete ships for the war effort. This new type of vessel required 300 tons of concrete, poured in three sections: the bottom, the sides, and the decks. Each section had to dry before the next section could be poured. The ship had to "set" for a month before launching. The photograph above shows the Liberty Shipyard's third way during construction; the company had four ways in total. Dredges and steam shovels were used to level the property. Construction of the interior of the *Cape Fear*'s hull can be seen in the photograph below. (Both, Bill Reaves Collection, NHCPL.)

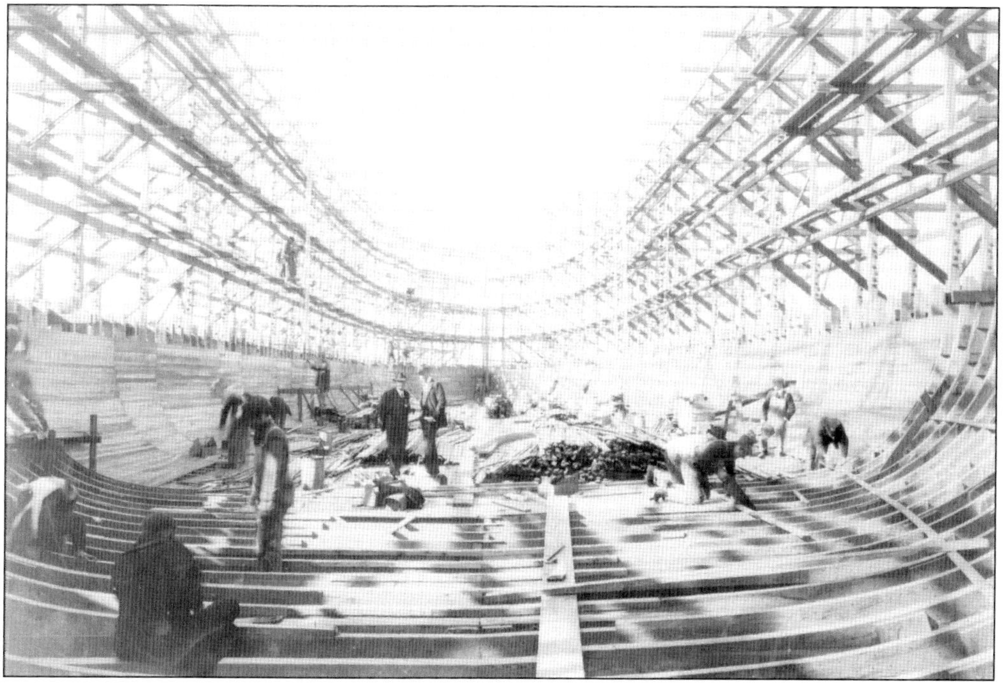

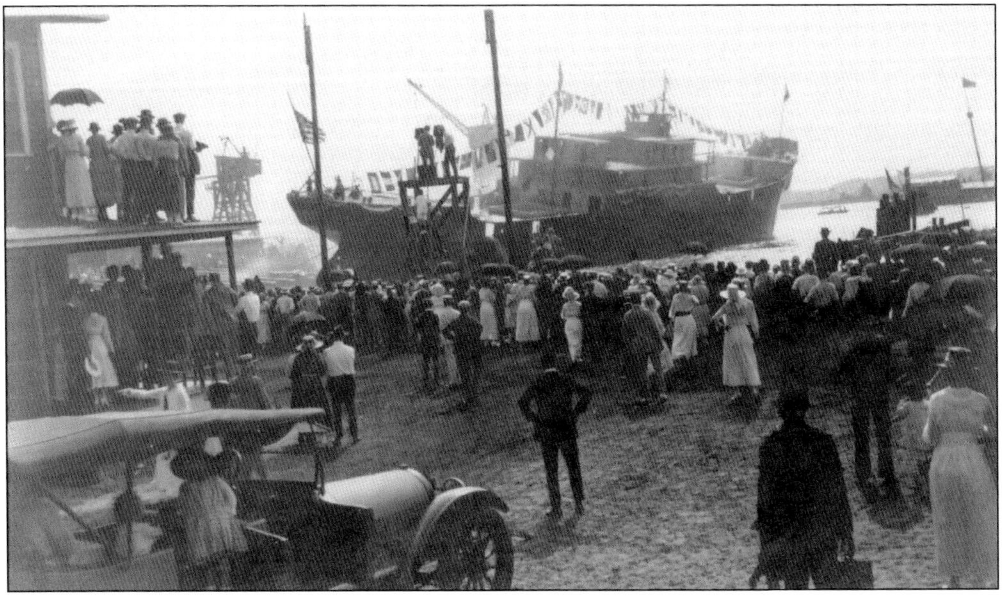

In July 1918, spectators dressed up for the launching of the *Cape Fear* at the Liberty Shipyard. As the vessel slid sideways into the Cape Fear River, it splashed many of the onlookers. It was the first concrete ship built in North Carolina, and the third in the United States. Its length was 266.5 feet, its breath of beam was 46 feet, and the depth of its hold was 24 feet. When a second concrete vessel was launched a few months later, the shipyard had fulfilled its contract with the US Shipping Board. As a result of the end of World War I, and with no more contracts in sight, the Liberty Shipyard closed.

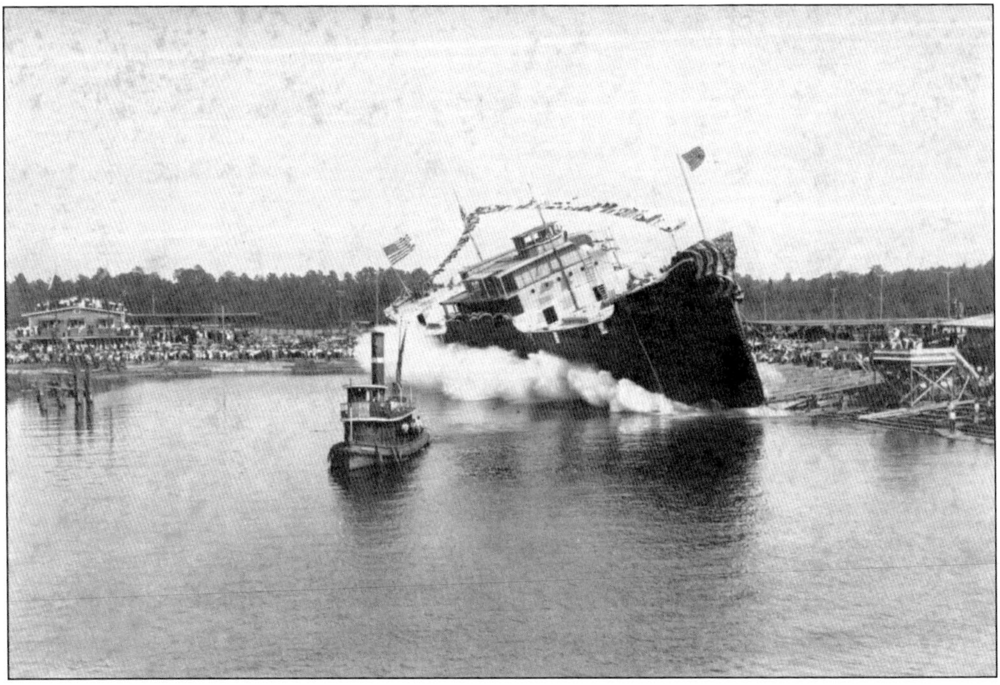

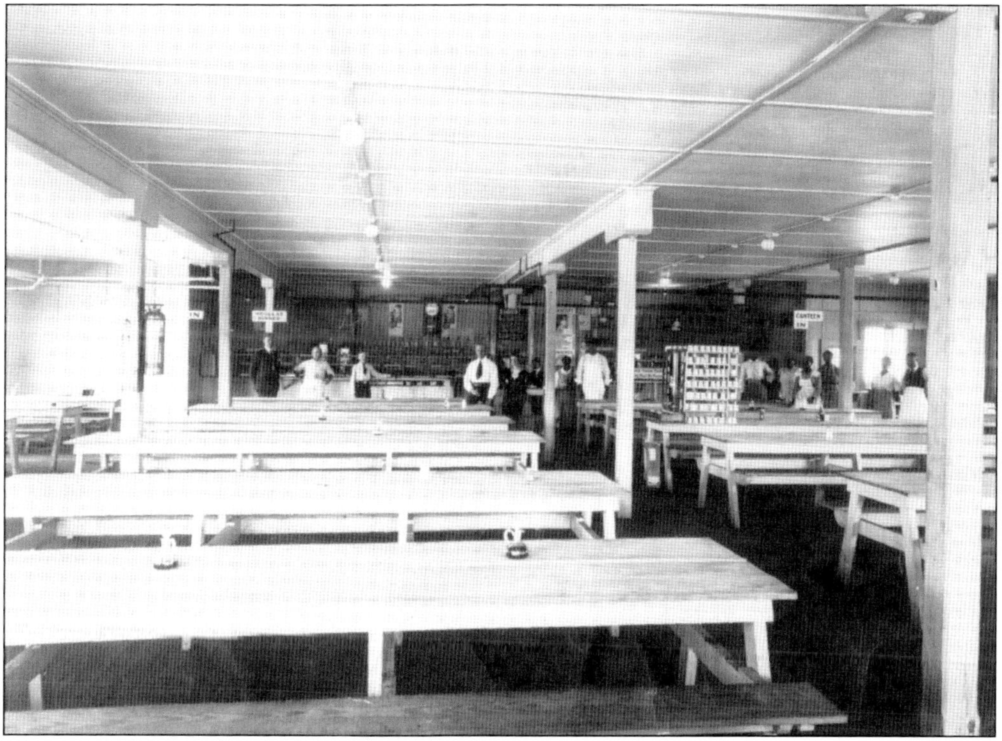

The Liberty Shipyard provided employment for many Wilmingtonians. Seen here in the shipyard commissary, Marion Reaves is the young boy wearing the shirt and tie, third from left. For working the lunch shift, he was paid 50¢ and received a hot meal. (Bill Reaves Collection, NHCPL.)

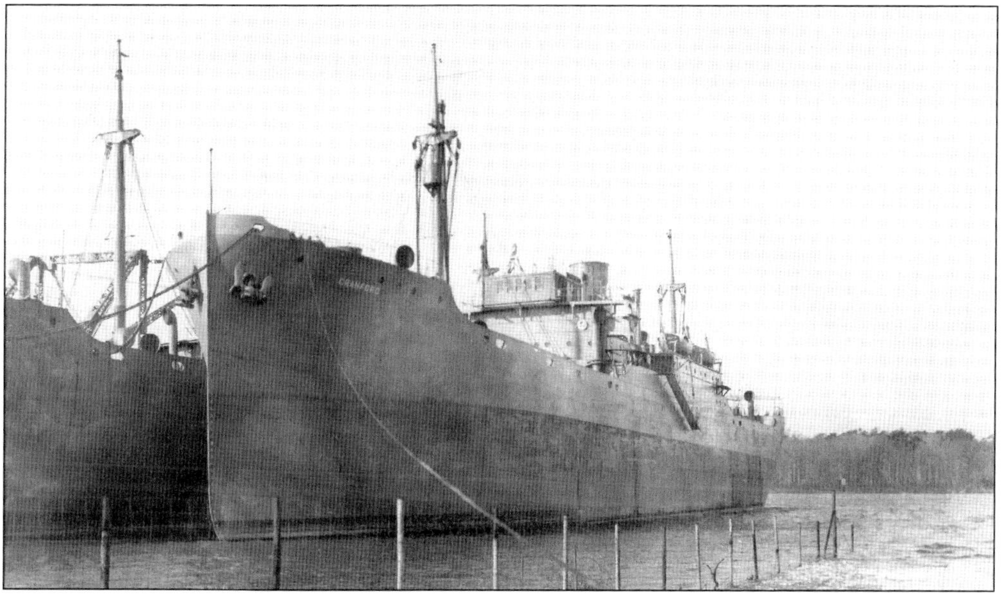

From 1917 to 1921, the Carolina Shipbuilding Company occupied a 100-acre site on the riverfront at Sunset Park. In order to build 12 or more 9,600-ton steel cargo vessels, the shipyard employed so many workers that a hotel was erected in the yard to prevent a housing shortage. The *Cranford*, named for Cranford, New Jersey, was the first ship to be launched, on Labor Day 1919.

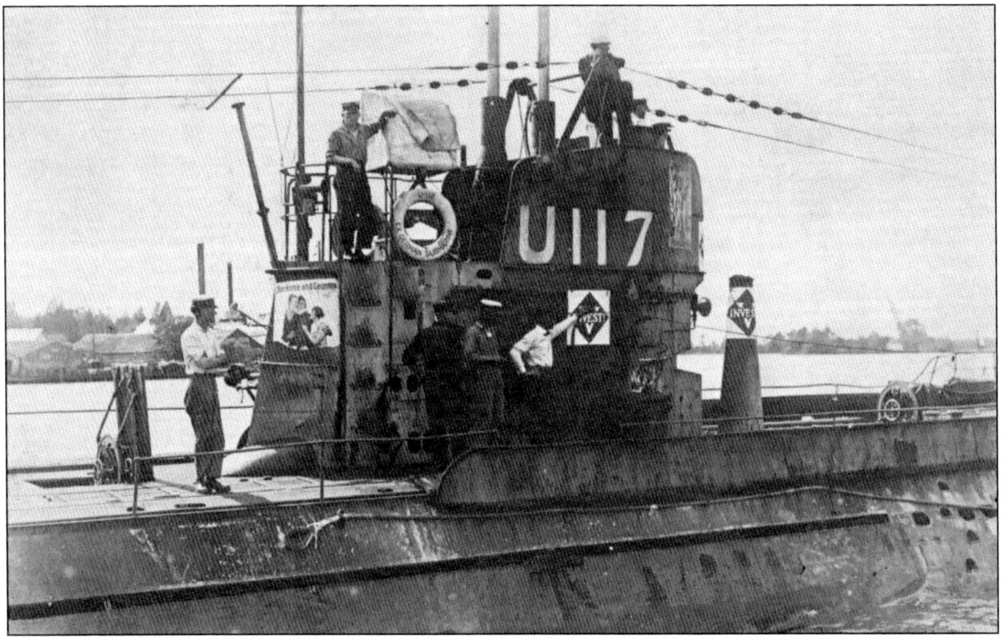

The German submarine U-117 was a long-range minelayer submarine built during World War I for the Imperial German Navy. In August 1918, the German U-boat laid mines off the North Carolina coast near Cape Hatteras. She torpedoed a British steamer and then returned to Germany, wreaking havoc on other Allied vessels along the way. After the armistice, she surrendered in England. She was then displayed as a war trophy at US ports. A curious crowd gathered at the waterfront on May 19, 1919, to view the German U-boat. One sign on the boat featured a veteran with his wife and child. It read, "For Home and Country." The lettering on the life preserver identified the boat as a "U-117 ex German submarine." Another notable sign was emblazoned with the phrase "Invest in Victory." (Both, Bill Reaves Collection, NHCPL.)

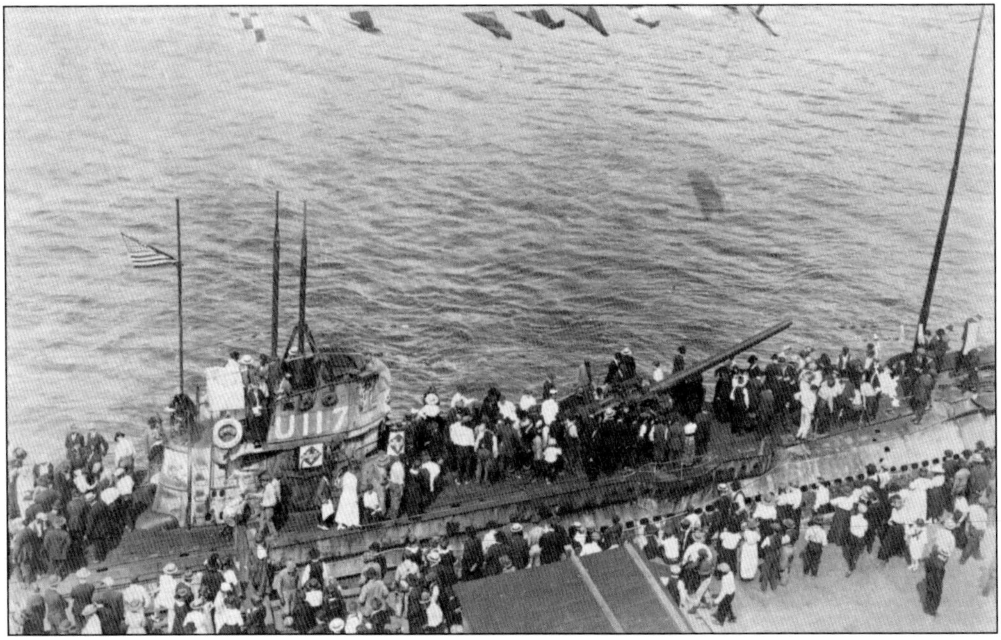

Three

1920–1945

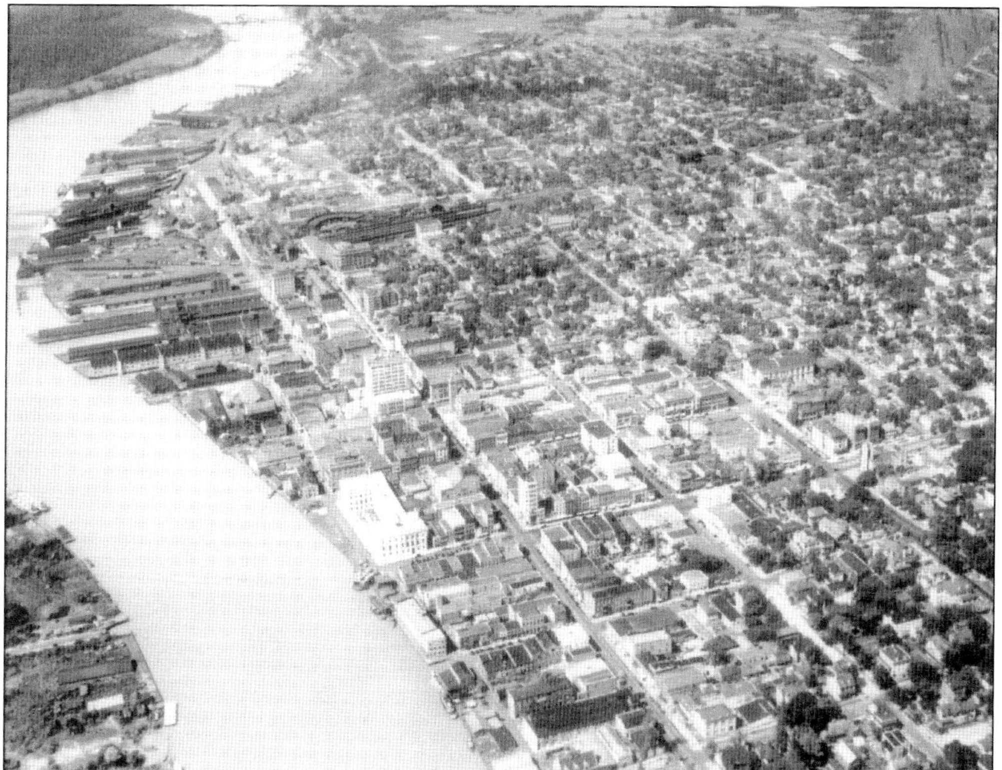

In 1920, the population of Wilmington was 33,372. It was a compact city where most residents walked or took the streetcar to work, much of which happened on the waterfront. This aerial photograph, taken in 1924, shows the waterfront from the foot of Orange Street to the Hilton Bridge. (Jim Pleasants Collection, NHCPL.)

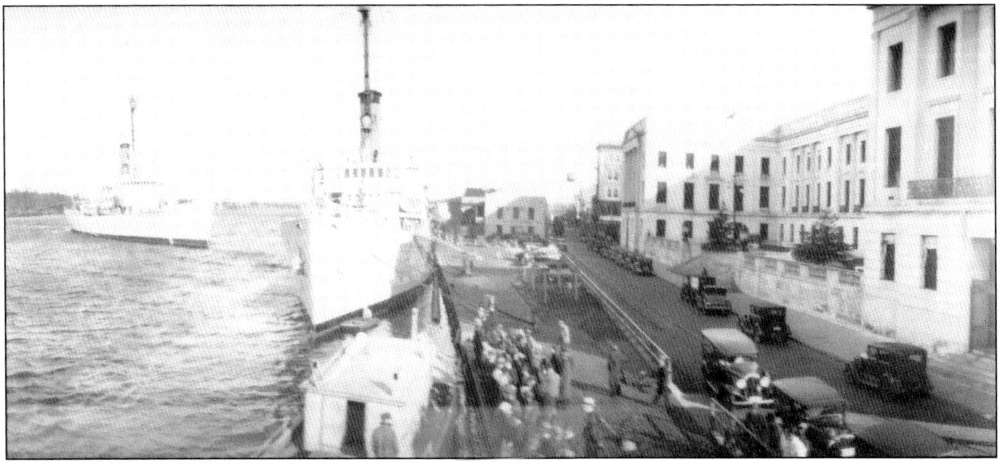

Louis T. Moore was the secretary of the Wilmington Chamber of Commerce during the Roaring Twenties, the Great Depression, and World War II. He tirelessly promoted all port city endeavors. Using his box panoramic camera, he photographed hundreds of area events and places. His work appeared in brochures, pamphlets, magazines, and other promotional materials. The collection is now available at the New Hanover County Public Library. In the photograph above, the USCGC *Modoc* and the USCGC *McAdoo* rendezvous at the government dock. The photograph below shows a tugboat pushing a barge into the northern part of the harbor. Both photographs were taken about 1928. (Both, Louis T. Moore Collection, NHCPL.)

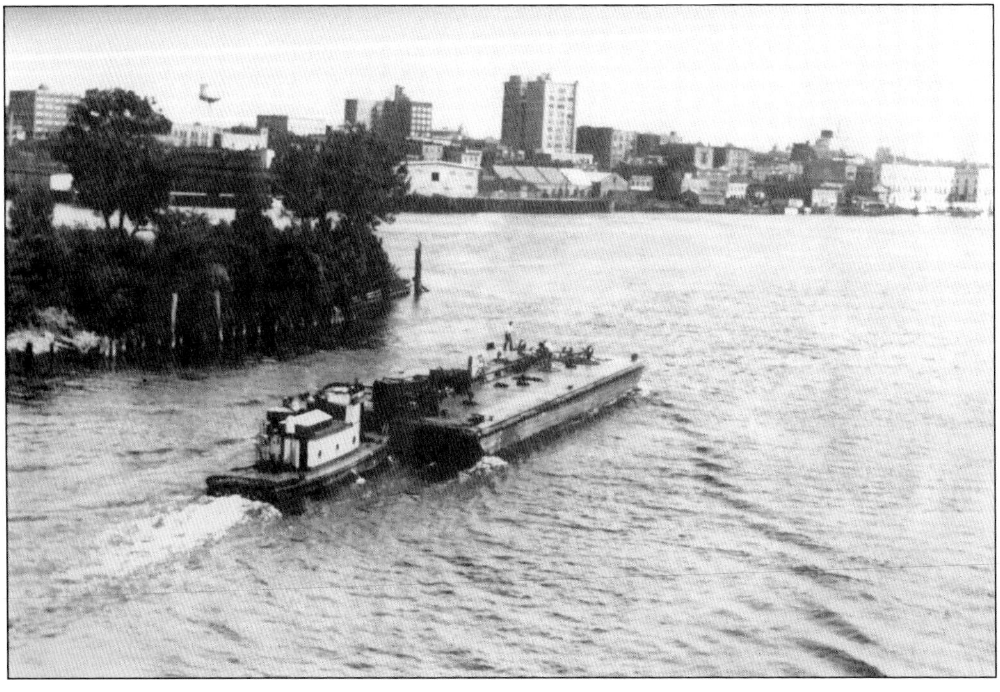

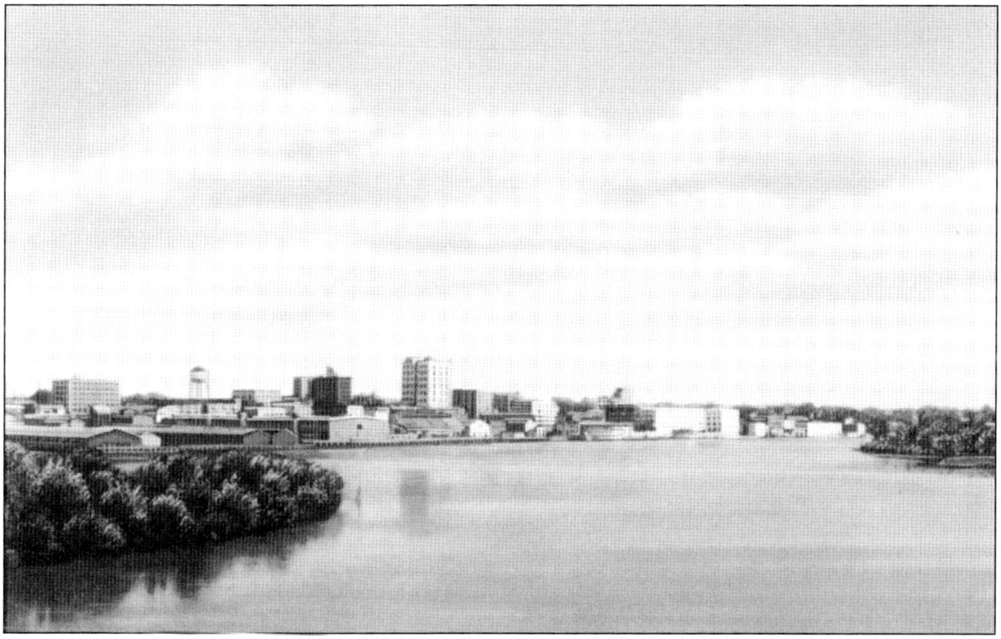

Many of the photographs that Louis T. Moore took for the Wilmington Chamber of Commerce were made into postcards. This linen postcard, dated 1932, shows a view of the harbor from the west branch of the Cape Fear River, with Point Peter on the left. Linen postcards were printed on paper with a high rag content and a rough finish.

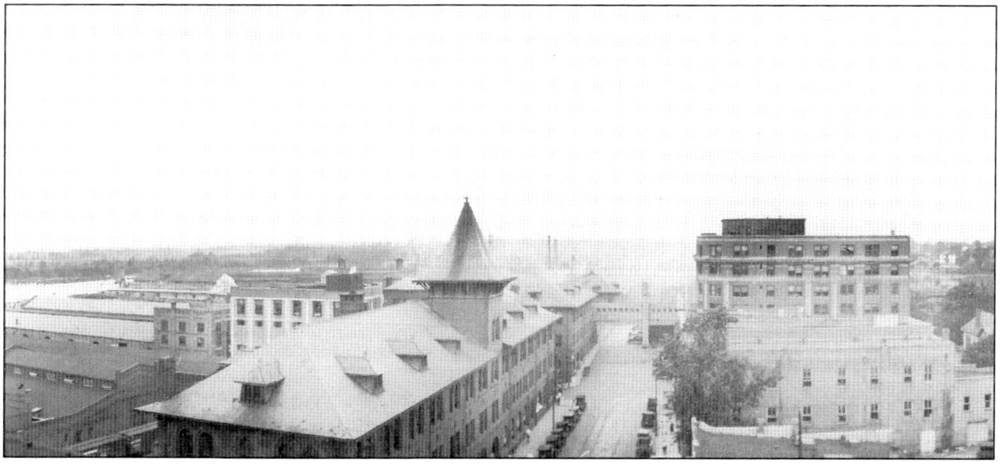

This photograph, taken about 1930, is a view of Front Street, looking north from Walnut Street. The Atlantic Coast Line Railroad office buildings are on the west side of Front Street. The tallest building on the right is Union Station. The bridge over the street took passengers from the station to the concourse, where they boarded the train. (Louis T. Moore Collection, NHCPL.)

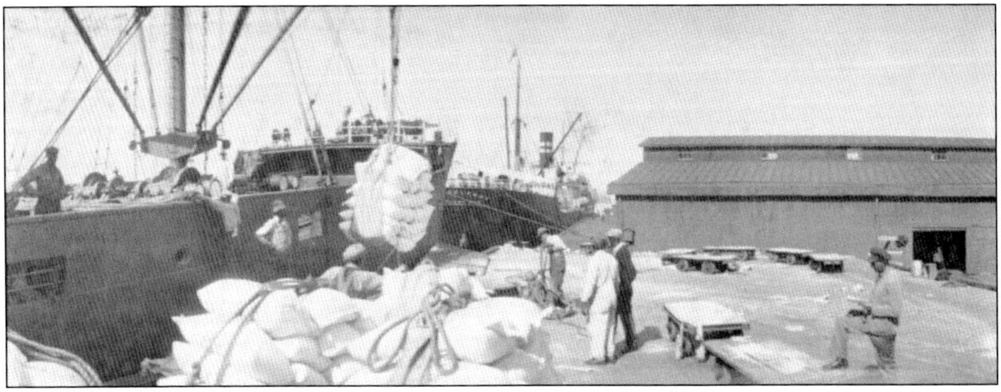

Louis T. Moore took these photographs of an unknown dock about 1930. In both images, African American longshoremen are unloading sugar from the Norwegian freighter *Bidarnes*. They use dollies and hand trucks to transport the sugar into the warehouse, where it was stored until it was sold. The sugar, which was produced in Cuba, was then transferred to freight cars and shipped by rail to markets on the East Coast. (Both, Louis T. Moore Collection, NHCPL.)

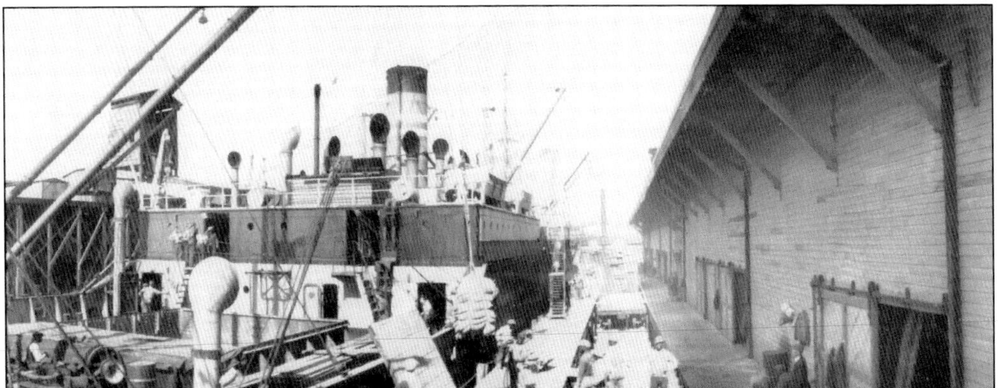

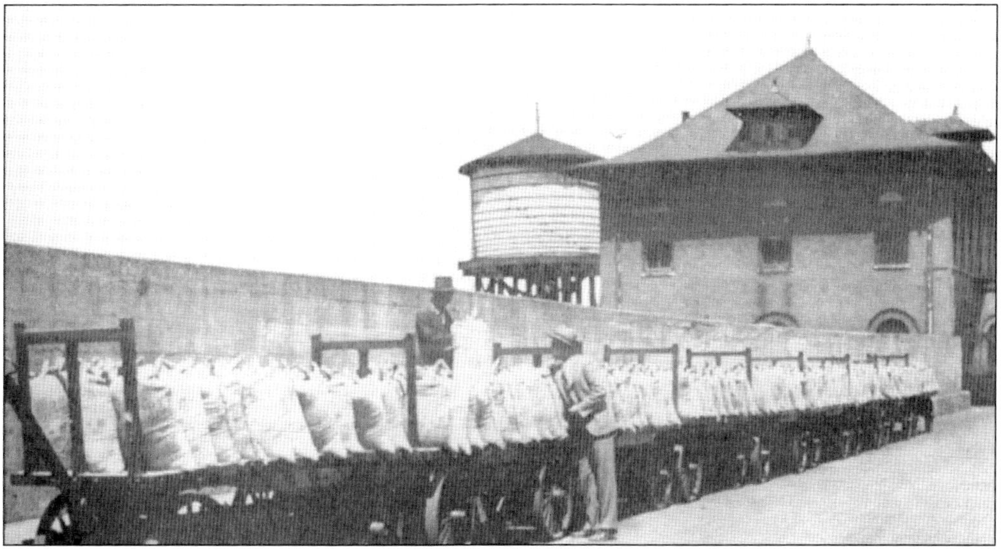

A supervisor is inspecting a bag of fertilizer in this 1927 photograph, which was taken in the railroad freight yard. That same year, the Atlantic Coast Line and Seaboard Air Line railroads together hauled $20 million worth of fertilizer to states up and down the Atlantic Seaboard. (Louis T. Moore Collection, NHCPL.)

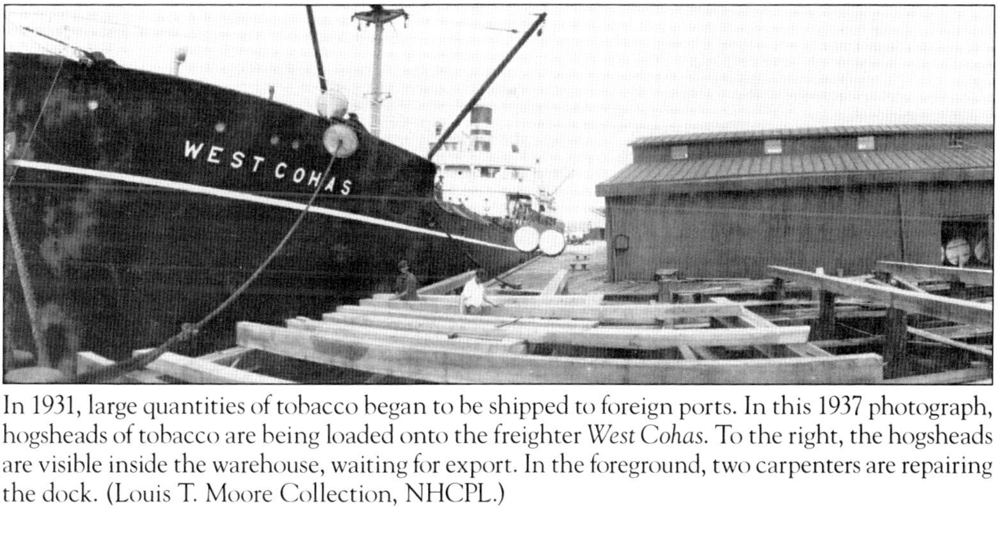

In 1931, large quantities of tobacco began to be shipped to foreign ports. In this 1937 photograph, hogsheads of tobacco are being loaded onto the freighter *West Cohas*. To the right, the hogsheads are visible inside the warehouse, waiting for export. In the foreground, two carpenters are repairing the dock. (Louis T. Moore Collection, NHCPL.)

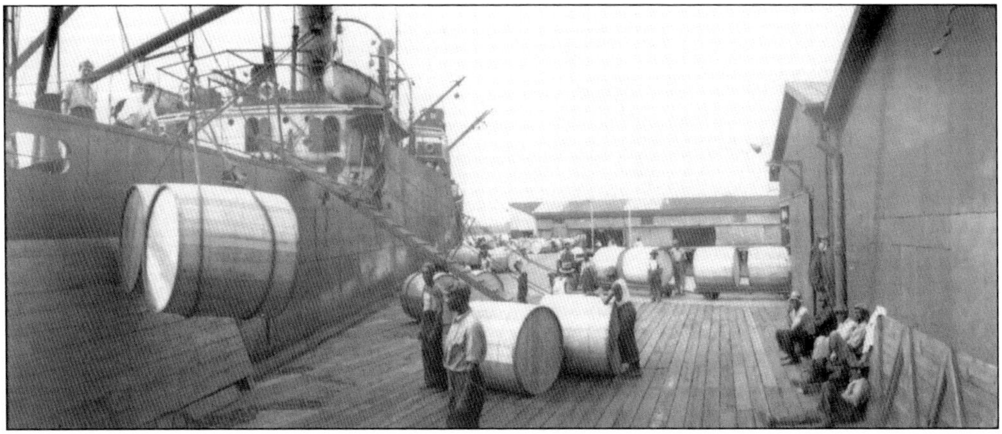

North Carolina was one of the largest tobacco-producing states in 1937, when this photograph was taken. Longshoremen can be seen loading hogsheads of tobacco onto a freighter. As a unionized group, they worked long hours and made good wages. A hogshead is four feet long and four feet in diameter. (Louis T. Moore Collection, NHCPL.)

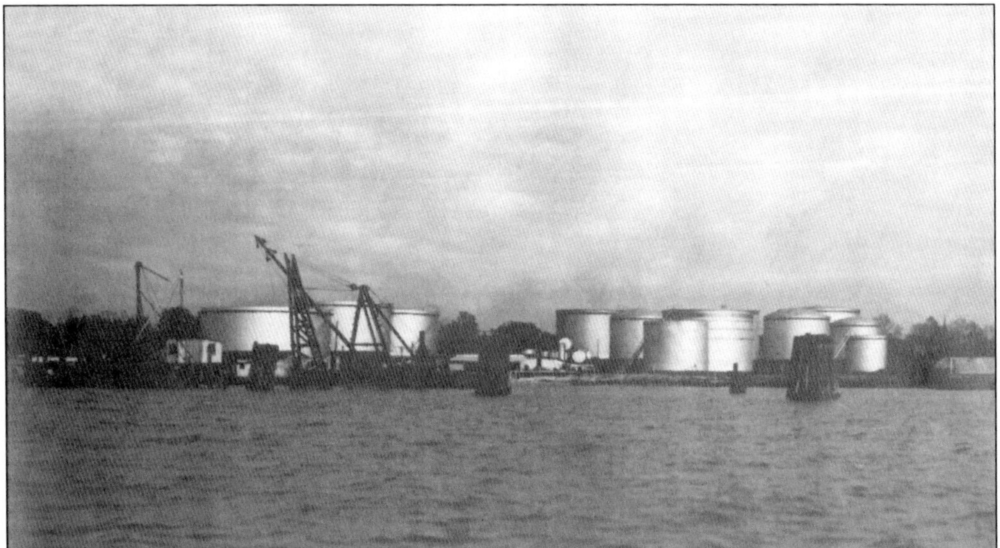

This photograph, taken in 1938, shows the Cape Fear Terminal Company, located at the foot of Wright Street. At the time, there were nine oil producers and shippers in the harbor, and Wilmington was ranked as the second-largest petroleum products port on the Atlantic Seaboard. As much as 75 percent of North Carolina's gas and oil consumption passed through the port. (Louis T. Moore Collection, NHCPL.)

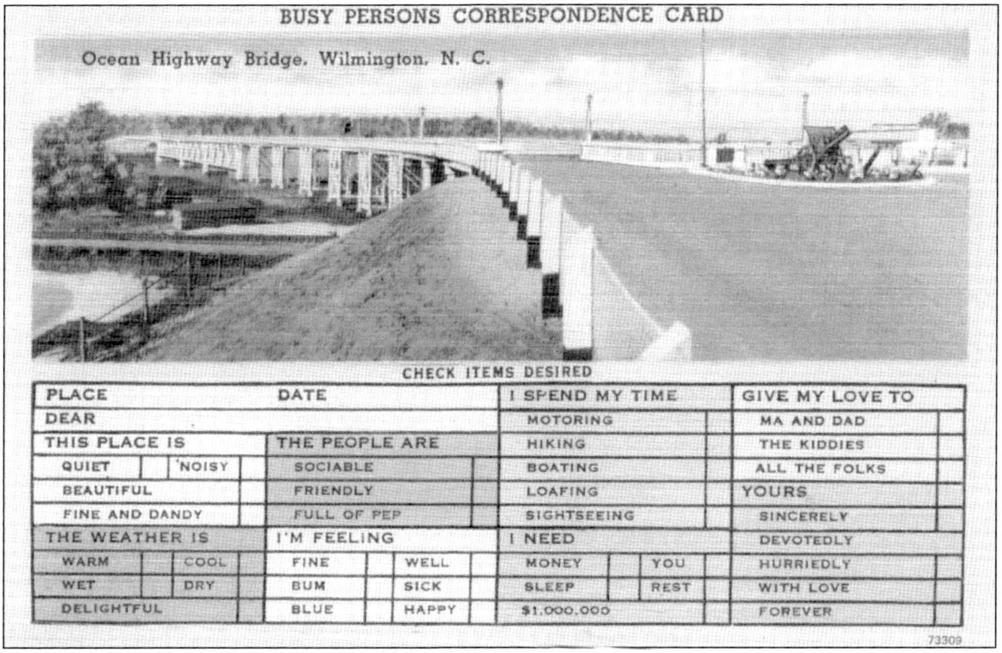

This humorous postcard was printed after the Atlantic Highway Bridge, or the Northeast Cape Fear River Bridge, was built in 1929. For the first time in history, people could drive their vehicles across the river. At the same time, another bridge was built across the Northwest Cape Fear River. The two bridges cost in excess $1.2 million.

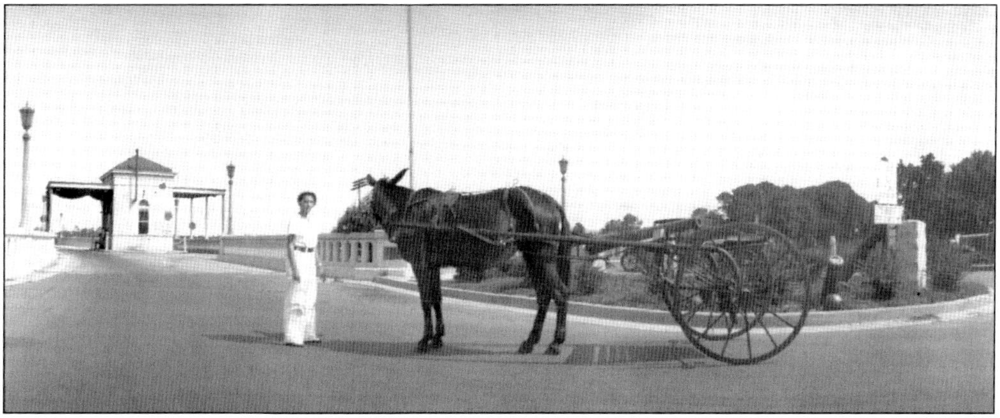

Bonds were sold to pay for the construction of the bridges, and a toll was collected on the east side of the bridges to pay off the bonds: 25¢ for a car (no matter how many passengers), 5¢ for pedestrians and bicycles, and 75¢ for large trucks. The cost for horses and wagons was not mentioned at the dedication. (Louis T. Moore Collection, NHCPL.)

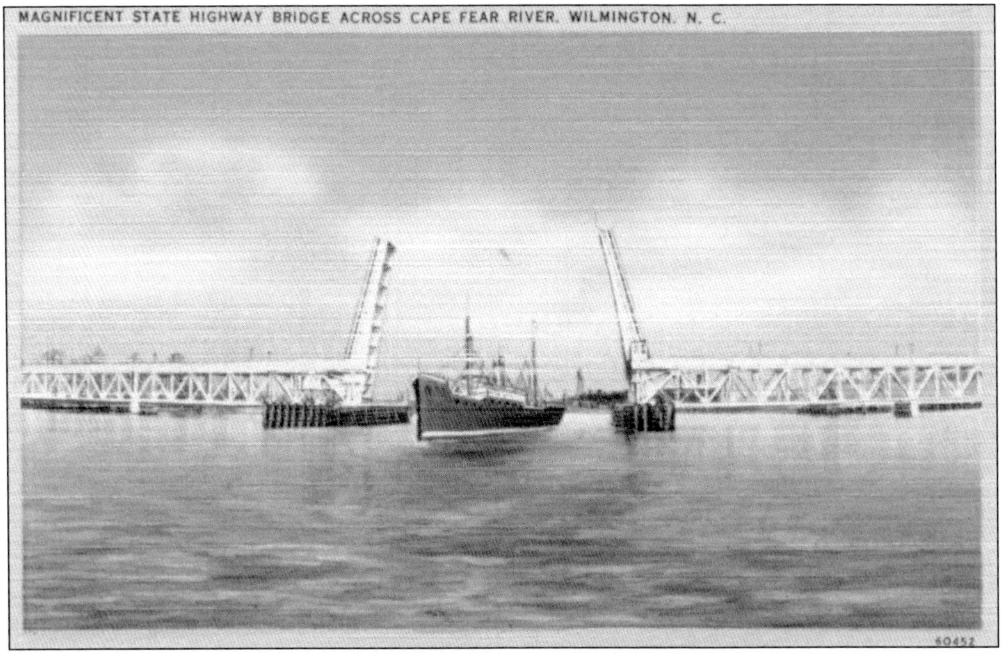

A freighter loaded with fertilizer passes through the span of the Northeast Cape Fear Bridge. When this postcard was issued, about 1940, Wilmington had 13 fertilizer factories, most of which were located north of the bridge. The bonds that had been issued to build the bridge were paid off in 1935. At the time, an estimated two million vehicles had crossed the bridge since its opening.

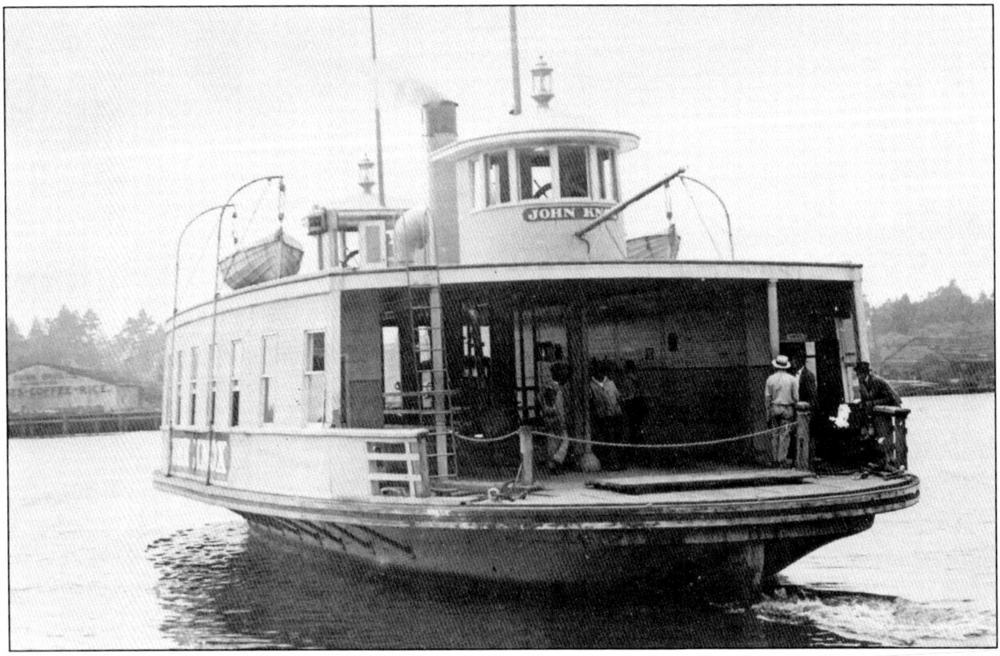

For 175 years, ferries crossed the Cape Fear River from the foot of Market Street to Eagles Island. In 1919, modern ferry slips were dredged on either side of the river, and 20-minute round-trip service began with the *John Knox* and the *Menantic*, which ran simultaneously. In 1935, the ferries were permanently retired when the bonds that had funded the twin bridges were paid off.

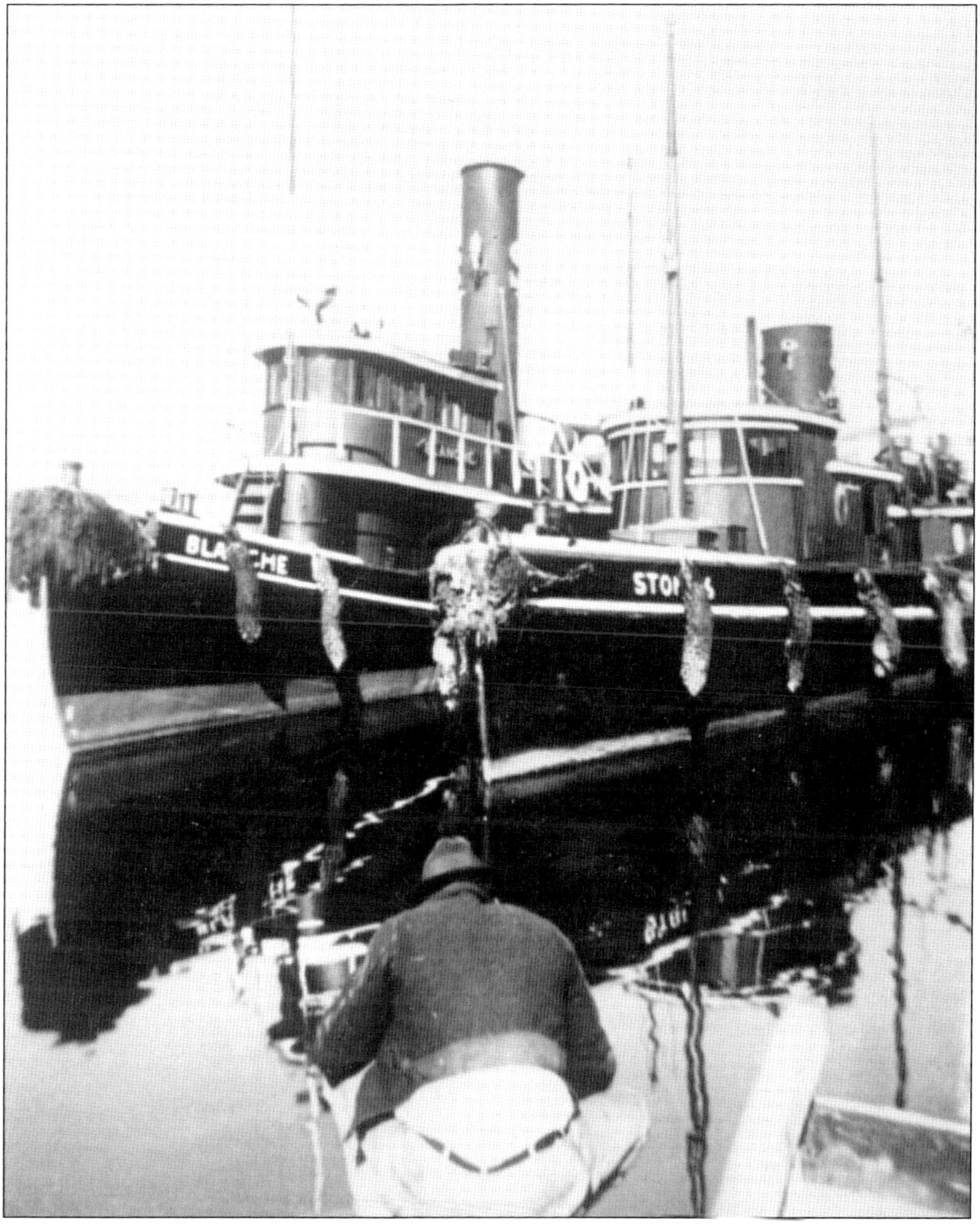

Tugboats are small, but their looks are deceiving. They are powerful enough to move vessels many times their size. In addition to assisting oceangoing ships as they enter or depart the port, they are used in tricky salvage operations. From the mid-19th century, the Wilmington harbor has been awash in brightly painted tugboats. Before diesel engines, they were powered by steam, for which they were called "steam tugs" before the term "tugboat" became more popular. Tugboats were constructed of wood or metal-sheathed wood because the resiliency of a wooden hull prevented damage to the tugboat as well as the other vessel in berthing operations. Moored on South Water Street for decades, the red-and-black boats of the Stone Towing Company are seen in this 1937 photograph. The company operated from 1895 to 1982, when its tugs were donated to become part of an artificial reef off Wrightsville Beach.

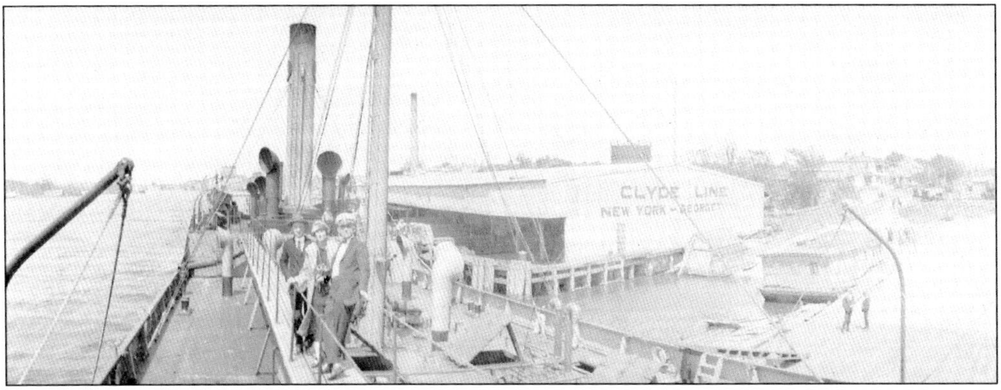

Passengers on board a Clyde Line steamer are pictured here as they enter the port. The company ran steamers in and out of Wilmington on a regular basis until 1938. In the 1920s and 1930s, many people preferred sailing to trains. The steamers stopped at most harbors from New York City to Georgetown, South Carolina. The Clyde Line terminal was located at the foot of Queen Street. (Louis T. Moore Collection, NHCPL.)

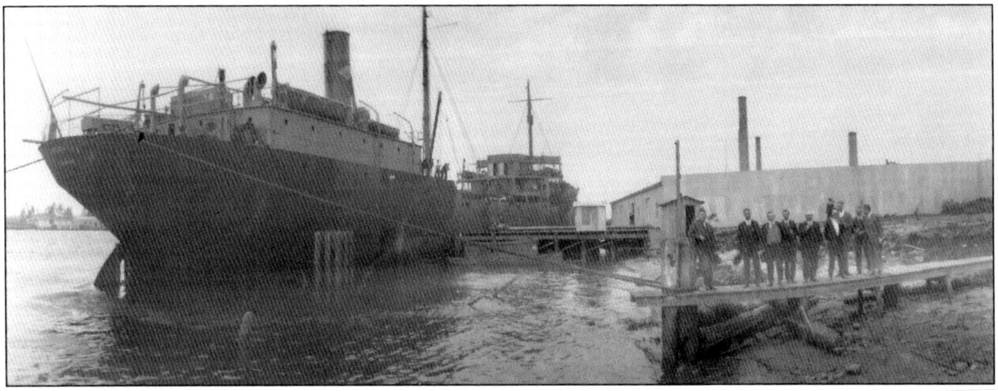

Employees of the Chadbourn Lumber Company Saw and Planing Mills pose at the company dock on the east bank of the Cape Fear River, between Queen and Wooster Streets. A freighter is docked at the sawmill in this photograph, taken by Louis T. Moore around 1925. The log way, which can be seen at center, carried the lumber from the mill to the vessel.

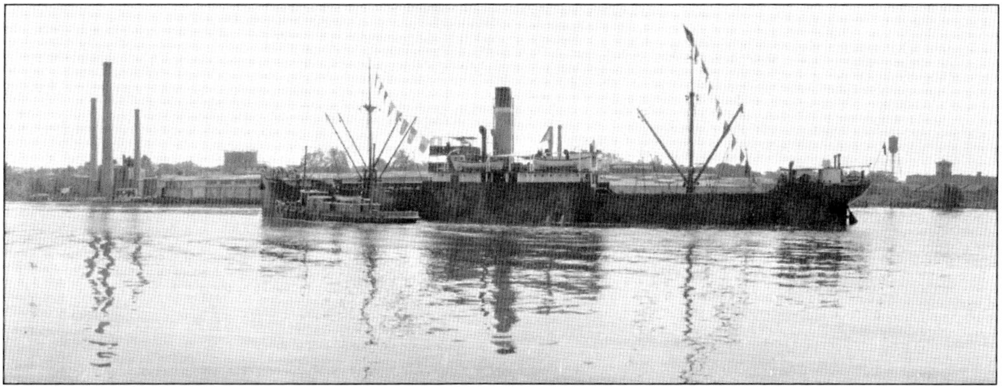

A note on the back of this photograph reads, "Freighter being towed into port on a national holiday." It is passing the foot of Queen Street. The three smokestacks at left belonged to the Tide Water Power Company, located at the foot of Castle Street until 1955. (Louis T. Moore Collection, NHCPL.)

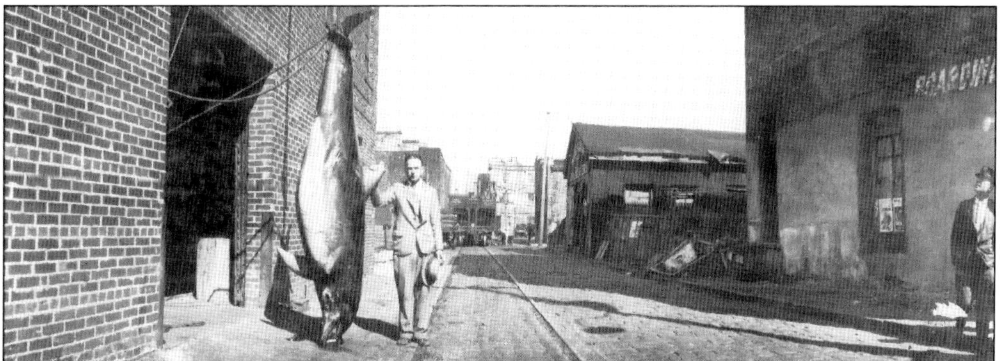

Albert Franklin Fales is pictured here at the entrance to his father's business, the J.B. Fales Fish House, located at 116 South Water Street. Capt. Will Moore had harpooned this porpoise, which measured 18 feet, on June 23, 1932. Fish houses were prevalent along the waterfront. (Louis T. Moore Collection, NHCPL.)

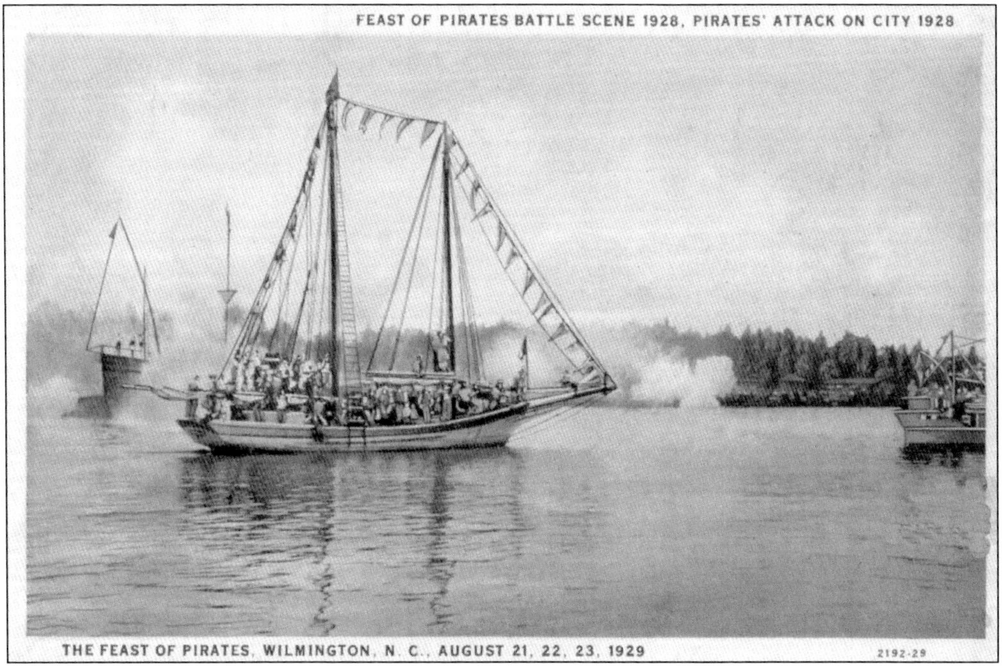

Although the Feast of Pirates was held for only three years, from 1927 to 1929, it was so popular that attendees talked about it for the rest of their lives. This 1929 postcard shows a mock battle between decorated fake pirate ships in the harbor. After the battle, the pirates came ashore and took the city hostage for three days of merriment.

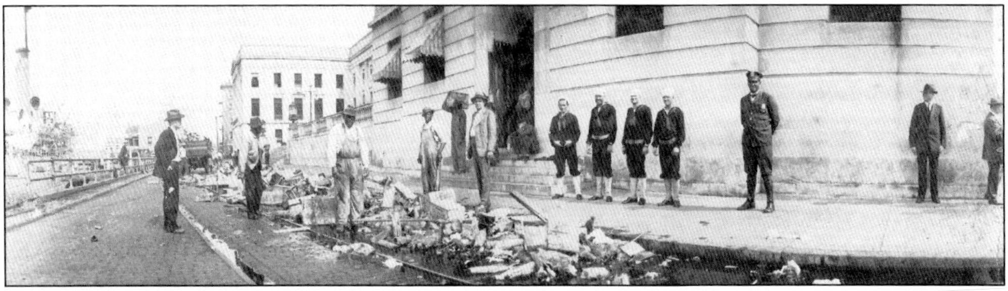

On January 6, 1933, US Revenue agents supervised the destruction of 600 cases of illegal whiskey. The expensive liquid was washed into the Cape Fear River. Most of the onlookers are smiling at the camera, while the man sitting on the steps hangs his head in disbelief. (Louis T. Moore Collection, NHCPL.)

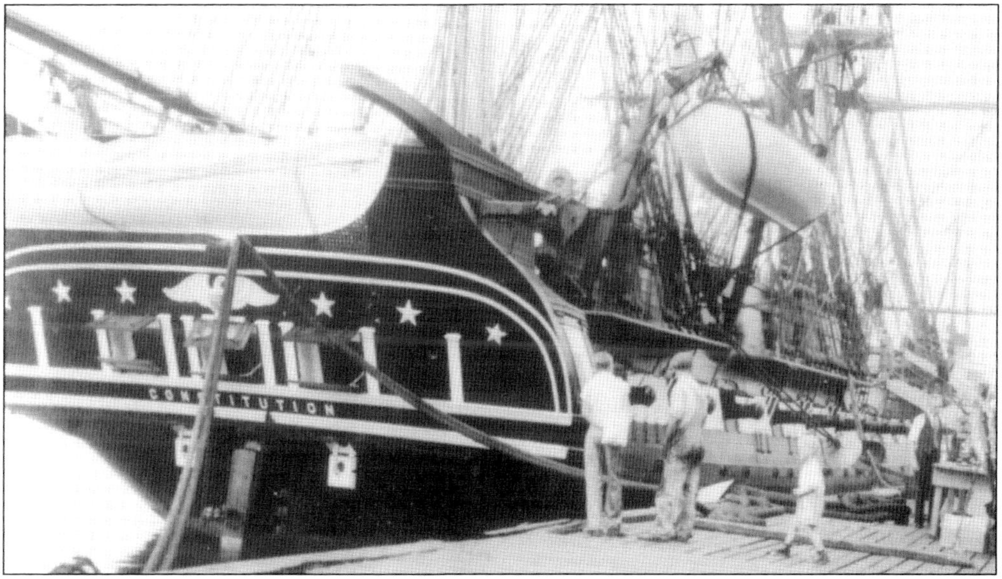

James Walton took this photograph of the wooden-hulled, three-masted USS *Constitution* when it visited Wilmington on November 21, 1931. Pres. George Washington named the frigate, commissioned in 1798, after the Constitution of the United States. During its eight-day stay in Wilmington, 42,000 people from all over North Carolina visited the ship.

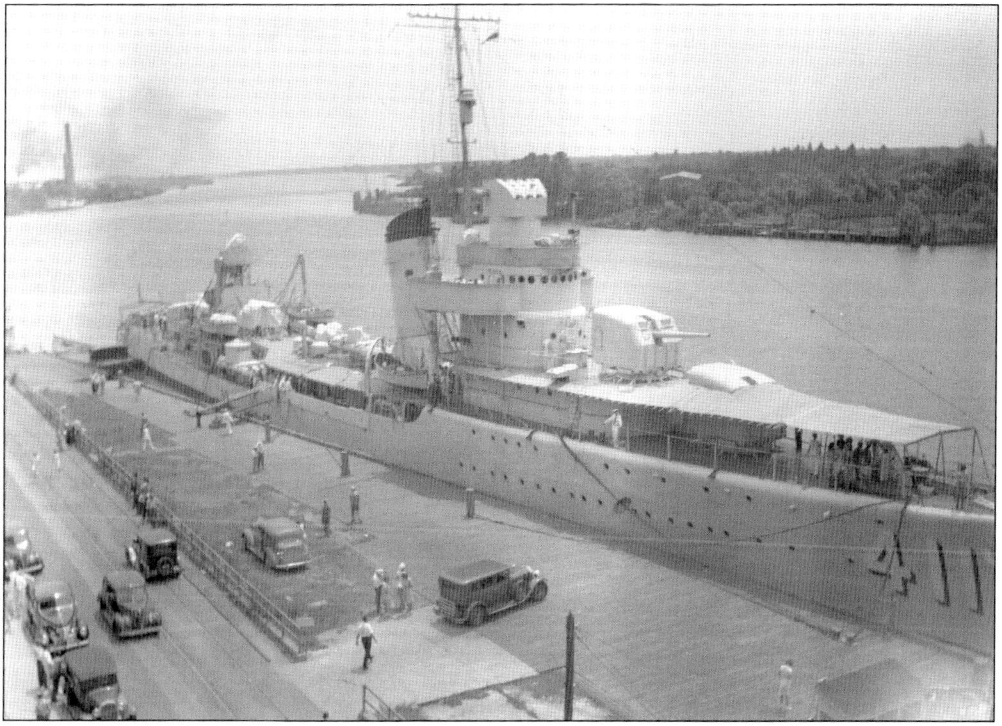

Helen Lovering took this photograph of the destroyer USS *Blue* when it docked at Wilmington in 1937. Newly commissioned, the destroyer spent its first year in training exercises on the East Coast. The *Blue* survived the bombing of Pearl Harbor but was scuttled after being hit by torpedoes at Guadalcanal. (Lovering Collection, NHPCL.)

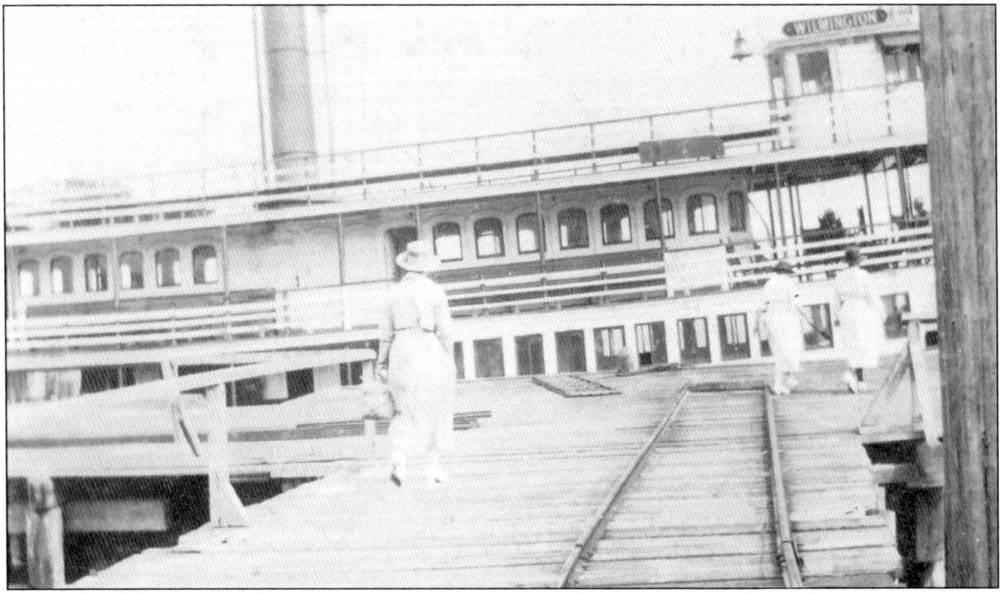

Marion Reaves took this photograph of three women boarding the steamer *Wilmington* in 1920. The women are dressed almost identically, in white dresses, white shoes, and hats. The photograph could have been taken at one of three places—Wilmington, Carolina Beach, or Southport. The steamer made daily trips to all three. (Bill Reaves Collection, NHCPL.)

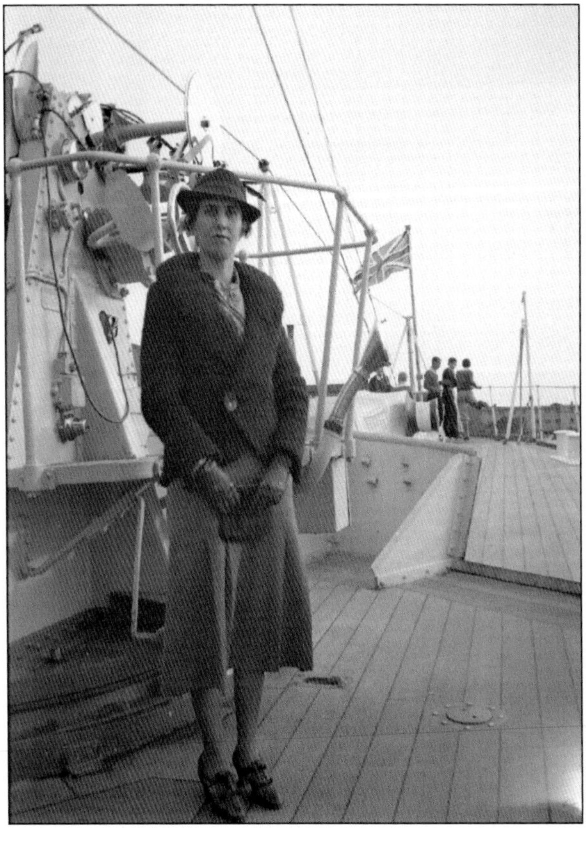

Helen Lovering poses on the HMS *Scarborough* in the 1930s, when the British vessel arrived on a goodwill visit to the port city. Built in 1931, the *Scarborough* joined the North American and West Indies Squadron. During peacetime, she visited coastal ports where large warships were unlikely to frequent. She saw duty during World War II, including the invasion of Normandy. (Lovering Collection, NHPCL.)

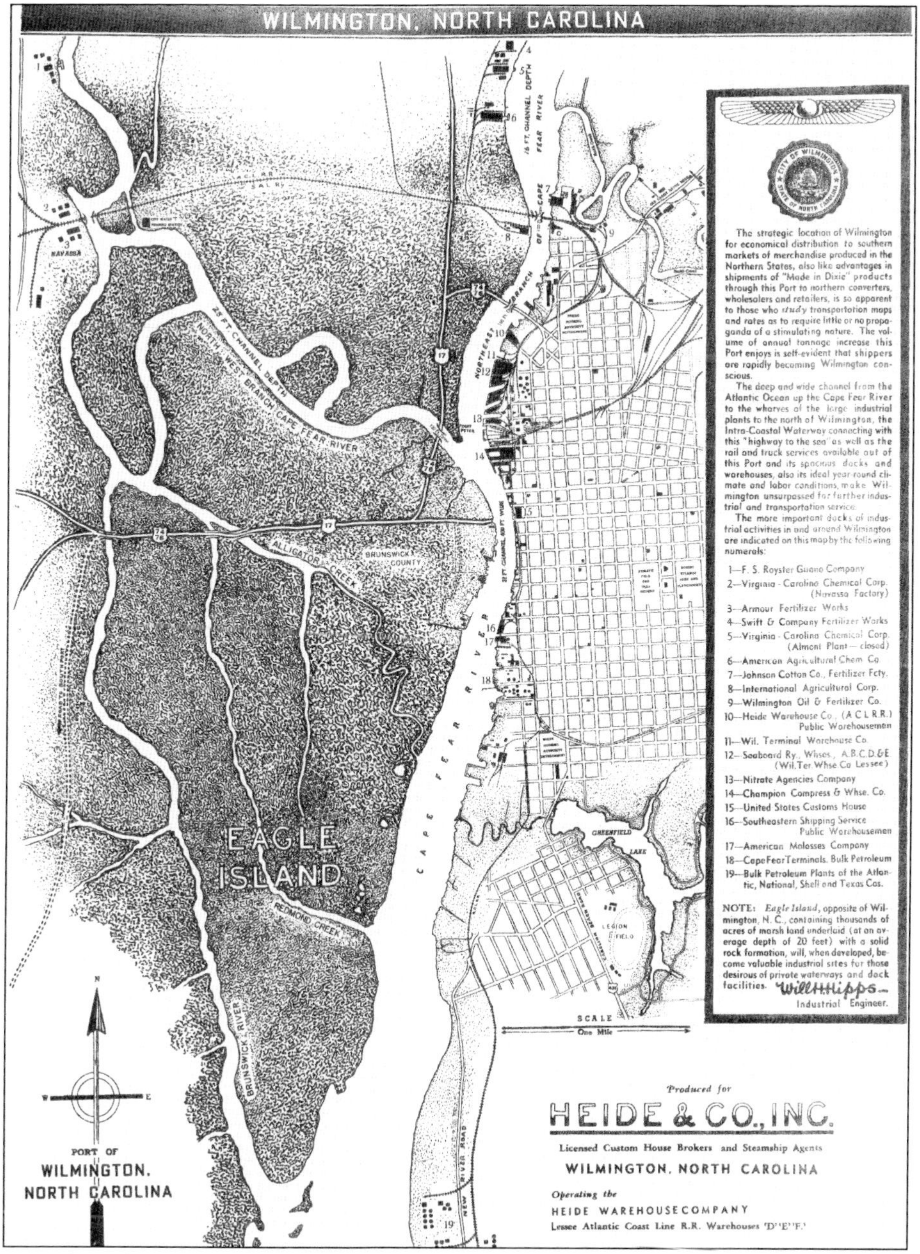

In 1939, when this map was created, Wilmington had a population of 33,407. At the time, the Wilmington Chamber of Commerce described the port as follows: "Wilmington's exportations and importations are large and ever-growing, which mark a successful port. As a cotton port, it handles a satisfactory volume. Wilmington ranks as the second largest fertilizer and petroleum products port on the Atlantic Seaboard. Its volume of petroleum products is such that practically 75% of the state's consumption passes through the port. Wilmington also has a tremendous volume of molasses importation, which serves half a dozen states, as well as an enormous amount of lumber handled in both coast-wise and foreign trade. Recent increase of port volume had been evidenced in large tobacco exports and growing imports of sugar, with vast shipments of bromine and distribution of petroleum products."

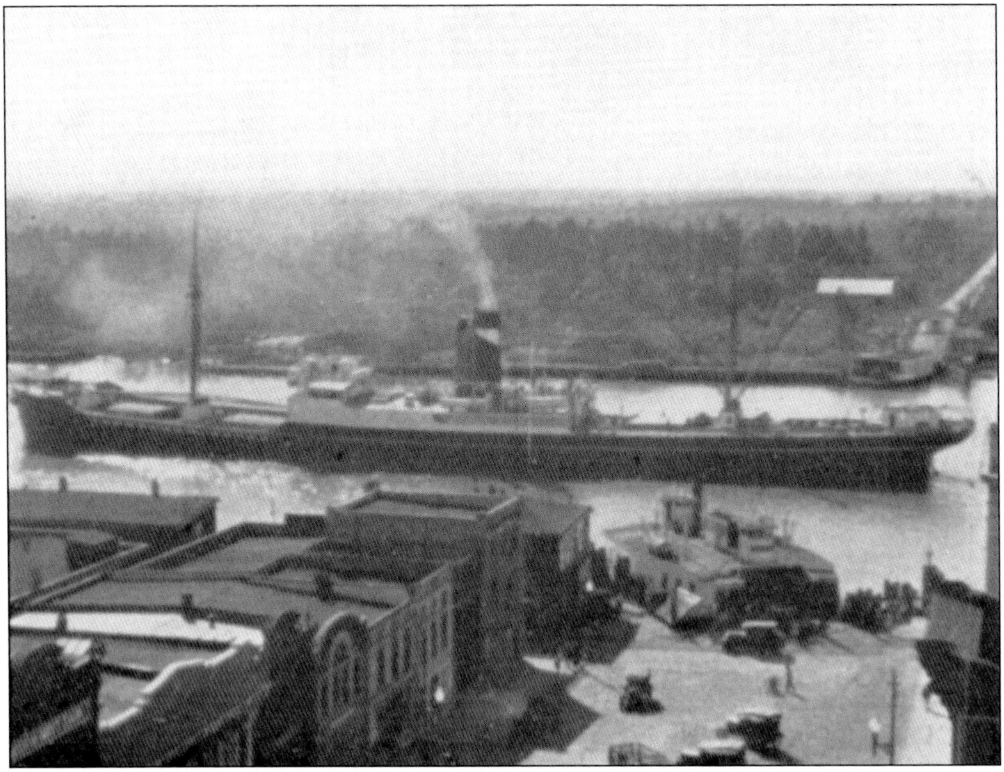

The caption for this 1933 photograph reads, "A Typical Day in the Wilmington Harbor." A freighter loaded with tobacco passes the foot of Market Street. The ferry *John Knox* is unloading automobiles at the ferry landing. Louis T. Moore took this photograph from the Atlantic Trust Building, located at the northeast corner of Front and Market Streets.

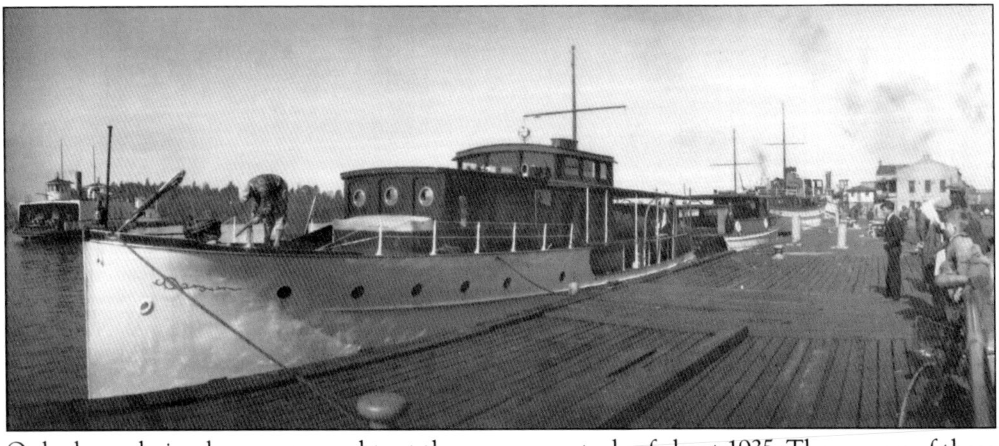

Onlookers admire three motor yachts at the government wharf about 1935. The owners of these yachts could have been visiting the city on their trip along the Atlantic Intracoastal Waterway. Wilmington was a popular port of call for travelers on the waterway, which runs from Maine to Florida. (Louis T. Moore Collection, NHCPL.)

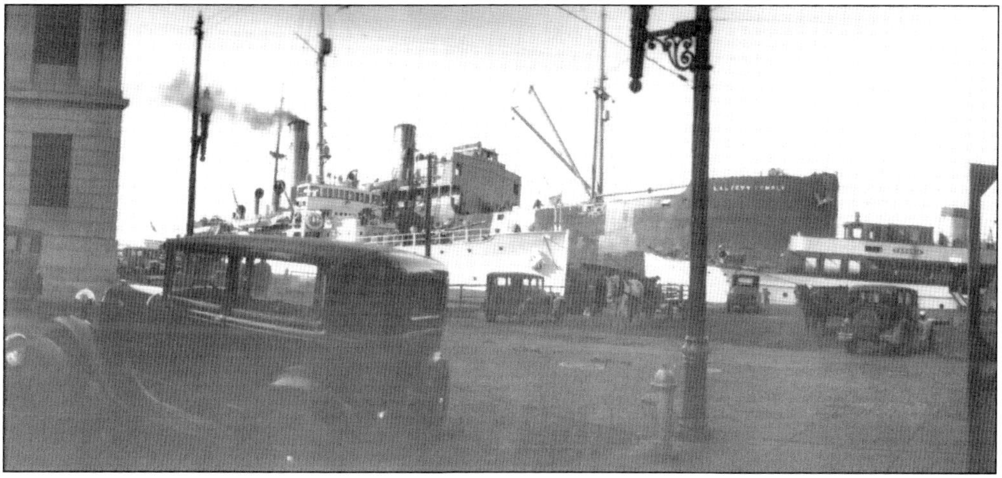

A freighter heading upriver passes the USCGC *Modoc*, which is moored next to a yacht at the government dock in front of the customhouse. When Louis T. Moore took this photograph about 1930, horses and wagons and several automobiles were parked on Water Street.

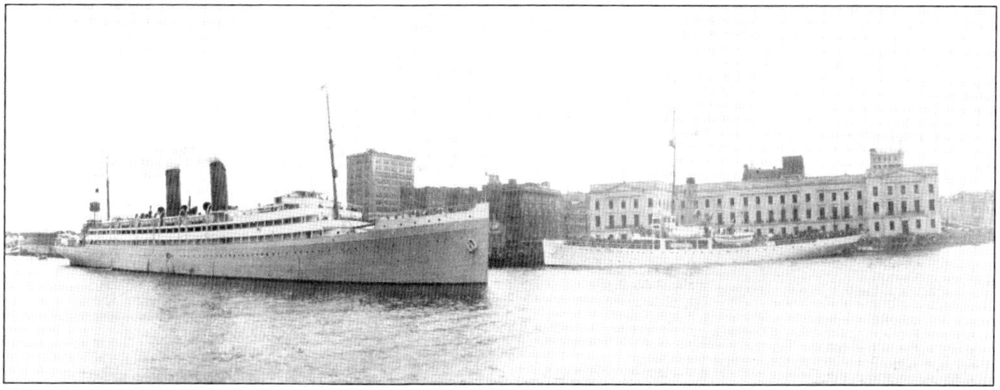

The cruise ship *Port Hamilton* sails downriver past the *Modoc* and the customhouse. The liner was underway to Hamilton, Bermuda, where it was based. The cruise liner called at ports from New York to Fort Lauderdale, Florida, before ending the trip in Bermuda. (Louis T. Moore Collection, NHCPL.)

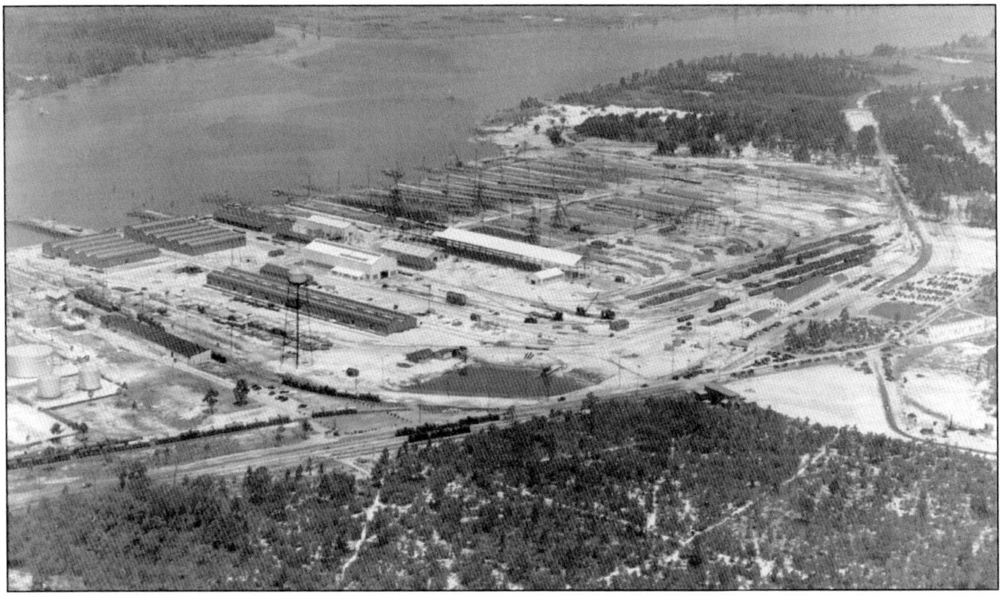

These photographs show the construction of the North Carolina Shipbuilding Company. The aerial view above looks north, upriver, and the aerial view below looks south, downriver. Located three miles south of the heart of downtown Wilmington, the shipyard occupied over 150 acres by the end of World War II. The $20,393,358 shipyard had six shipways. The rectangular buildings were fabrication shops, machine shops, and ship sheds. The shipyard lived up to its motto, "To Build Good Ships Quickly." In just five years, from 1941 to 1946, a total of 243 ships were built here. The first 126 vessels were Liberty ships, 27 of which were eventually lost as a result of the war. Built to carry cargo, one ship took an average of 415,391 man-hours to complete.

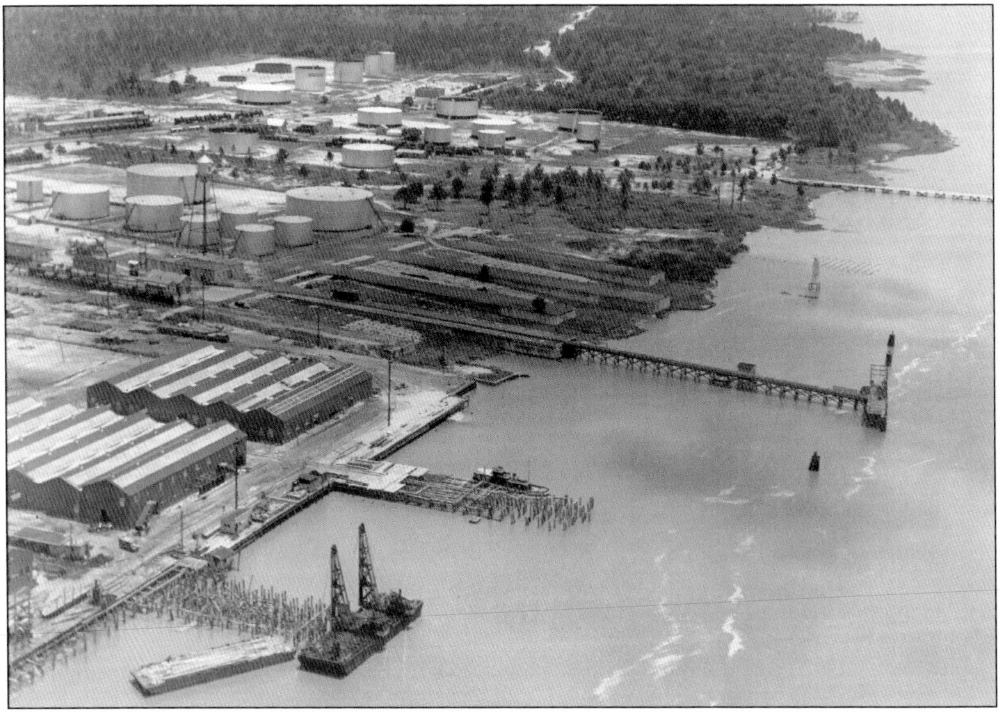

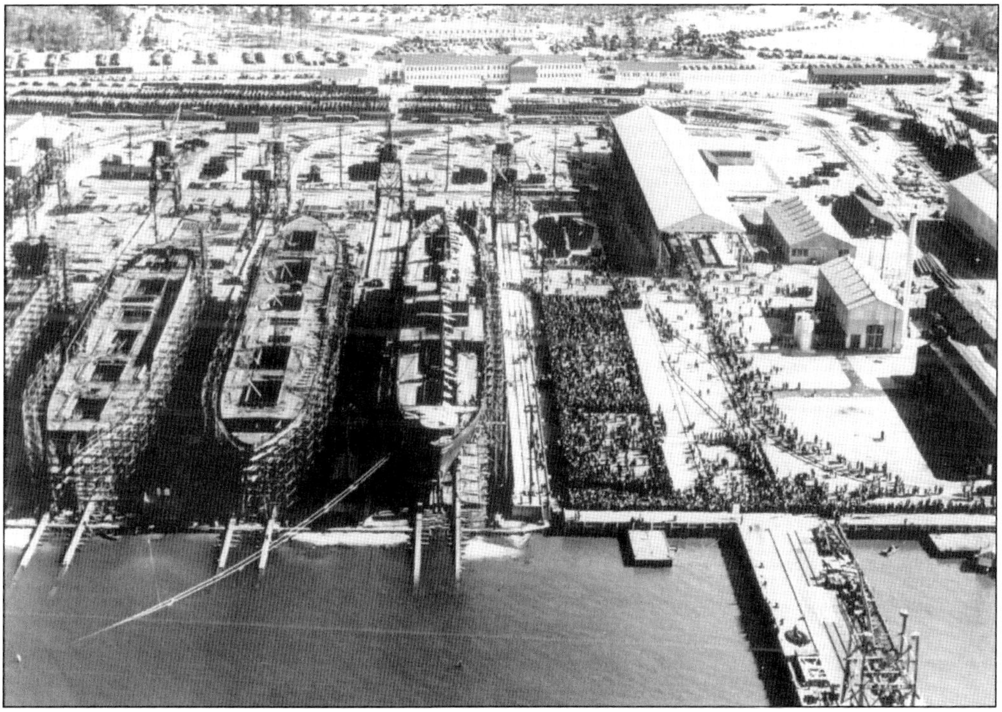

This aerial photograph shows four ships under construction, with hundreds of employees in the yard. Employment at the shipyard reached a peak of 21,000 on March 11, 1943. The majority of workers came from within 200 miles of Wilmington. The port city was known as the "Defense City" during the war.

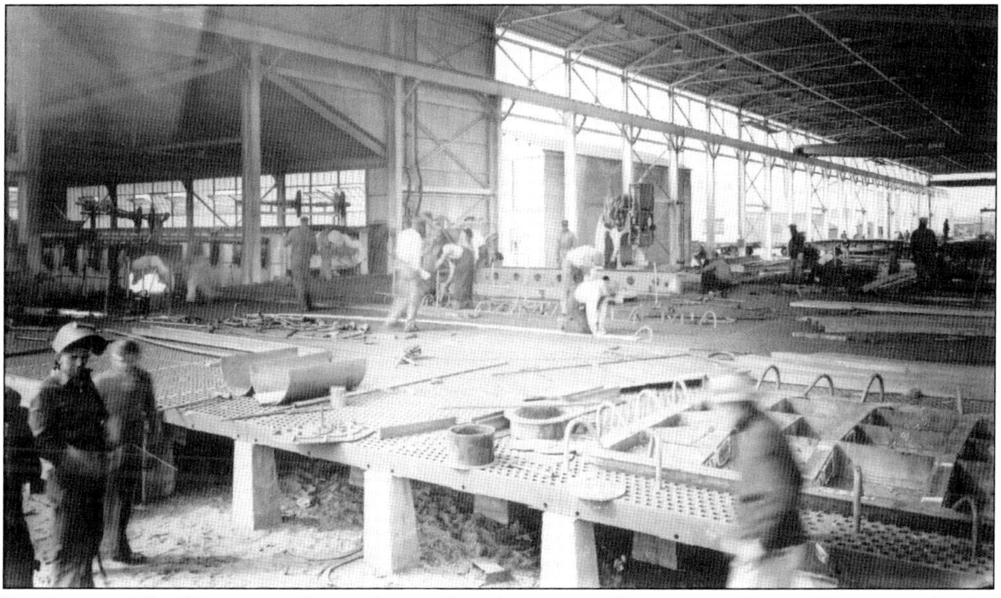

Inside one of the fabrication shops, shipyard workers are in the process of assembling parts for the next vessel. Trade schools were established in the early days of the shipyard. The welding school alone trained 7,247 workers. Other schools trained electricians, steam engineers, plumbers, sheet metal workers, and pipe coverers.

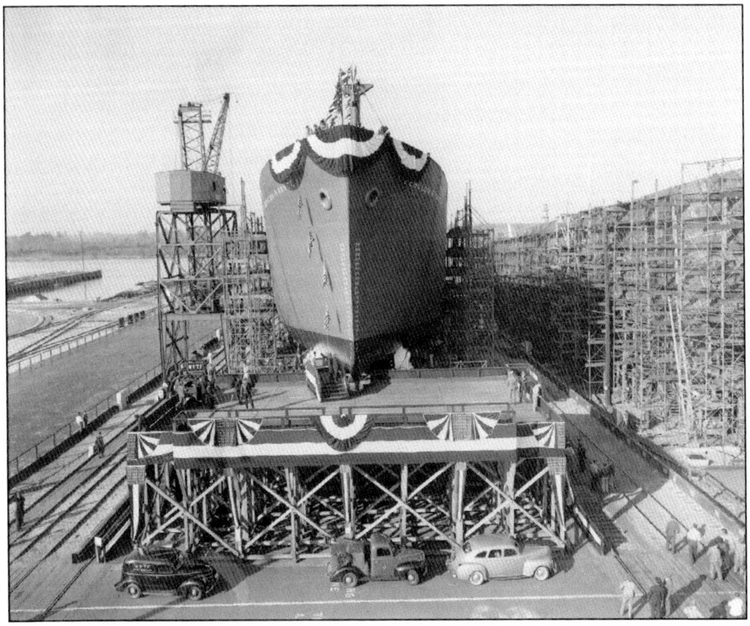

On December 6, 1941, a matter of hours before the Japanese attack on Pearl Harbor, the first Liberty ship was launched. The *Zebulon B. Vance* was named in honor of North Carolina's Civil War governor. As North Carolina's first lady, Alice Wilson Broughton christened the vessel. The *Vance* began her war service as a freighter and ended it by transporting war brides back to the United States.

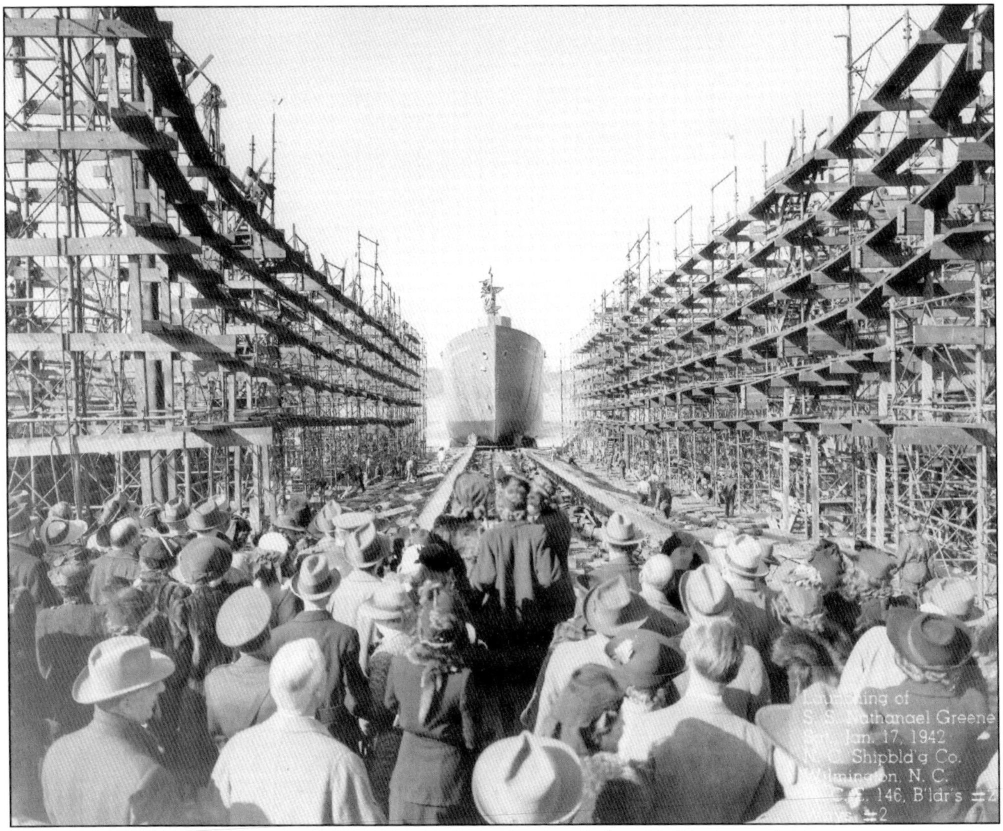

Hundreds of spectators turned out for the launching of the SS *Nathanael Greene* on Saturday, January 17, 1942. It was the second Liberty ship built at the shipyard, and it took less than eight months from the time of laying the keel to this well-attended launching.

The SS *Northern Light* is seen here in the Cape Fear River after launching. Preempted by the US Navy, she was renamed the USS *Paramint*. The wording on the vessel's side was typical of several methods used by the North Carolina Shipbuilding Company to advertise charitable giving. As the USS *Paramint*, she was later involved in the Bikini Atoll atom bomb experiment.

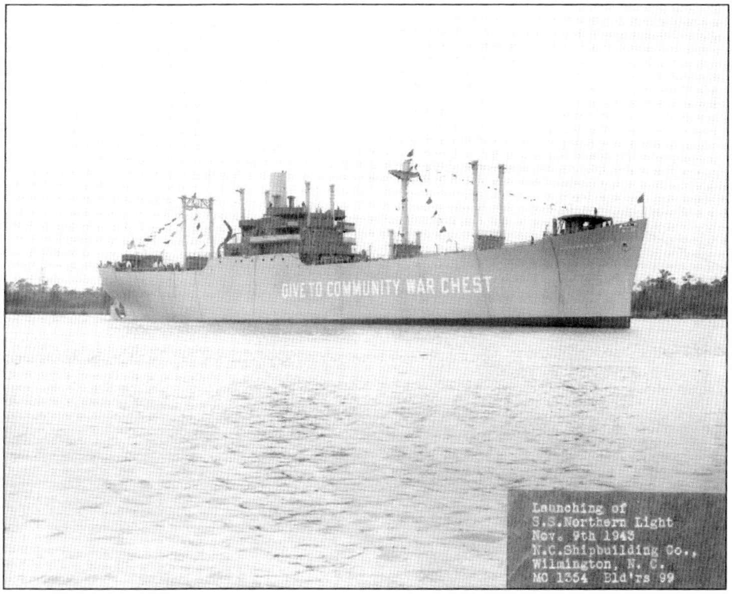

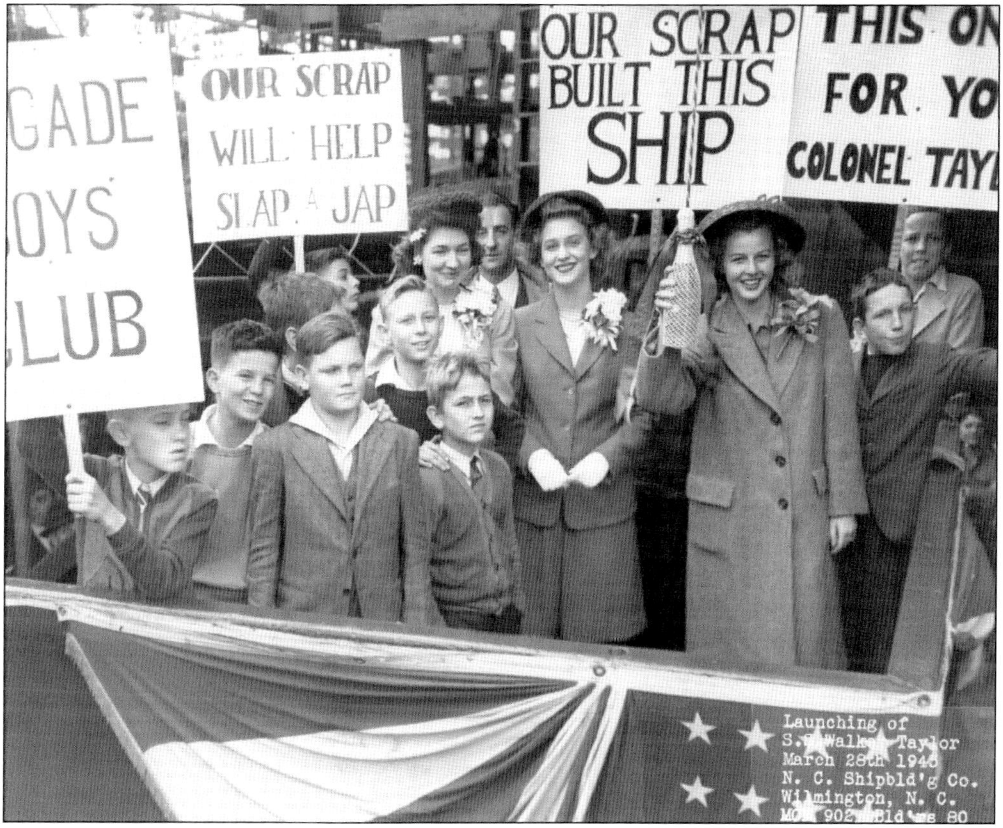

Surrounded by young men from the Boys' Brigade Club, Frances Taylor (right, holding champagne bottle) was the sponsor for the launching of the SS *Walker Taylor* on March 28, 1943. The ship was named in honor of her grandfather Col. Walker Taylor, who founded the beloved institution for underprivileged boys.

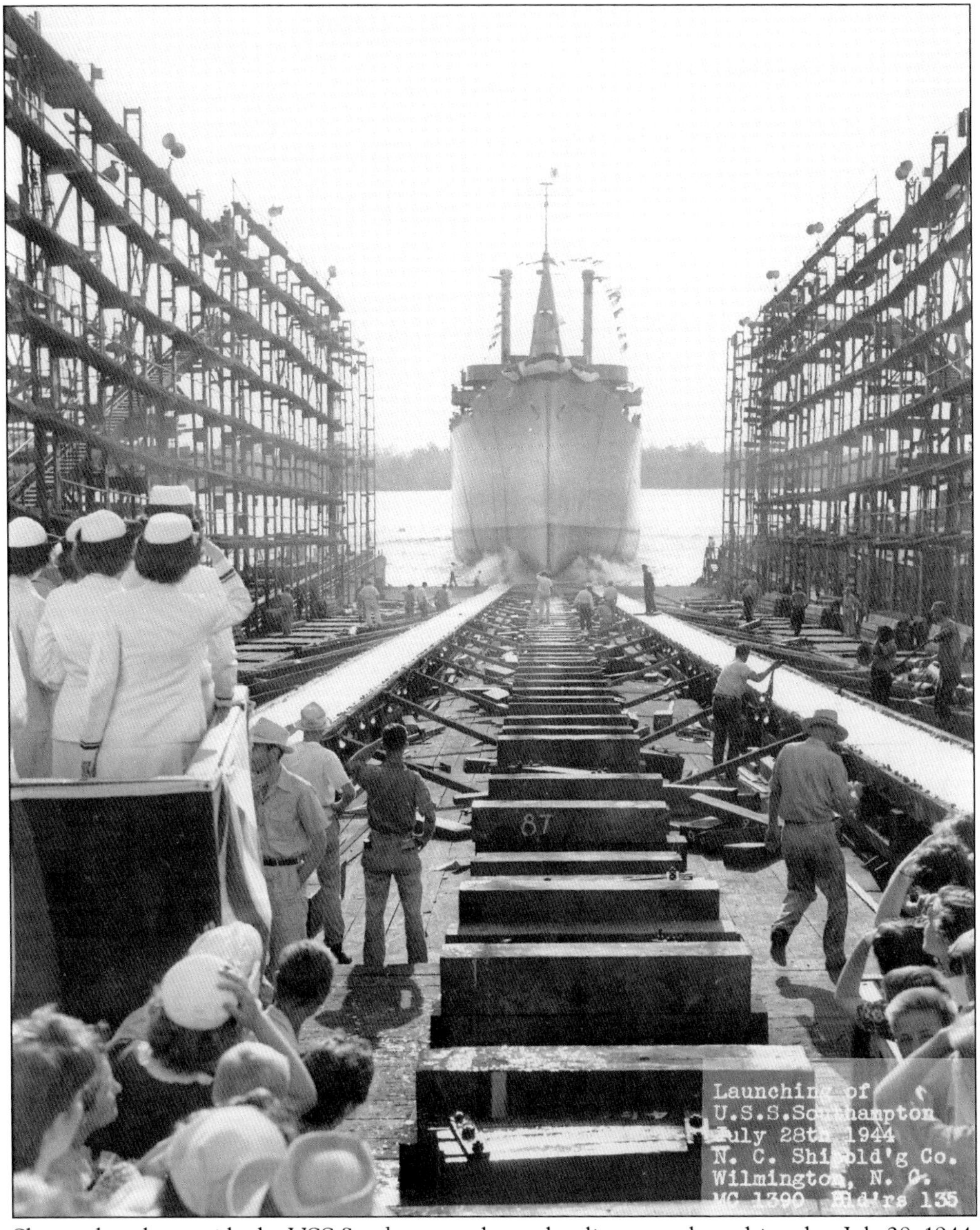

Shipyard workers guide the USS *Southampton* down the slipway on launching day, July 28, 1944. Named in honor of Southampton County, Virginia, the *Southampton* was a Tolland-class attack transport vessel of the Navy. She was active in the Pacific, taking part in the Battle of Iwo Jima. After serving for the duration of the war, the *Southampton* was decommissioned on June 21, 1946, when she was sold and renamed the SS *Flying Clipper*. On the dais at left, several members of the US Naval Reserve (Women's Reserve) salute as the Liberty ship slips into the Cape Fear River. During World War II, women were recruited to serve as Women Appointed for Volunteer Emergency Services (WAVES). The word "emergency" reflected the acceptance of women due to the unusual circumstances of wartime, acknowledging that, after the war, their naval service would no longer be needed. However, women have continued in service since that time.

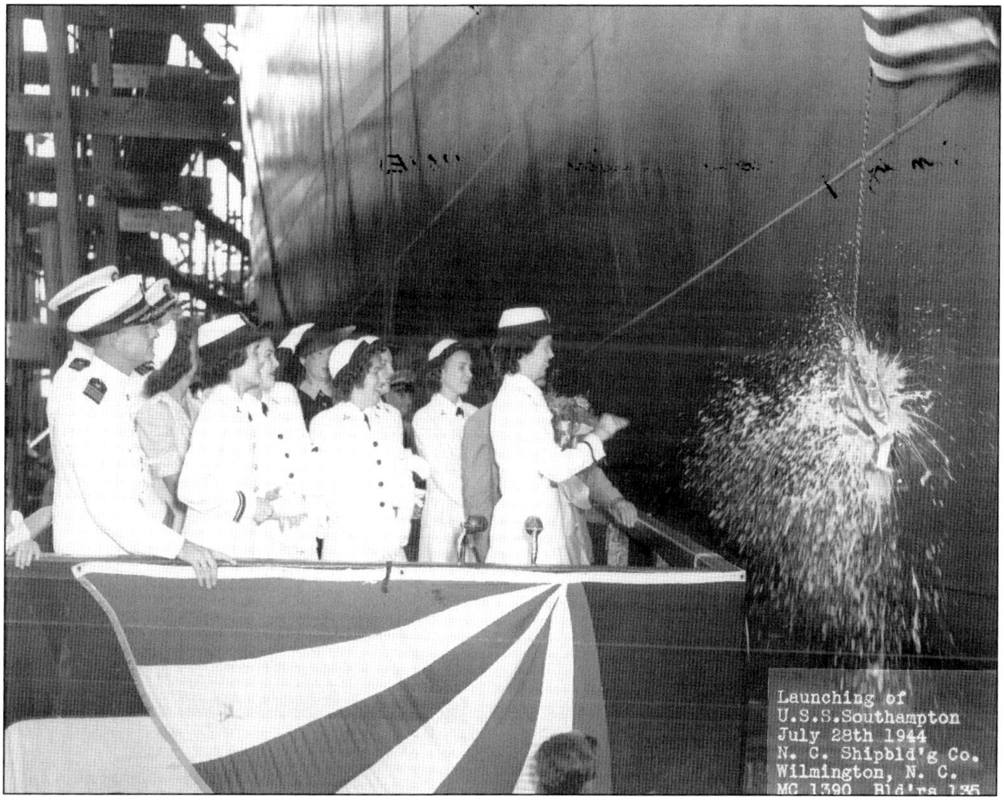

Ensign Rama V. Blackwood (far right) of the US Naval Reserve (Women's Reserve) christened the USS *Southampton* on July 28, 1944. Ensign Blackwood was chosen as the sponsor in honor of the second anniversary of WAVES, organized on July 30, 1942. The need for more service people brought about this major social change.

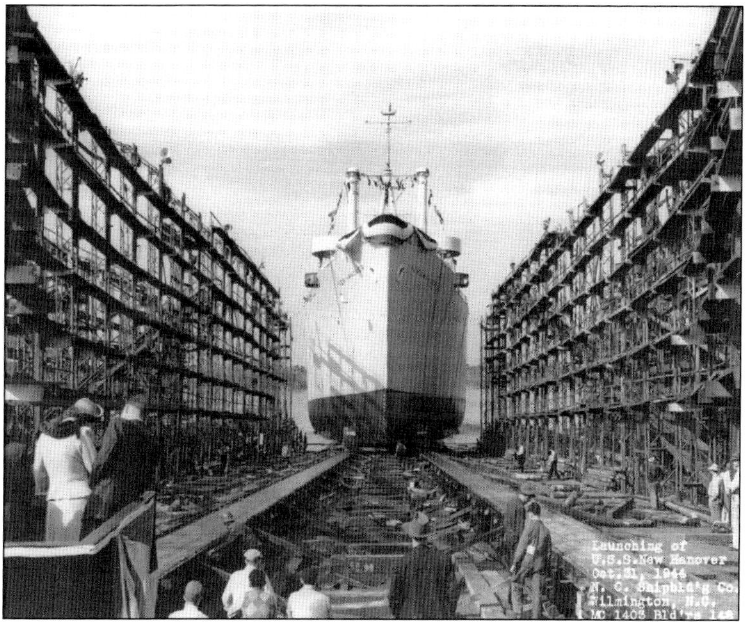

Wilmingtonians were proud to have a ship named for their home county. The USS *New Hanover* was launched on October 31, 1944, in the third year of the war. As the 148th vessel to be built at the shipyard, the *New Hanover* survived 30 air attacks by the Japanese before being decommissioned on July 30, 1946. She was bought and sold several times, until she was scrapped in 1970.

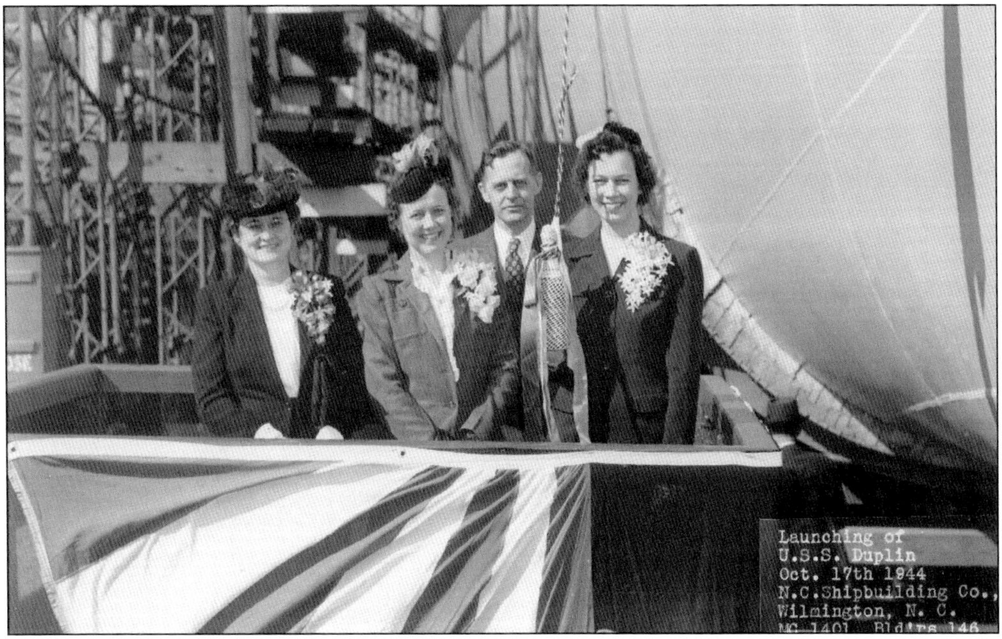

Mary Jennette (above, right) of Faison, North Carolina, was the sponsor for the launching of the USS *Duplin* on October 17, 1944, an honor she received for selling the most war bonds in Duplin County. Standing next to her is W.S. McMahon, the assistant secretary of the shipbuilding company. The photographer wrote the following note on the back of the photograph below: "This picture is unique in that no sponsor appears even as the vessel is christened. Miss Jennette apparently did not trust Mr. McMahon to prevent the remnants of the champagne bottle from flying back, for she ducked so deeply as to be hidden by the bunting."

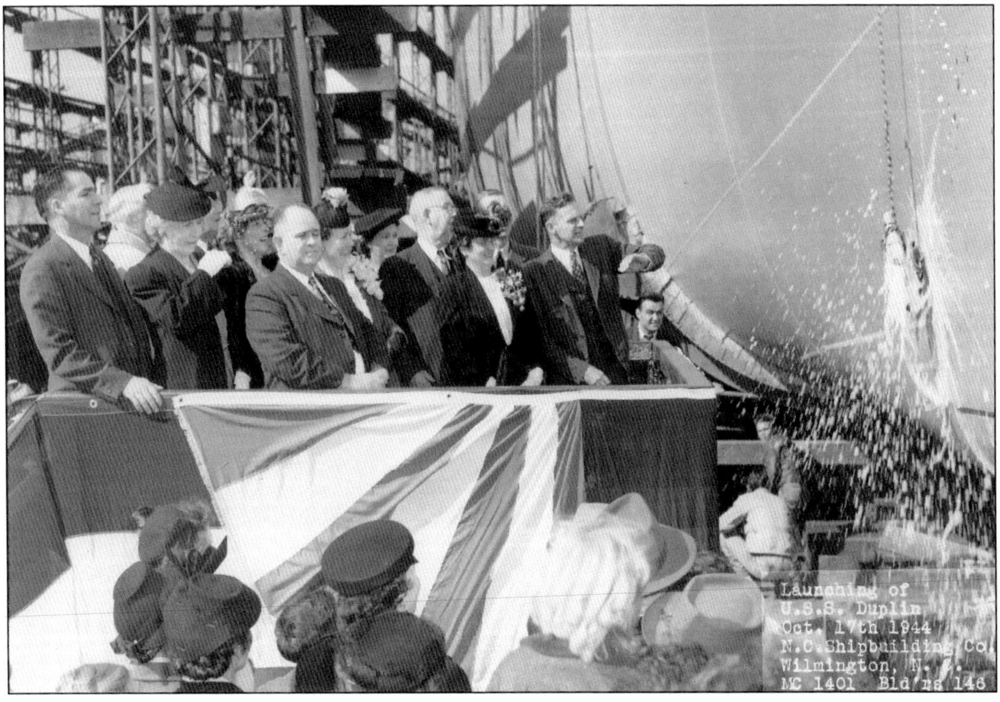

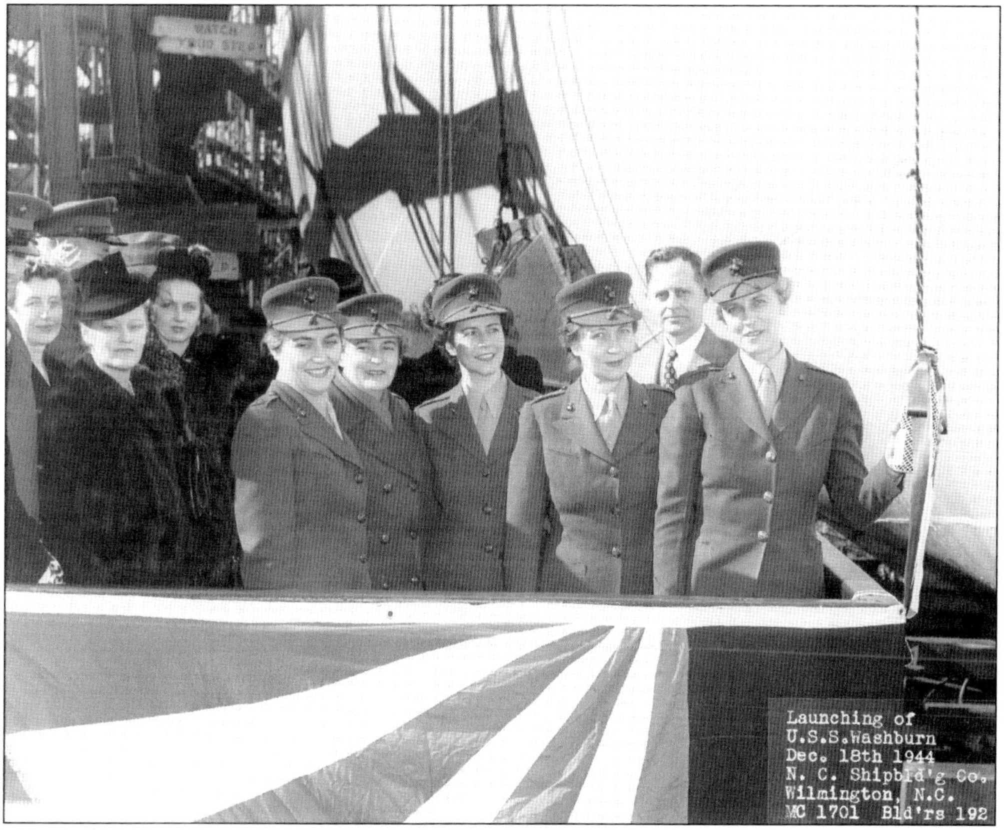

Maj. Katherine A. Towle, US Marine Corps Reserve (far right), was the sponsor for the launching of the USS *Washburn* on December 18, 1944. The shipyard selected Major (later Colonel) Towle, who had been in command of female Marines at Camp Lejeune, in recognition of her outstanding war service. As colonel, Towle later became the commanding officer of all female Marines.

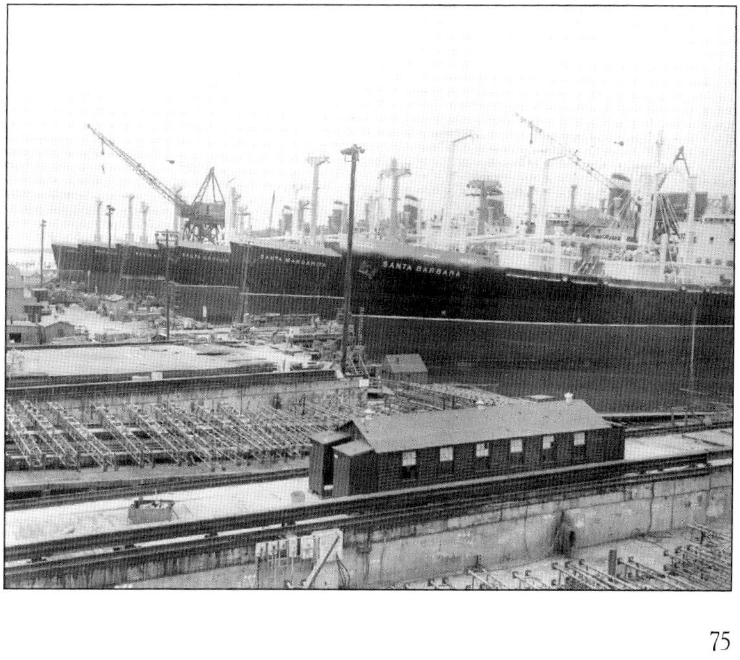

Designed and built for Grace Line, Inc., six C2-S-AJ4 passenger-cargo vessels are seen here at the North Carolina Shipbuilding Company outfitting piers on May 16, 1946. The *Santa Barbara*, the *Santa Cecilia*, the *Santa Margarita*, the *Santa Maria*, the *Santa Luisa*, and the *Santa Isabel* were the last vessels built at the shipyard.

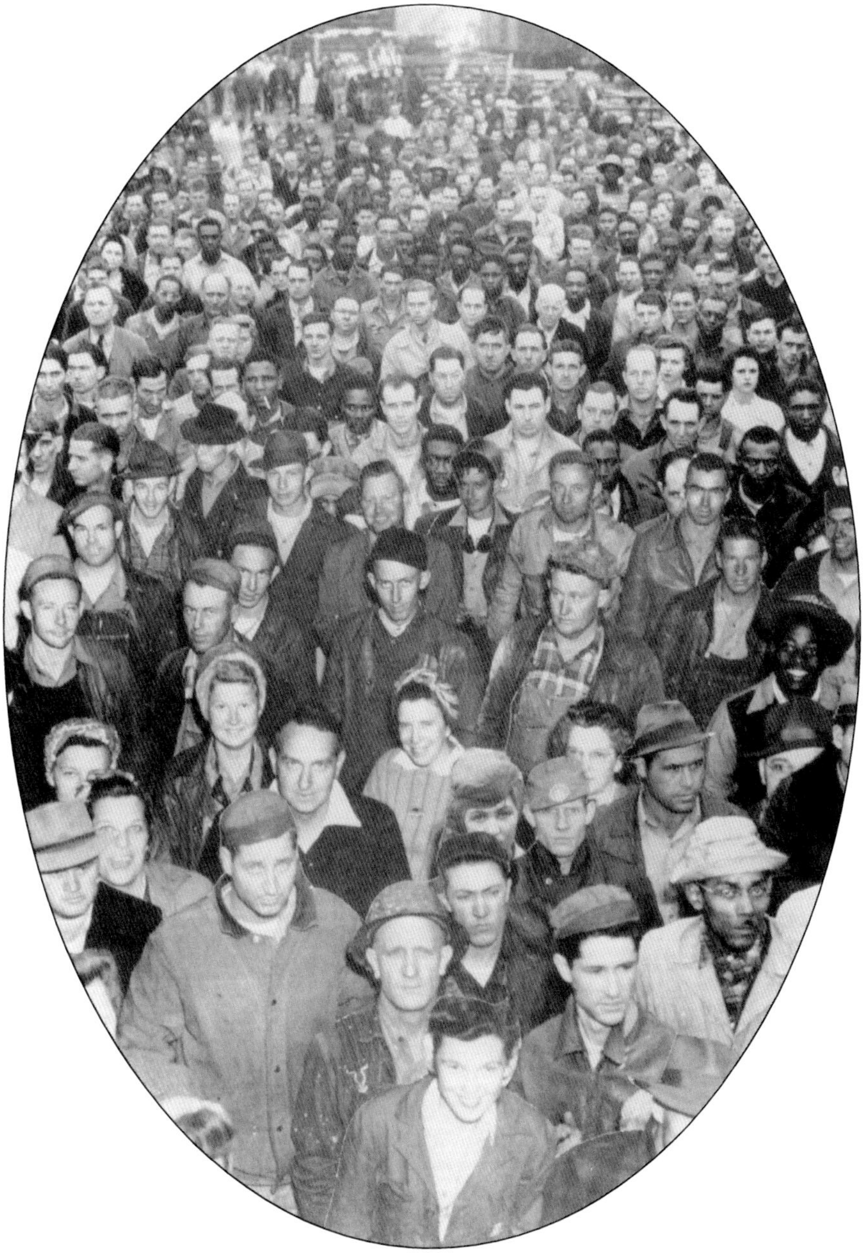

The shipyard employed so many people that the population of Wilmington grew by over 22,000 during the war years. Housing was a problem, so the government built apartments just for shipyard workers. Maffitt Village alone had 3,762 units. The Maritime Commission paid for 11 new city buses to transport the employees to work. During the war, 6,813 workers joined the armed forces or the Merchant Marines. More than 1,200 women worked at the shipyard. The on-site infirmary had 7 physicians and 17 nurses. Collectively, the shipyard employees bought over $20 million of war bonds and gave $239,000 in Community Chest campaigns. Shipyard management proudly said, "We take pride in the fact that in the space of five years, thousands of willing, non-professional shipbuilders have built a modern plant, solved the problems of training and changing requirements and man power drains and have built ships of a quality recognized throughout the world."

Four

1945–1975

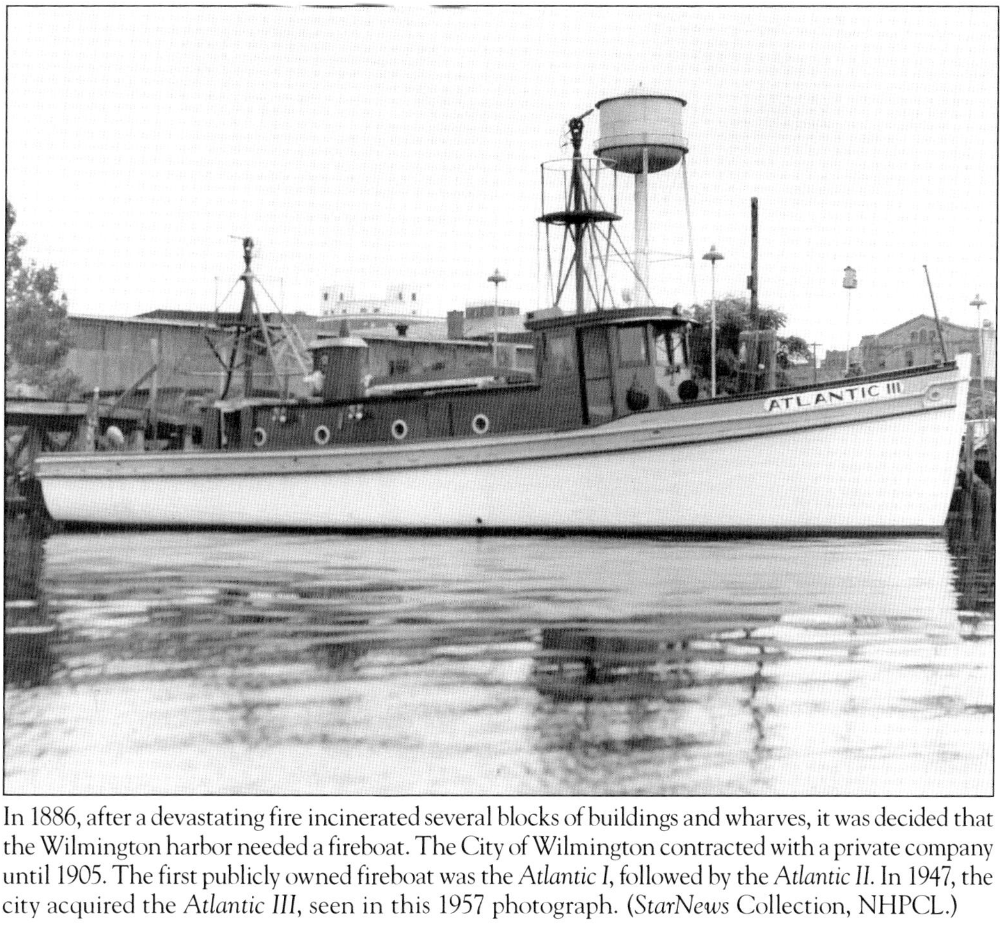

In 1886, after a devastating fire incinerated several blocks of buildings and wharves, it was decided that the Wilmington harbor needed a fireboat. The City of Wilmington contracted with a private company until 1905. The first publicly owned fireboat was the *Atlantic I*, followed by the *Atlantic II*. In 1947, the city acquired the *Atlantic III*, seen in this 1957 photograph. (*StarNews* Collection, NHPCL.)

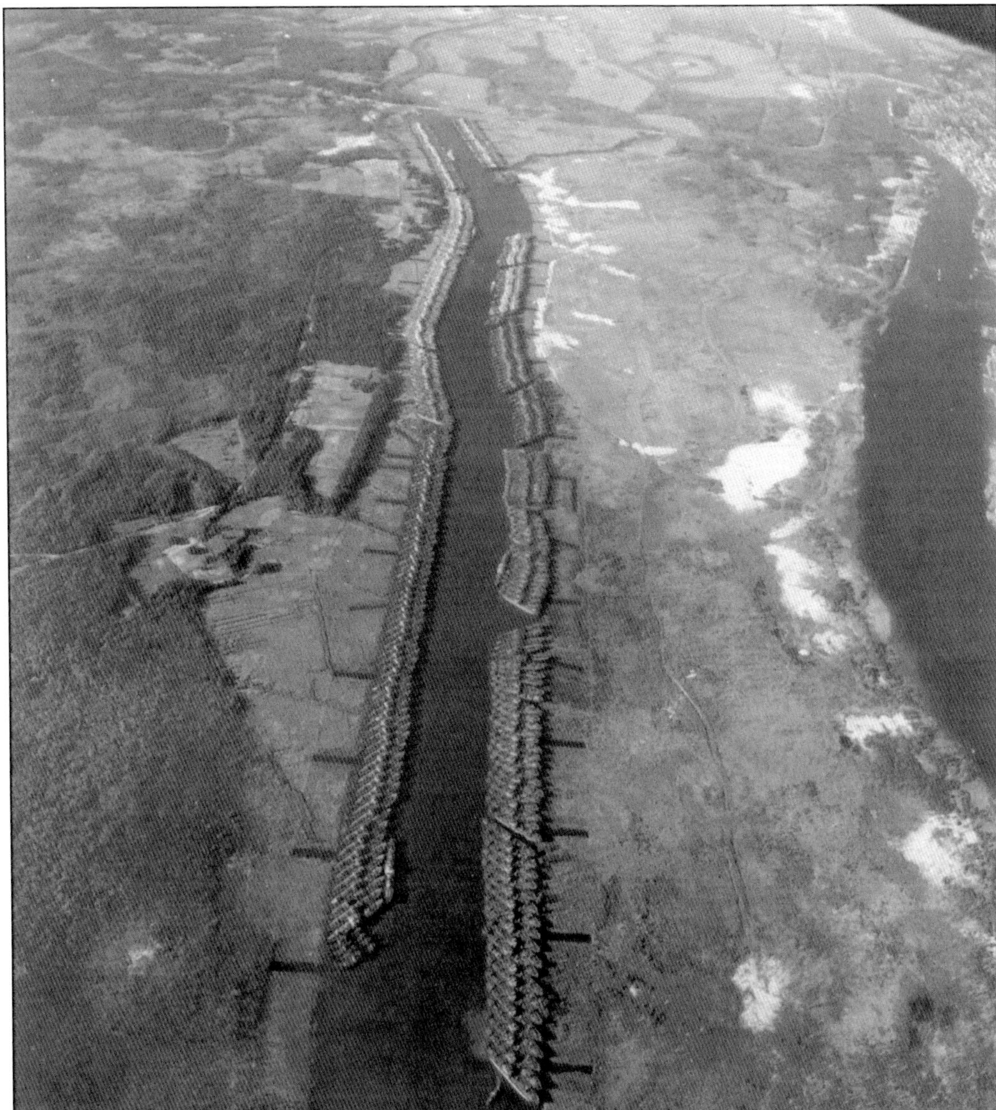

This aerial photograph was taken in the 1950s. The Cape Fear River and downtown Wilmington are at right, and the Brunswick River is shown lined with hundreds of ships of the reserve fleet. After World War II, the US Maritime Administration selected the Brunswick River as one of several locations for mothballing surplus troop transport vessels. On August 12, 1946, the first transport arrived at the Brunswick River facility, named the US Maritime Commission Reserve Fleet Basin. Vessels were removed from time to time, to go back into naval service, to be sold to foreign countries, or to scrap. Some were taken out of mothballs for service in the Korean War. In 1958, the number of ships peaked at 649. The last ship to leave was the SS *Dwight W. Morrow*, in early 1970.

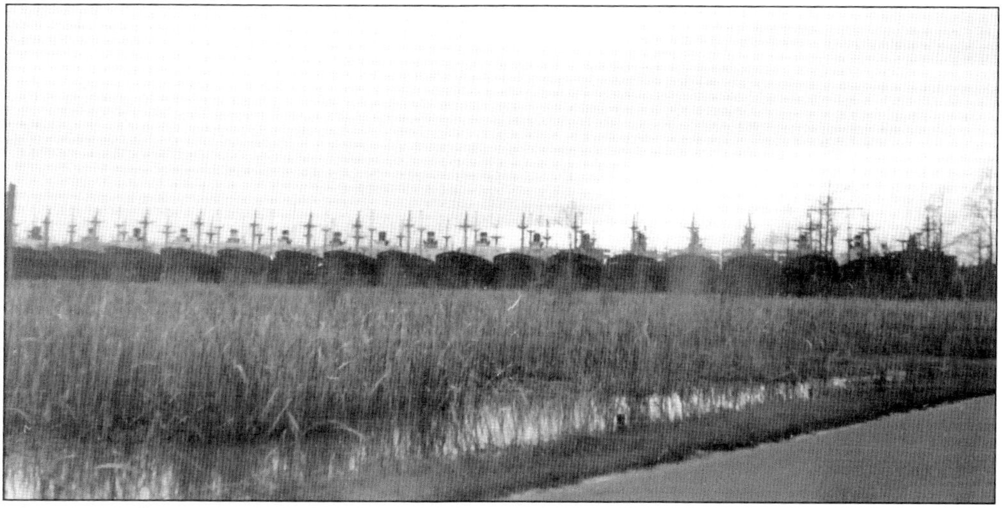

The reserve fleet was also known as "the mothball fleet," because the vessels were set aside and preserved in case of need, or "the ghost fleet," because boaters and fishermen said the ships looked haunted, especially on a misty day. Children loved to be taken into the layup basin, where they were told tales of World War II. In 1954, during Hurricane Hazel, some of the vessels became unmoored and entered the Cape Fear River, resulting in considerable damage. Afterward, engineers came up with a new, more secure way to anchor the ships, which were a fixture of the harbor for 24 years. (Both, *StarNews* Collection, NHCPL.)

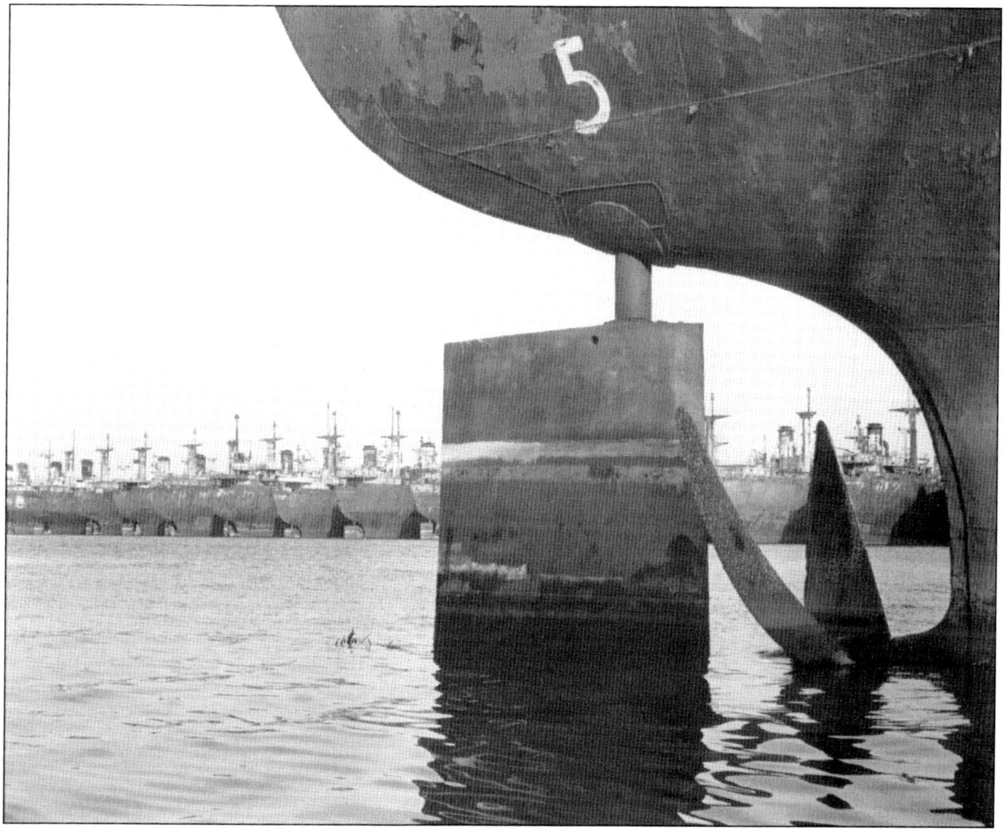

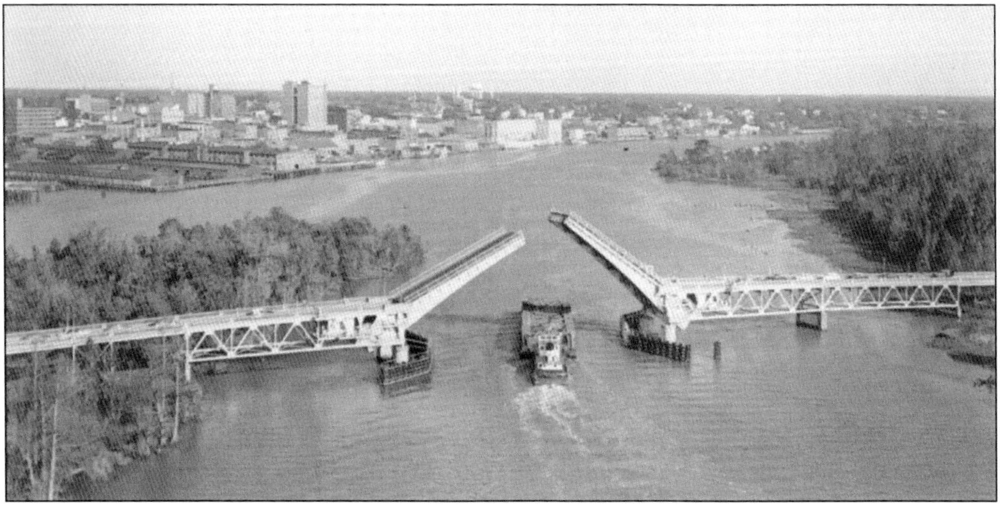

After World War II, Wilmington had 54 wharves, piers, and docks. Docking facilities could handle as many as 16 oceangoing vessels simultaneously. Imports far outnumbered exports, however, and Wilmington's status as a port was reduced from an international to a regional level, at which point it became an import distribution center. This postcard with a bird's-eye view of the Wilmington harbor is dated 1955.

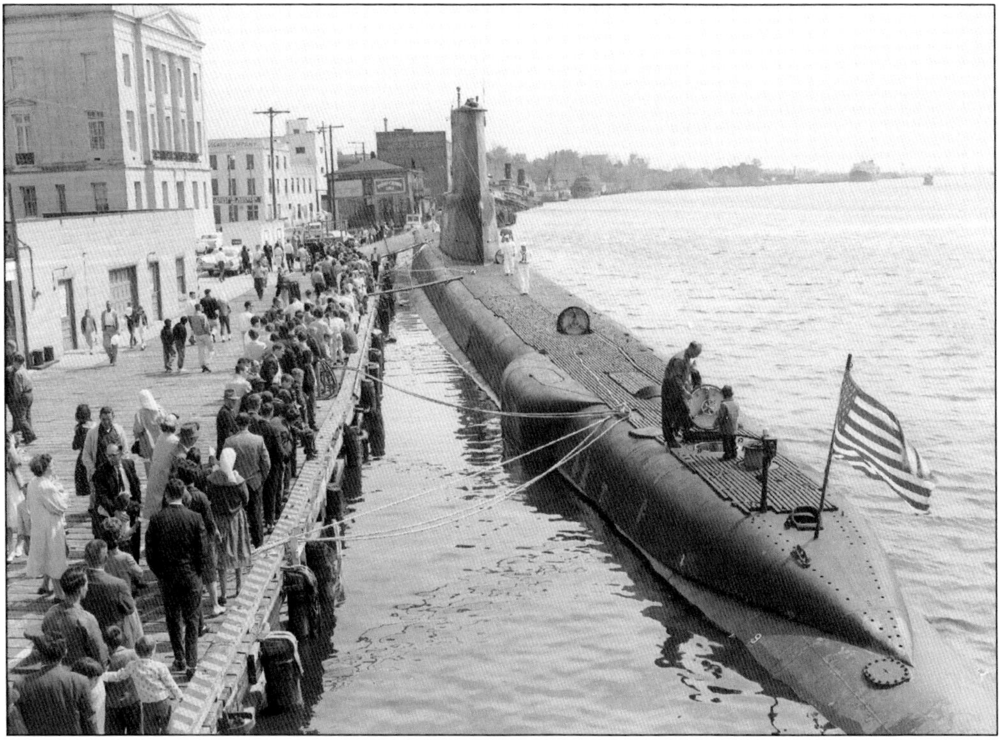

Wilmingtonians have always turned out in large numbers to see a visiting ship. Hugh Morton took this 1950s photograph of a crowd gathered to see the submarine *Sea Leopard*. Note that the government dock and bulkhead were still made of wood. A native of Wilmington, Morton took thousands of photographs of places and events all over North Carolina. (Hugh Morton Collection, University of North Carolina at Chapel Hill.)

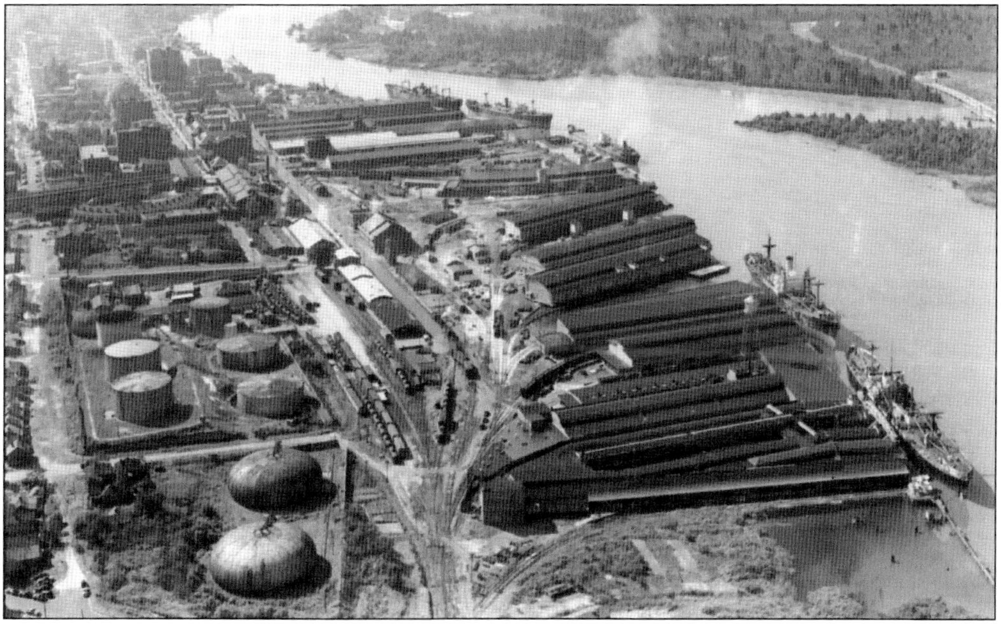

Hugh Morton documented the greatest fire in Wilmington history, on March 9, 1953. The fire started at 8:55 a.m. Within an hour, Morton was shooting aerial views of the conflagration at the Wilmington Terminal Company. Billowing thousands of feet into the air, the smoke could be seen from 25 miles away. With little time to spare, *Max Manus*, a Norwegian freighter, was towed away from the flaming dock. The crew of the fireboat *Atlantic III* was praised for its heroism in the blaze, which injured 21 persons and caused huge property losses. The fireboat plunged into the thick smoke, maneuvering between two slips where the flames could be pushed away from several warehouses. Morton took the photograph above sometime before the fire. (Both, Hugh Morton Collection, University of North Carolina at Chapel Hill.)

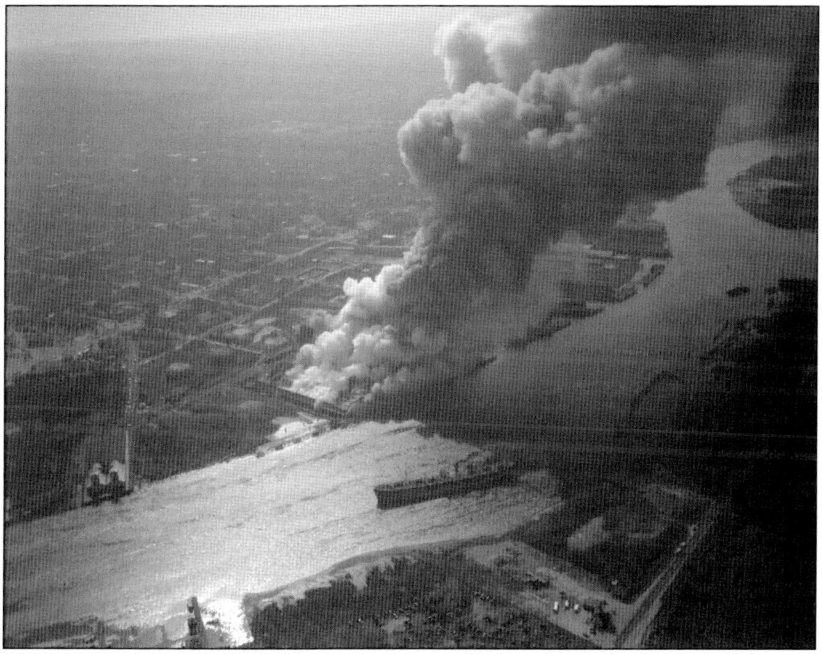

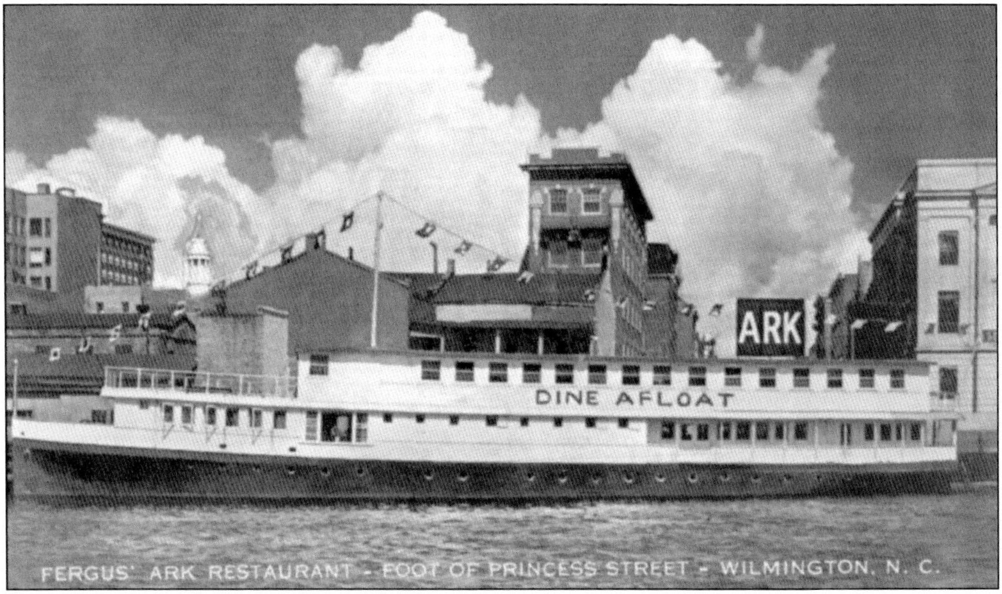

In 1951, Eldridge Fergus purchased a boat with a concrete hull that had been used from 1946 to 1949 as an office for the Brunswick River reserve fleet. Built in Wilmington in 1922, the vessel served as an army troop transport (1920s), a banana boat (1920s), a gambling boat (1930s), and a Coast Guard quarter vessel (1941) before returning to its home port. Fergus converted the boat into a floating restaurant that was moored at the foot of Princess Street. The postcard above is dated 1955. The photograph below, dated 1956, shows the location of the Ark Restaurant on the waterfront. At left is the USCGC *Mendota*, moored at the government wharf.

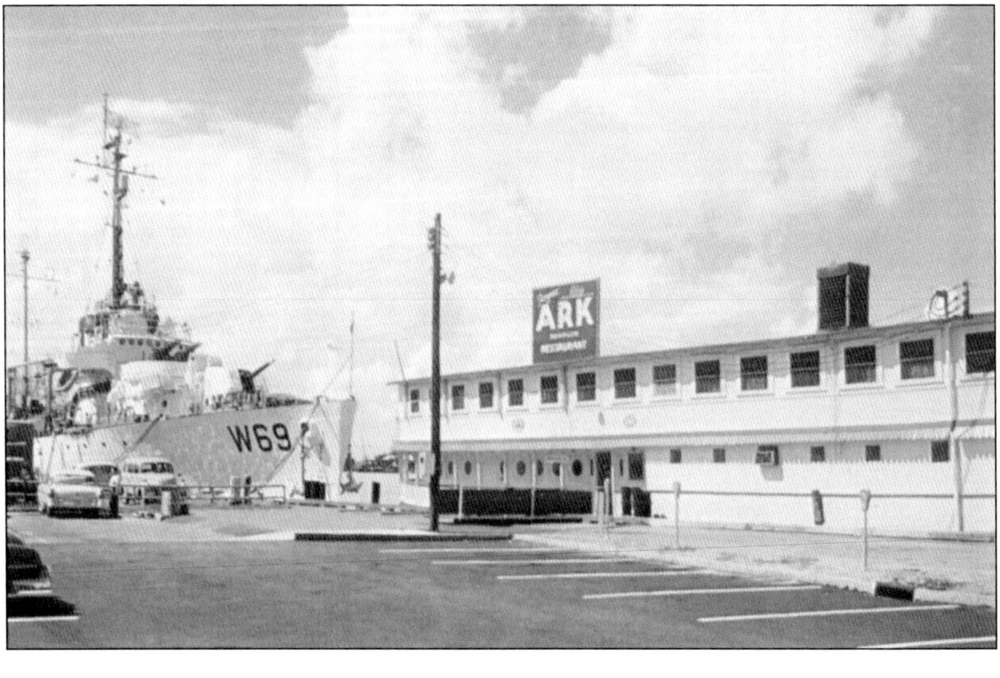

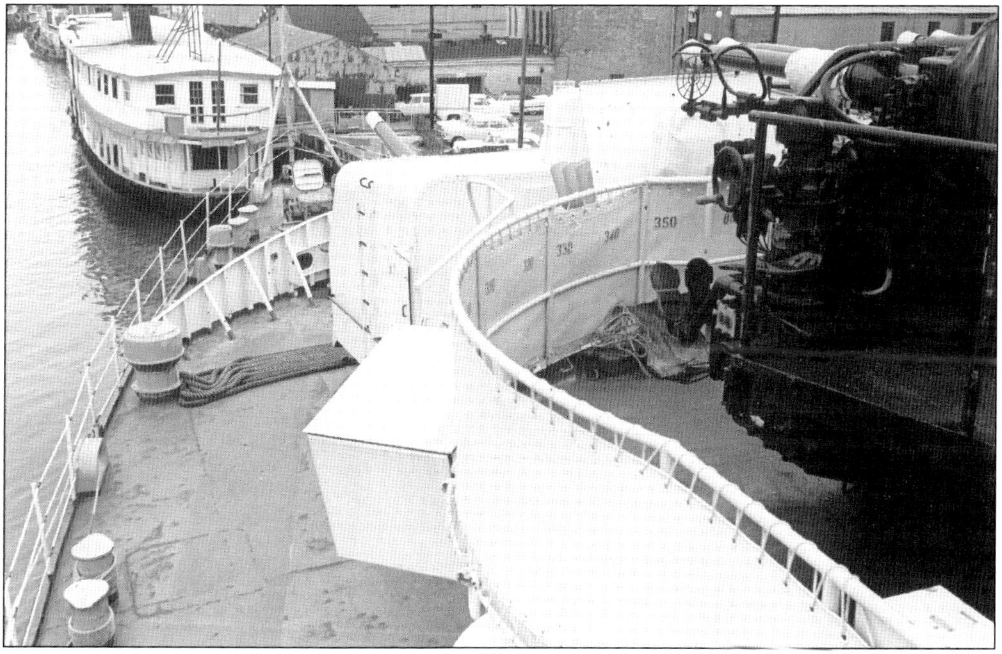

Fergus's *Ark* was located across the river from the battleship *North Carolina*, which sailed into Wilmington on October 2, 1961. The most difficult part of navigating the battleship to its berth was the turn that had to be made to enter the slip. At that point, the river was 550 feet wide, and the ship was 728 feet long. As the tugboats began to push the battleship, her bow got stuck in the mud, and her stern hit the *Ark* on the port side. Fergus claimed the *Ark* was the only vessel to be struck by a US battleship in US waters. He had a purple star painted at the point of impact. The photograph below was taken on December 5, 1965, when the *Ark* was being towed away to Florida, where it was reborn as another floating restaurant.

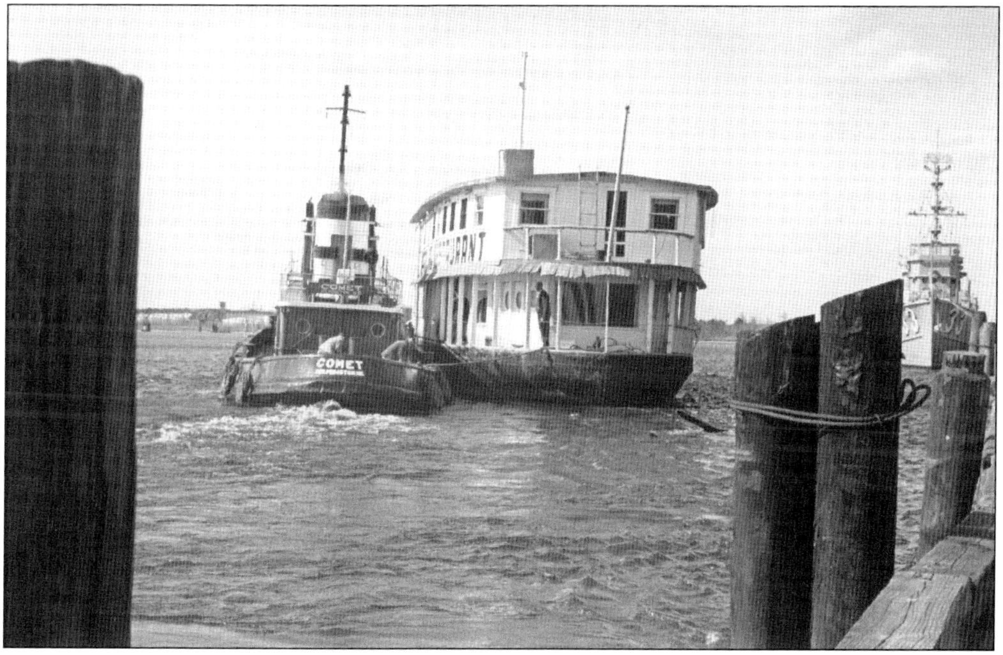

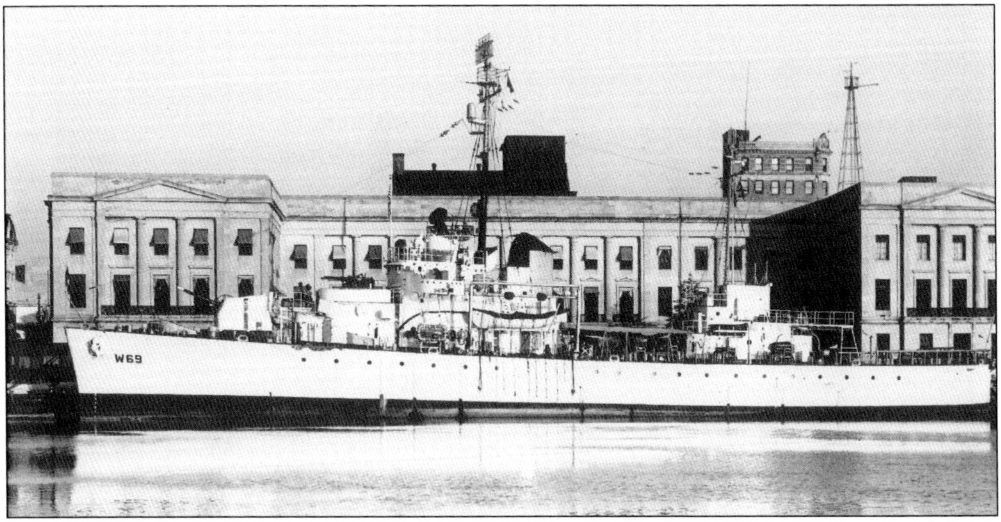

Over the years, Coast Guard vessels stationed in Wilmington have enforced tariff and trade laws; apprehended pirates, smugglers, rumrunners, and drug runners; conducted search-and-rescue operations; dismantled ice floes and conducted iceberg patrols; aided weather forecasting; served with Navy units in wartime; protected the environment; and provided homeland security. These photographs show the USCGC *Mendota*, which was stationed in Wilmington from 1947 to 1972. The photograph above was taken early in her service in Wilmington, whereas the photograph below shows a homecoming late in her Wilmington career. (Both, *StarNews* Collection, NHCPL.)

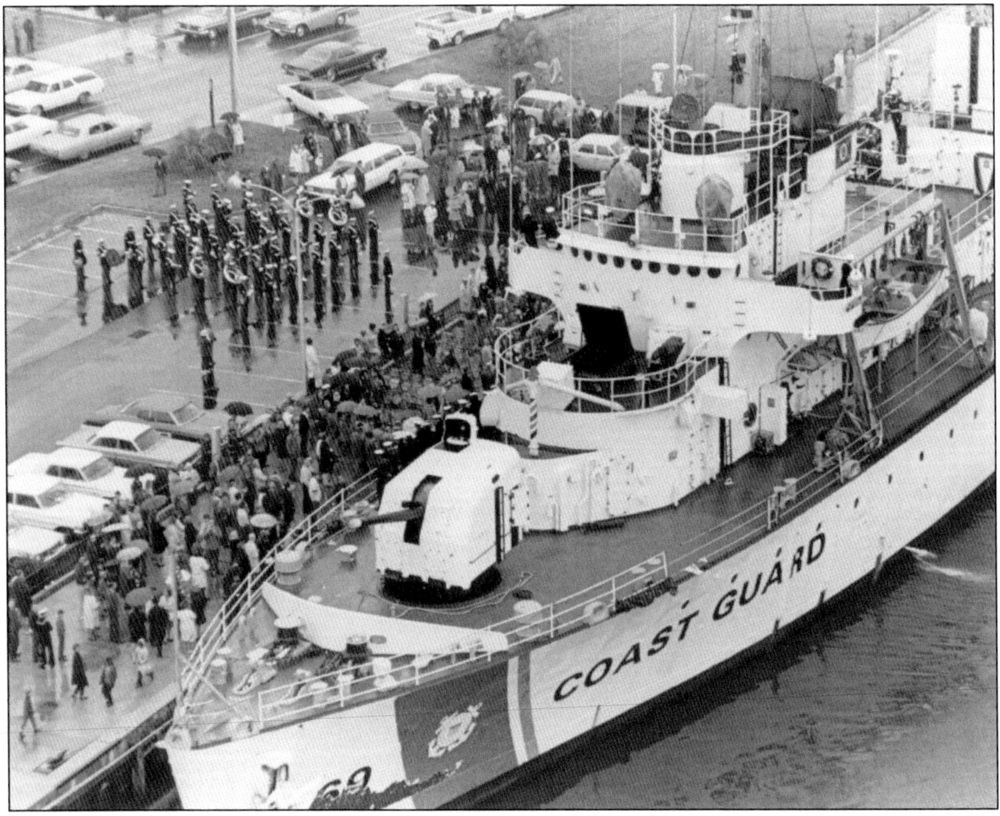

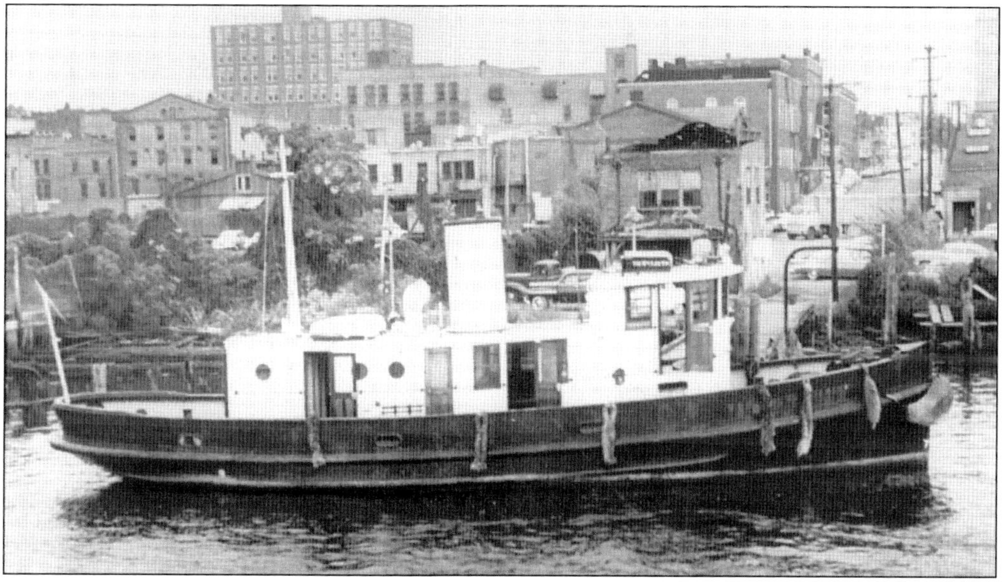

The photograph above shows the *Atlantic III* moored at the fireboat station house of the Wilmington Fire Department. Located at the foot of Grace Street, the station was built in 1926 and torn down during urban renewal. The tall building in the background was the Hotel Wilmington, torn down in 1975. The photograph below shows the *Atlantic III* and the *Atlantic IV* side by side at the fireboat station dock, shortly before the retirement of the older tugboat. The *Atlantic IV*, a steel-hull tugboat, replaced the *Atlantic III* in 1961. Built in Bath, Maine, in 1932, the *Atlantic IV* had served as a floating medical examination room for the US Public Health Service as well as an icebreaker on the Chesapeake Bay before coming to Wilmington. After 25 years of service, the vessel was replaced in 1986. (Both, *StarNews* Collection, NHCPL.)

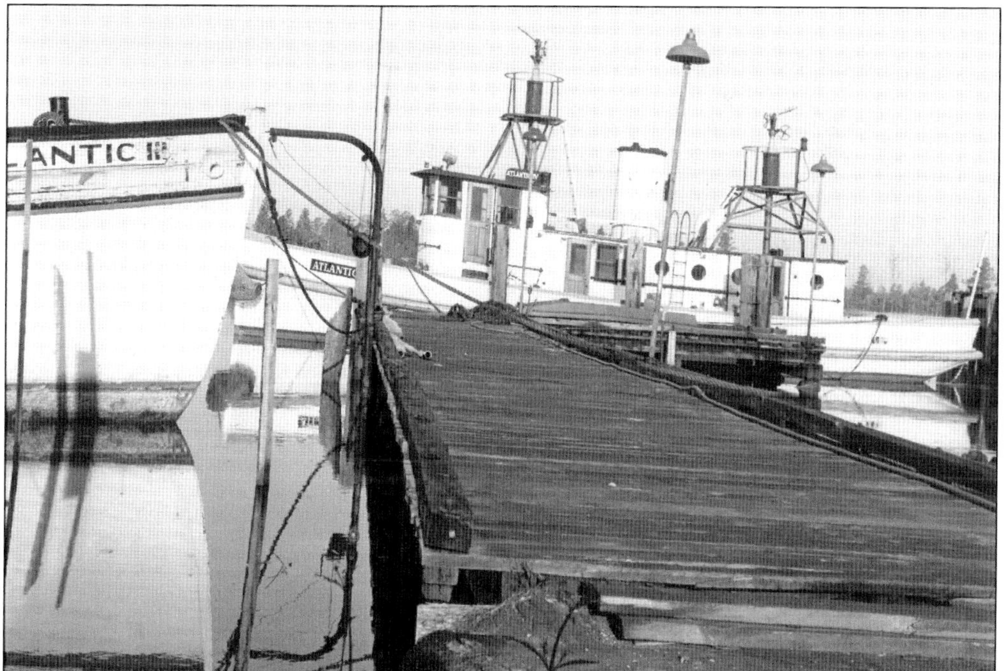

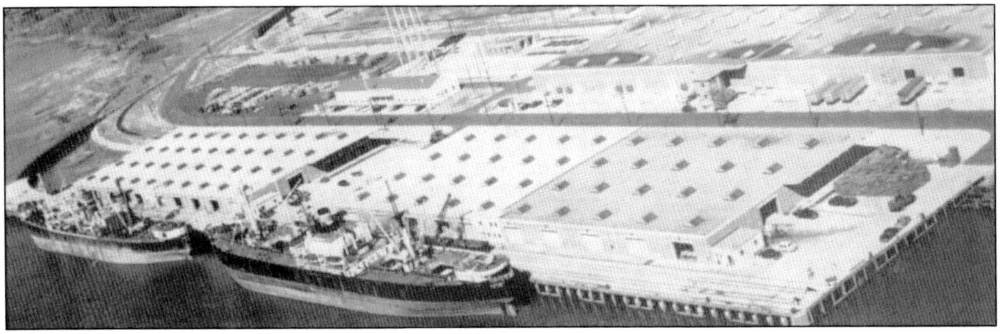

In 1949, North Carolina issued $7.5 million worth of bonds to build two ports: one in Morehead City and one in Wilmington. Two-thirds of the bonds were issued for Wilmington. In 1950, construction began at the former site of the North Carolina Shipbuilding Company. In Wilmington, the North Carolina Ocean Terminals are known as the state docks. Not long after opening, the state docks began controlling nine-tenths of shipping in the Wilmington harbor. The photograph above shows the state docks shortly after construction. Within nine years, the port had a 2,510-foot wharf that could accommodate five 5,500-foot vessels. The photograph below shows longshoremen unloading a vessel at night in 1969.

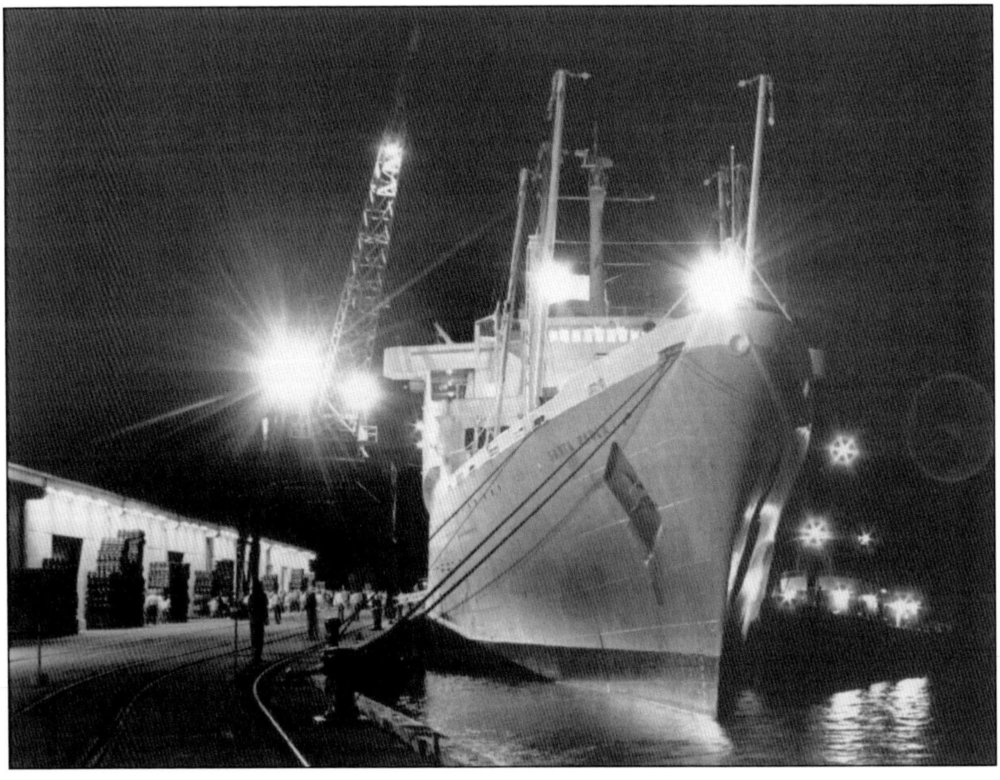

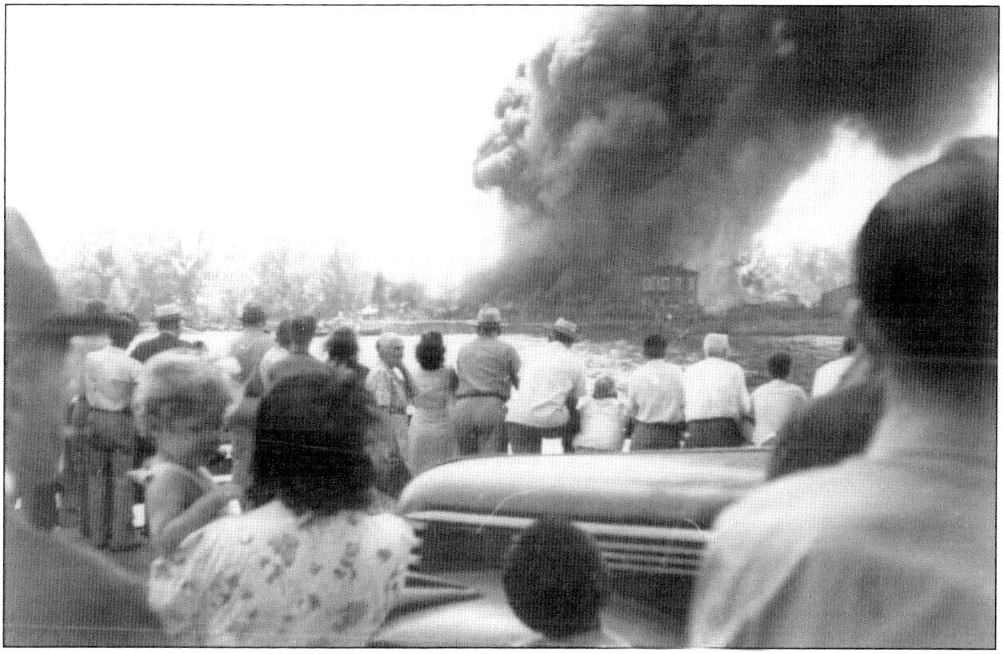

These photographs were taken by Charles M. Paty in 1946. He said, "Shortly after I was discharged from the US Navy I made a trip with my father to Wilmington. I was downtown and observed a very large fire across the river on Eagles Island. I whipped out my camera and started shooting." The photographs were taken on Water Street between Market and Dock Streets. Most of the buildings located directly across the river were burned. The area was mostly uninhabited until the battleship *North Carolina* sailed into Wilmington in 1961.

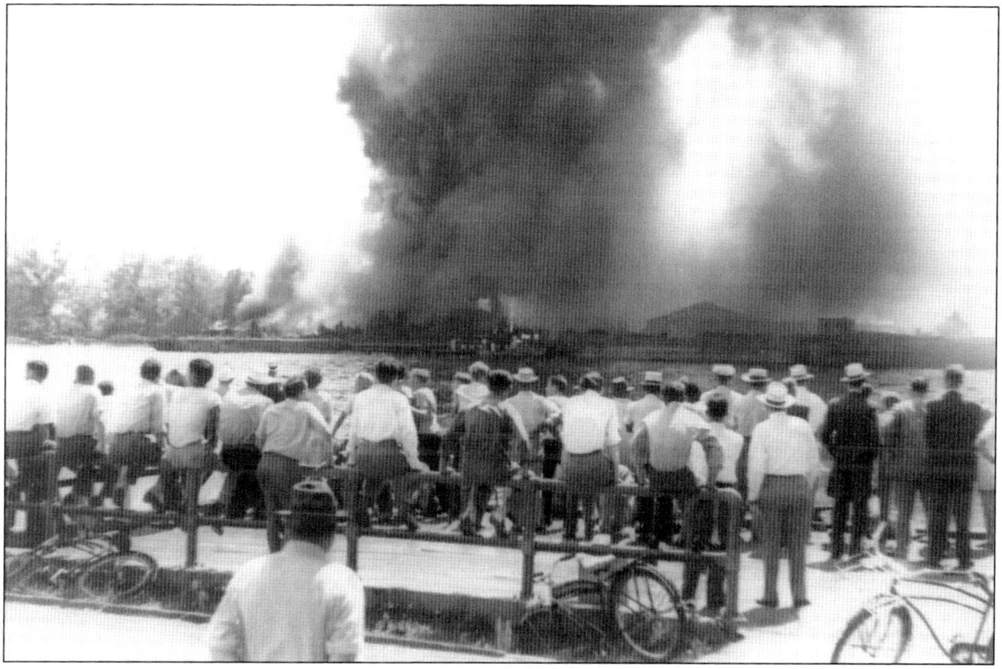

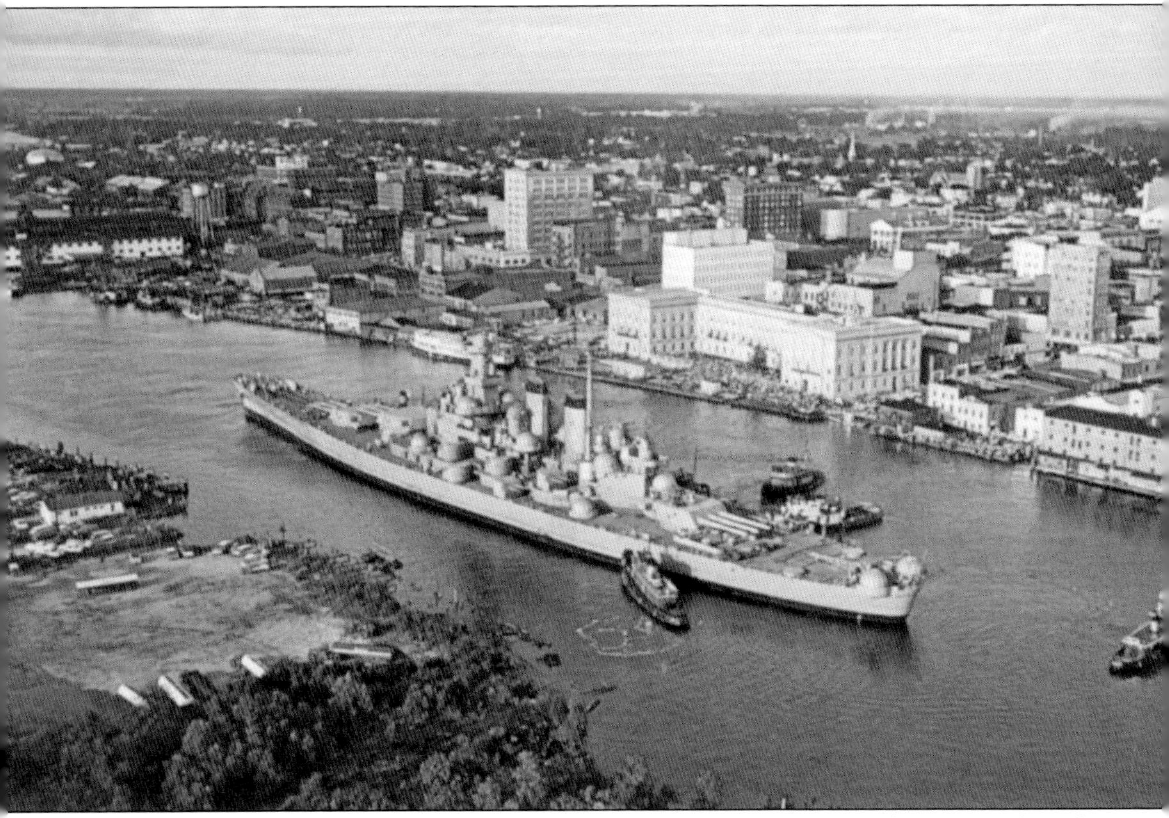

A grand statewide effort to commemorate World War II was completed in 1961, when the battleship *North Carolina* found a permanent berth on the west side of the Cape Fear River. A year after news had reached Wilmington that the battleship was going to be scrapped, James S. Craig suggested obtaining the battleship and moving her to Wilmington as a memorial to the 10,000 North Carolinians who had perished in the war. A Battleship Commission was formed, and, under the leadership of Wilmington native Hugh Morton, it succeeded in raising the funds to complete the project. Generous donations poured in from across the state, including pennies, nickels, and dimes collected by North Carolina schoolchildren. Thousands of citizens watched as the mighty ship arrived on October 2, 1961. The ship's fire control tower was taller than any of Wilmington's buildings, and the ship's length was greater than two city blocks.

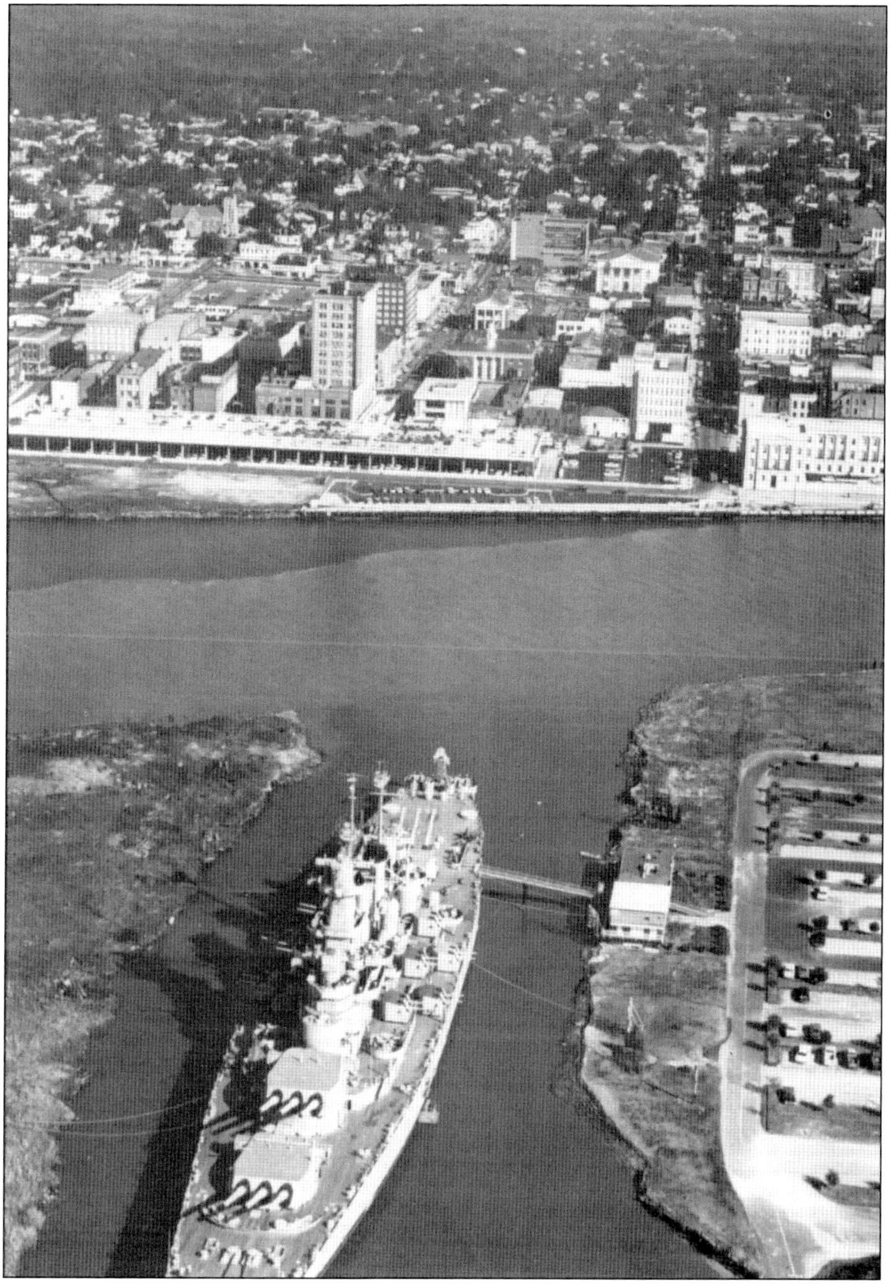

The battleship *North Carolina*, seen here in 1965, became a major tourist draw for the Wilmington harbor. North Carolinians had saved it, and now they wanted to visit it. At the same time, the City of Wilmington embraced a bold new plan called the Waterfront Renewal Project. The idea was to rejuvenate the harbor by tearing down old buildings and constructing new ones, most of which was funded by the federal Urban Renewal Administration of the Housing and Home Finance Agency. The large parking deck seen across the river from the battleship was one of these funded projects. At a cost of $635,000, it was built in hopes of bringing shoppers and tourists downtown. For 225 years, the harbor had been the center of commercial activity. The new plan looked to the river as the center of recreational activity.

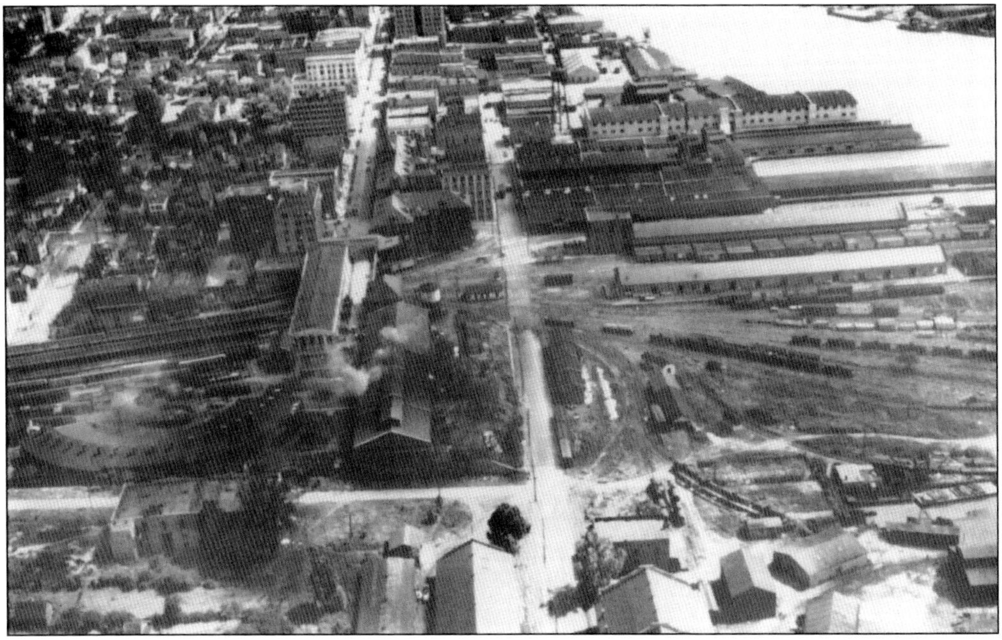

This is an aerial view of the Atlantic Coast Line Railroad (ACL) complex in the early 1950s. Wilmington was a railroad town through and through until December 10, 1955, known as Black Thursday, when the ACL announced it was going to relocate the company headquarters to Florida. By 1960, the transition was complete, and over 1,300 employees and their families had left Wilmington.

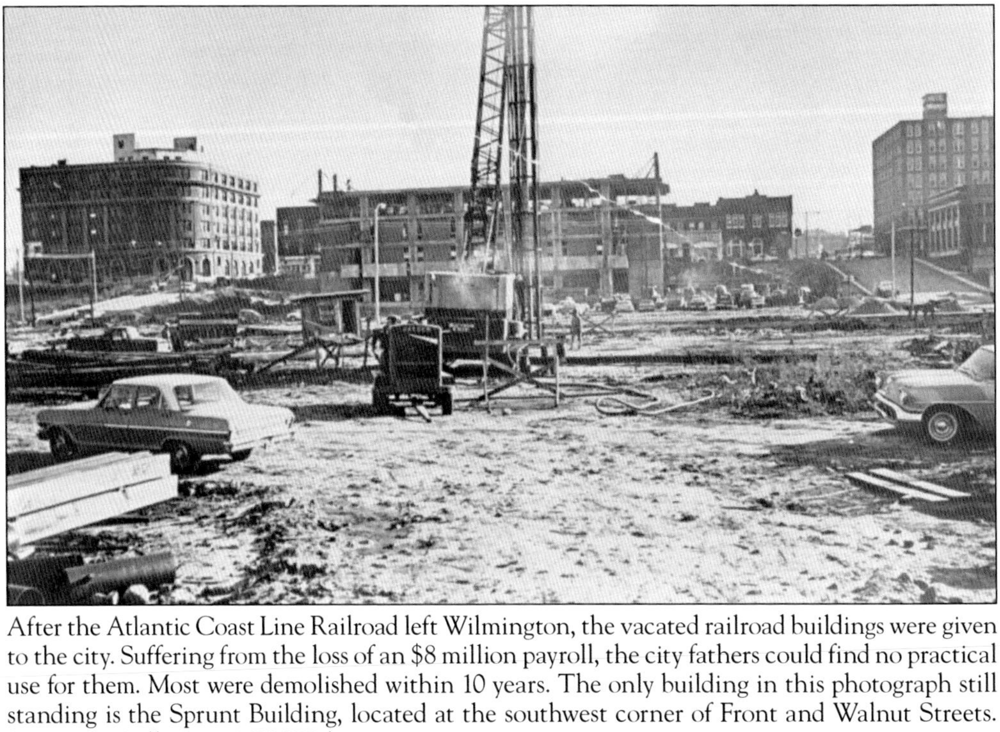

After the Atlantic Coast Line Railroad left Wilmington, the vacated railroad buildings were given to the city. Suffering from the loss of an $8 million payroll, the city fathers could find no practical use for them. Most were demolished within 10 years. The only building in this photograph still standing is the Sprunt Building, located at the southwest corner of Front and Walnut Streets. (*StarNews* Collection, NHCPL.)

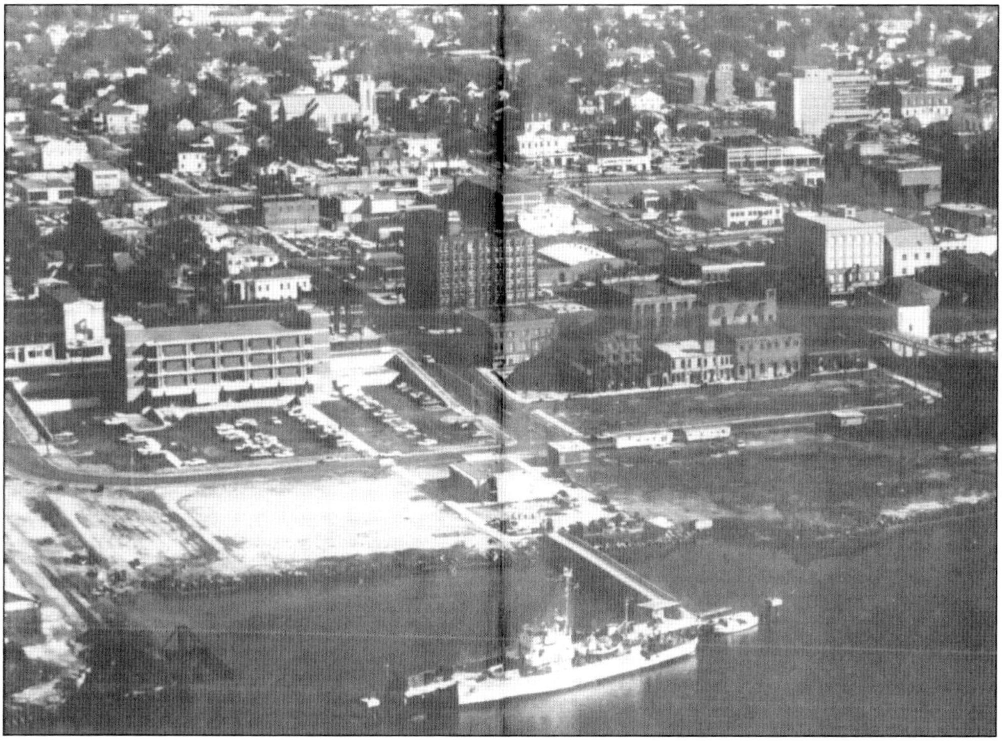

Part of the Waterfront Renewal Project included $1.075 million to construct a new campus for the Cape Fear Technical Institute. This aerial view was taken from the 1968 school yearbook. The school needed a waterfront location because it focused on marine technology. Students got hands-on training in commercial fishing, boatbuilding, marine salvage, diving, marine engineering, environmental protection, and fish farming. (Cape Fear Community College.)

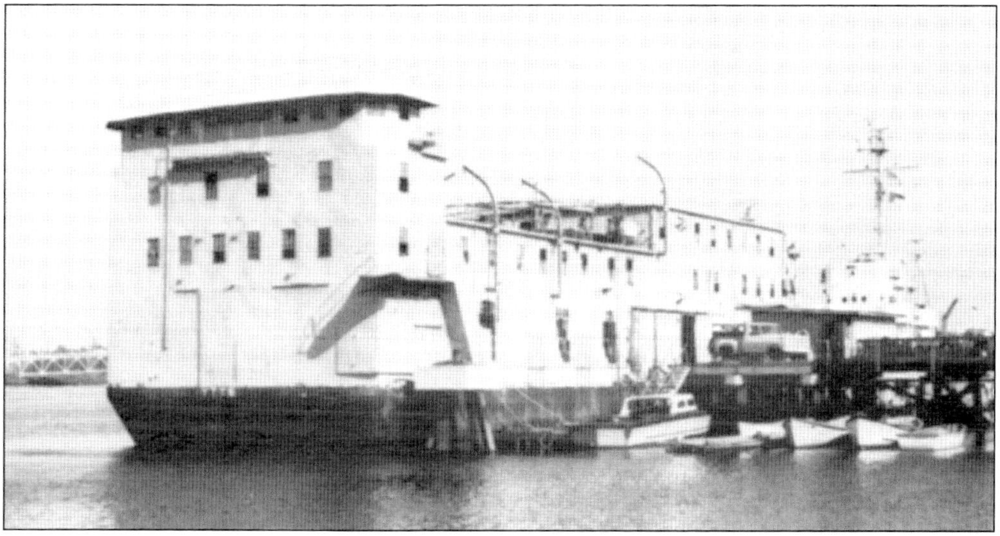

As the Cape Fear Technical Institute grew in popularity, it outgrew its classroom capacity. To solve this problem, the school acquired this World War II–era barge for use as a floating classroom. At 150 feet long, it had four decks and covered 28,000 square feet. Both students and faculty renovated the vessel, which was used for nearly five years. (Cape Fear Community College.)

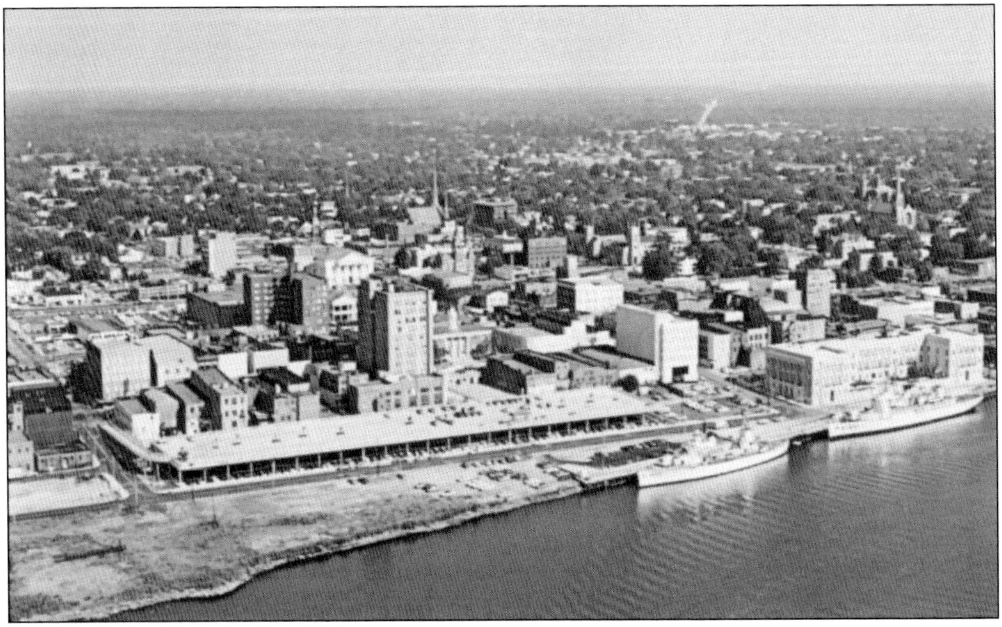

These postcards depict the changing landscape of the Wilmington waterfront in the early 1970s. The battleship and little else can be seen on the once-bustling Eagles Island. Site improvements on the east side of the river included grading and street repaving, as well as water, sewage, and drainage installations. The new 600,000-square-foot Coast Guard docking facility can be seen in the postcard above. In the postcard below is the Timme Plaza Hotel, built in 1970. A vital component of the city's urban renewal plan was a modern hotel. It had 156 guest rooms, a restaurant, a lounge, a large banquet room, a swimming pool, and plenty of parking. Hilton Hotels eventually purchased the hotel, which, as Hilton Riverside, has been remodeled and expanded.

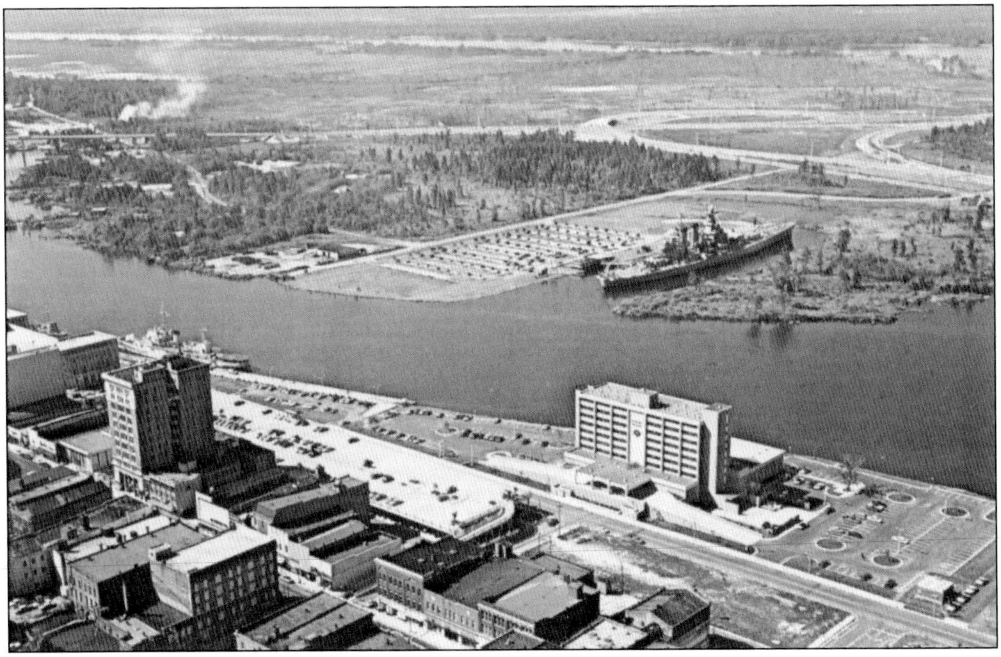

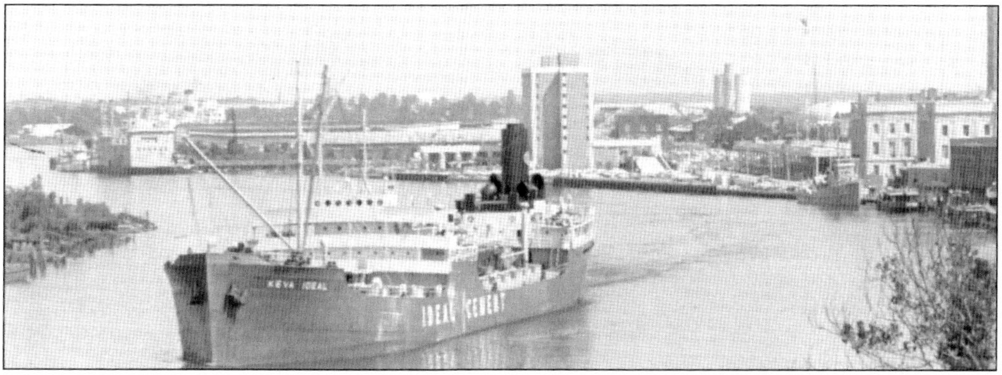

Along with urban renewal, waterborne commerce continued on the northern end of the harbor. In this 1971 photograph, an Ideal Cement Company vessel is heading downriver. The company was located on the Northeast Cape Fear River. The Alton Lennon Federal Building is in the background at right, and the tall building in the center is the Hilton Riverside Hotel. (*StarNews* Collection, NHCPL.)

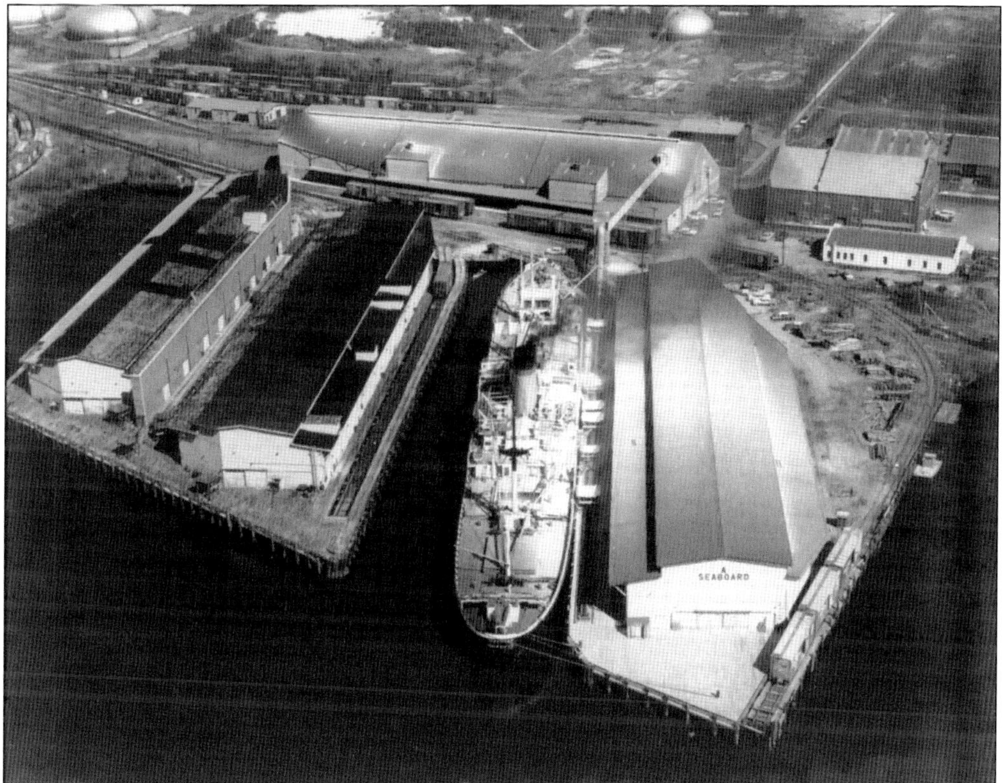

In 1962, photographer Joe Nesbitt took this aerial shot of the Seabord Air Line dock, which is located near the current site of the Wilmington Convention Center. The boxcars would unload onto freighters at water's edge. Occasionally, one would end up in the Cape Fear River. The vessel, named *Tzoynitep Neipaieyz*, hailed from Greece. (Joe Nesbitt Collection, NHPCL.)

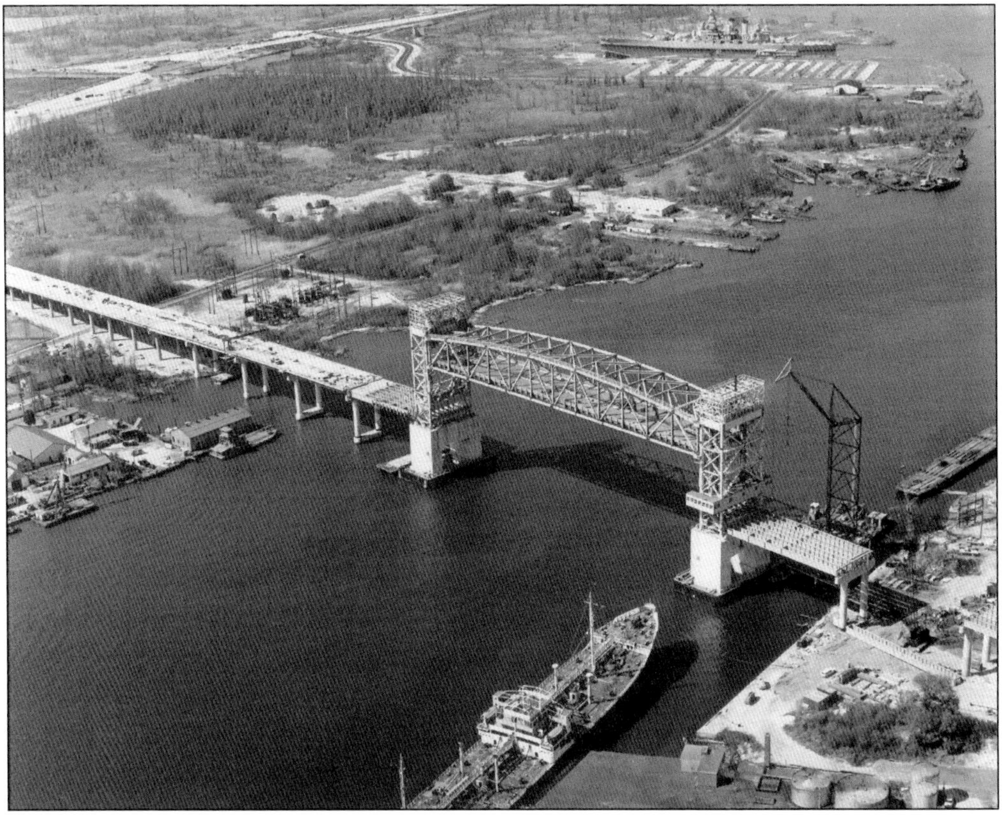

The first bridge to be constructed in Wilmington since the twin bridges of 1929 was the Cape Fear Memorial Bridge, named in honor of those who served in World War II. Construction began in 1966, when concrete was poured for the east tower pier. Elevator towers mark both sides of the main channel, from which a 400-foot lift span is raised to allow river traffic to pass underneath. Costing more than $16 million, the Cape Fear Memorial Bridge was dedicated in September 1969. The photograph below was taken during its first week of operation. (Both, *StarNews* Collection, NHCPL.)

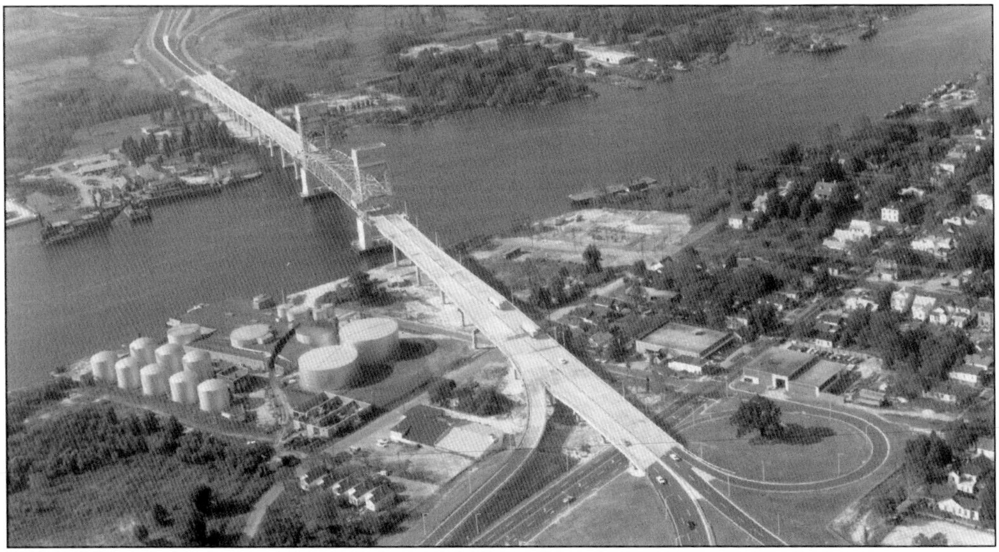

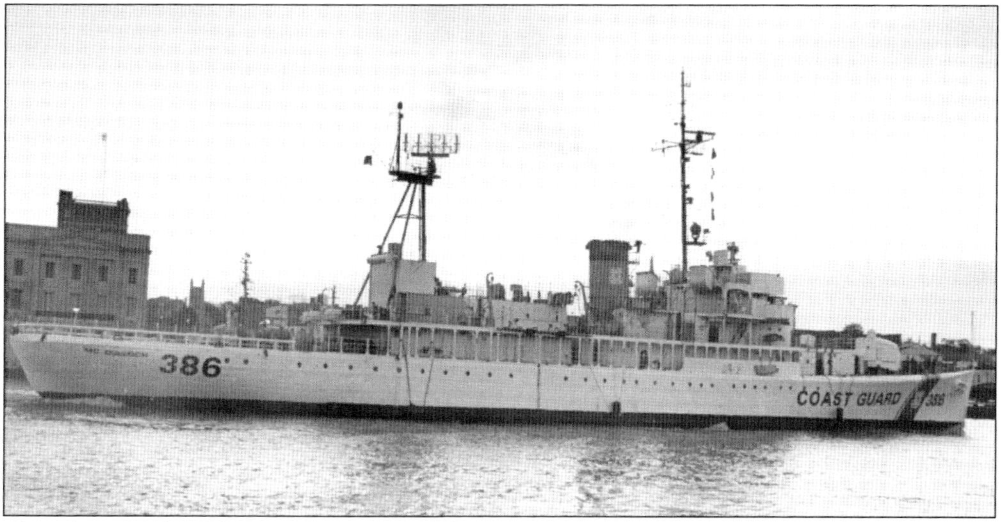

This photograph of the USCGC *McCulloch* was taken on February 8, 1972, near the end of her time in Wilmington. The cutter began service as a Navy torpedo boat tender in World War II. In 1946, she was transferred to the Coast Guard and refitted for ocean-station duty. Stationed in Wilmington from 1966 to 1972, she performed weather reporting as well as search-and-rescue tasks. (*StarNews* Collection, NHCPL.)

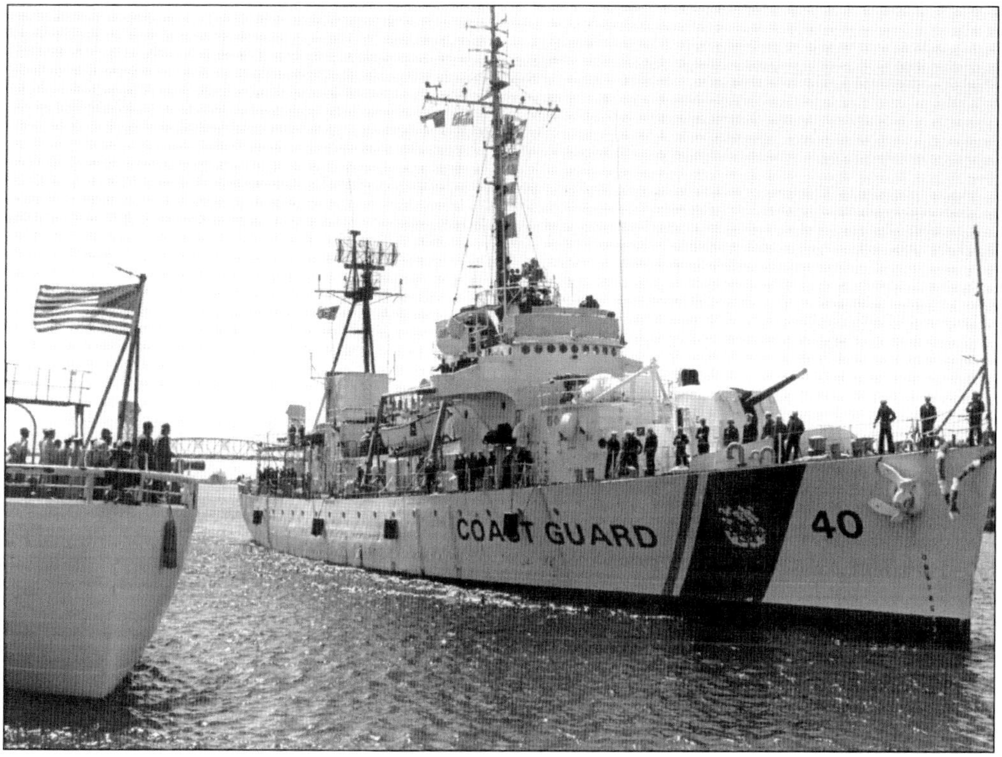

In this photograph, taken on March 24, 1972, the USCGC *McCulloch* leaves the harbor as the USCGC *Winnebago* sails upriver to begin duty in Wilmington. Stationed in Wilmington from March 1972 to February 1973, the *Winnebago* was used for law enforcement, ocean-station duty, and search-and-rescue efforts. (*StarNews* Collection, NHCPL.)

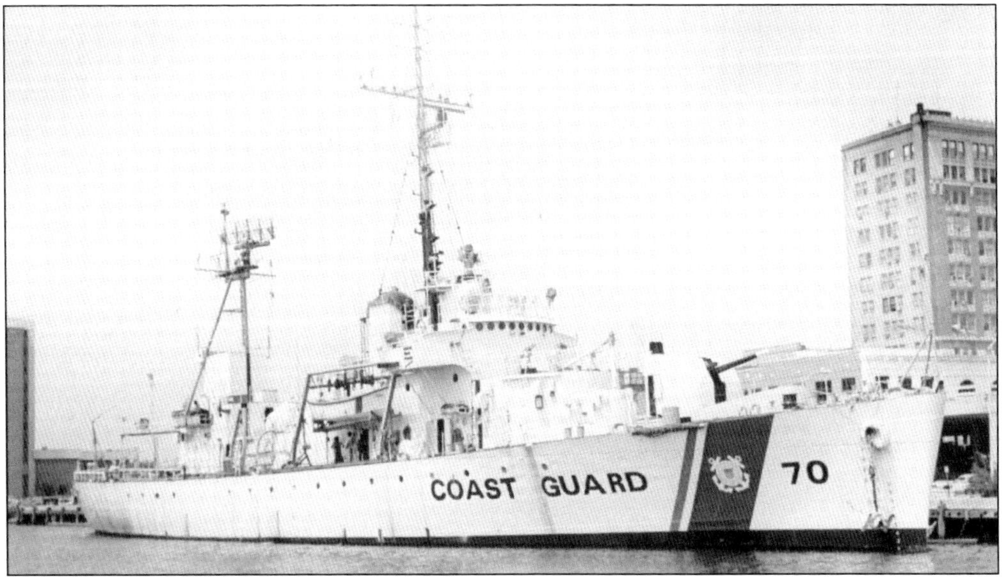

Before she came to Wilmington, the USCGC *Pontchartrain* was assigned to Coast Guard Squadron Three, Vietnam, from March 31 to November 9, 1970. She was stationed in Wilmington from 1971 to 1973. These photographs were taken as the cutter prepared to depart for a European cruise on June 4, 1973. Friends and family, as well as a few girlfriends, are gathered along the waterfront to bid farewell to the crewmen. The *Pontchartrain* was used for law enforcement, ocean-station duty, and search-and-rescue missions. She was decommissioned on October 19, 1973, then scrapped the next year. (Both, *StarNews* Collection, NHPCL.)

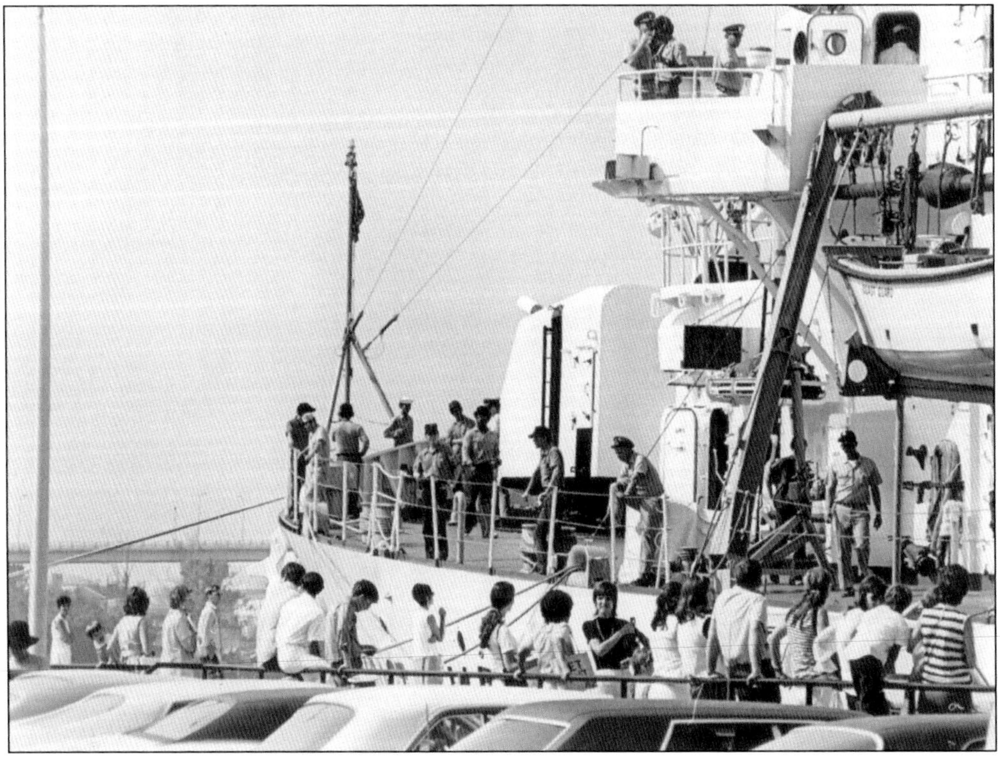

Five

1975–2013

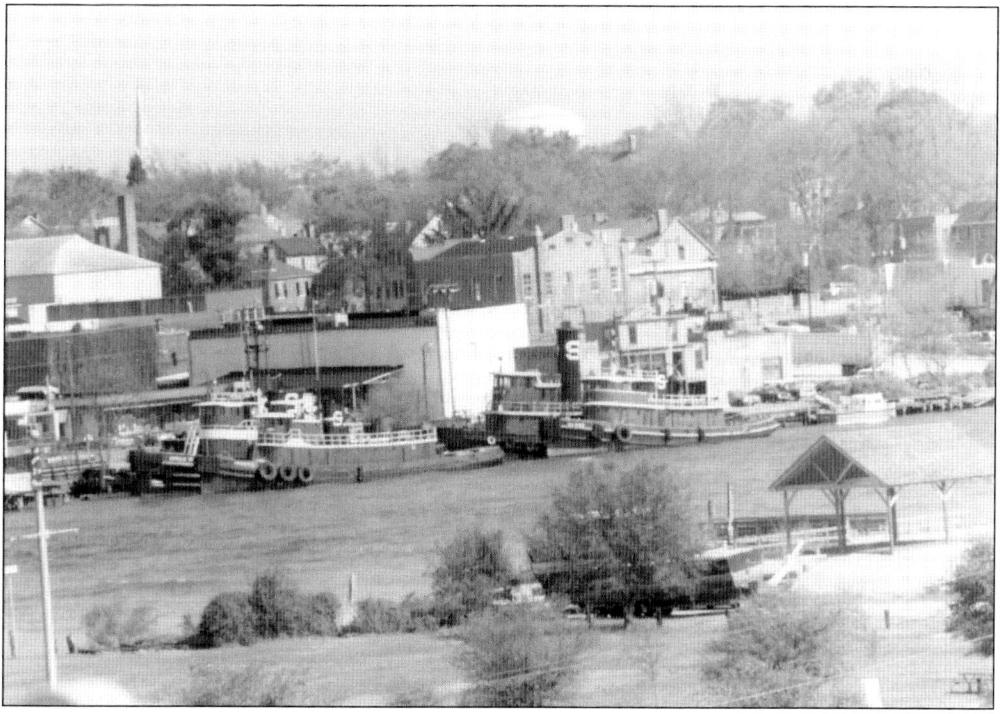

This photograph was taken from the battleship in 1975. The white building in the center surrounded by the Stone Towing Company tugboats was the old icehouse, built in 1845. Ice shipped from New England lakes and rivers was stored here until the invention of manufactured ice in the 1880s. R.C. Fergus & Sons Wholesale Seafood occupied the building at the time this photograph was taken.

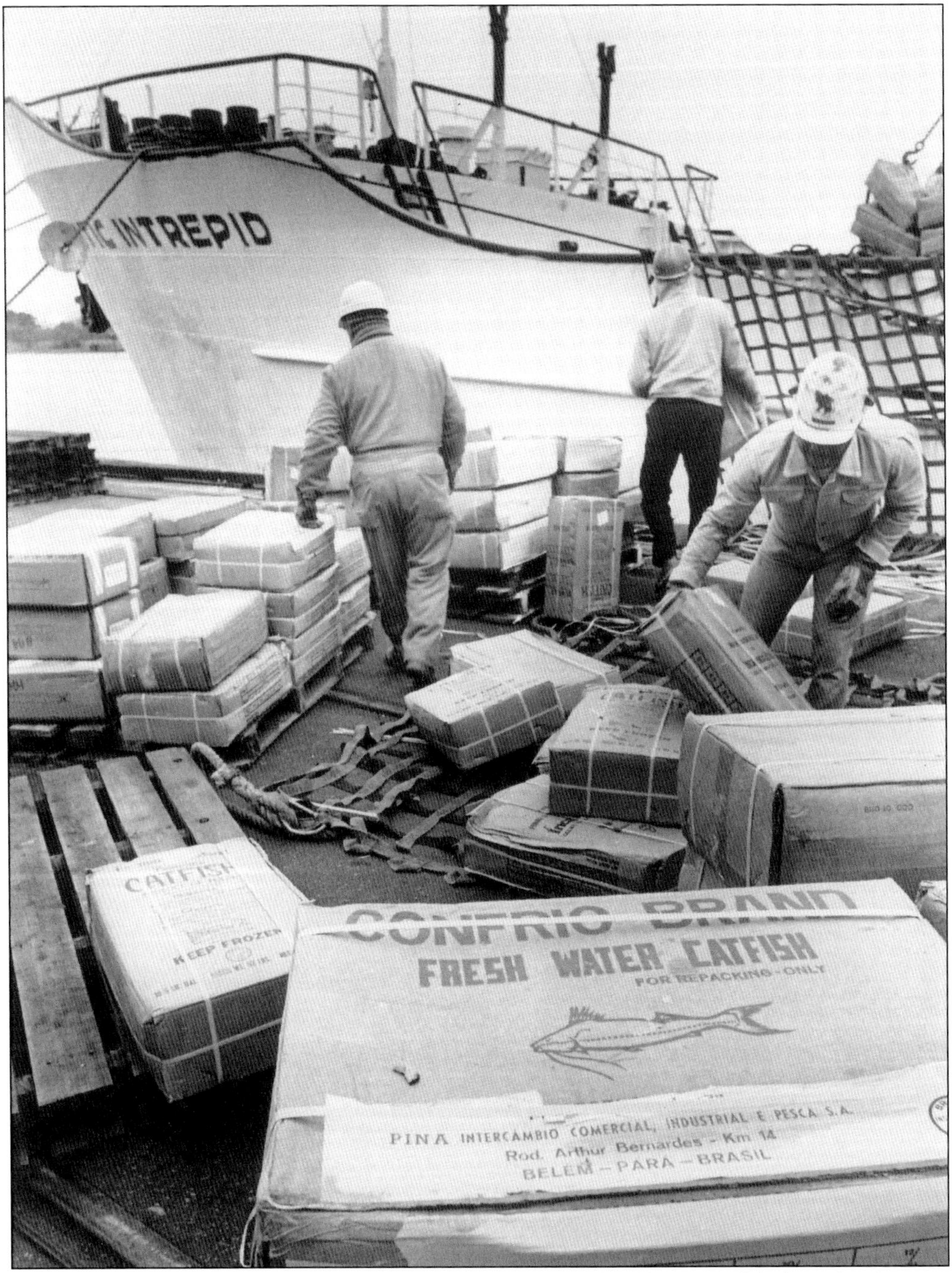

On December 4, 1976, longshoremen unloaded 447,547 pounds of frozen catfish from the Amazon at the North Carolina State Port at Wilmington. The fish were bound for Tennessee, Louisiana, and California. The boxes of fish were break bulk cargo, or non-containerized general cargo, stored in crates, barrels, pallets, or other units to be loaded onto or discharged from ships and other forms of transportation. Other kinds of break bulk cargo are iron, steel, machinery, linerboard, wood pulp, lumber, hogsheads, tobacco, pipes, and telephone poles—all of which can be placed in a container. (*StarNews* Collection, NHCPL.)

Joe Nesbitt took this aerial view of the North Carolina State Port at Wilmington in 1981. One ship is unloading at the port while another one at midstream is leaving the harbor after loading at the oil terminal. The Cape Fear Memorial Bridge can be seen in the distance. (*StarNews* Collection, NHCPL.)

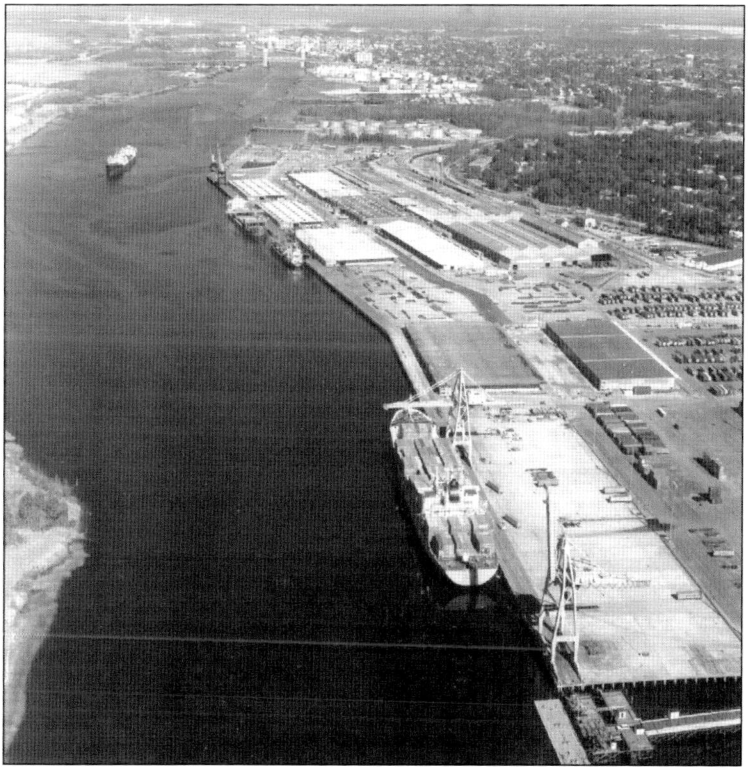

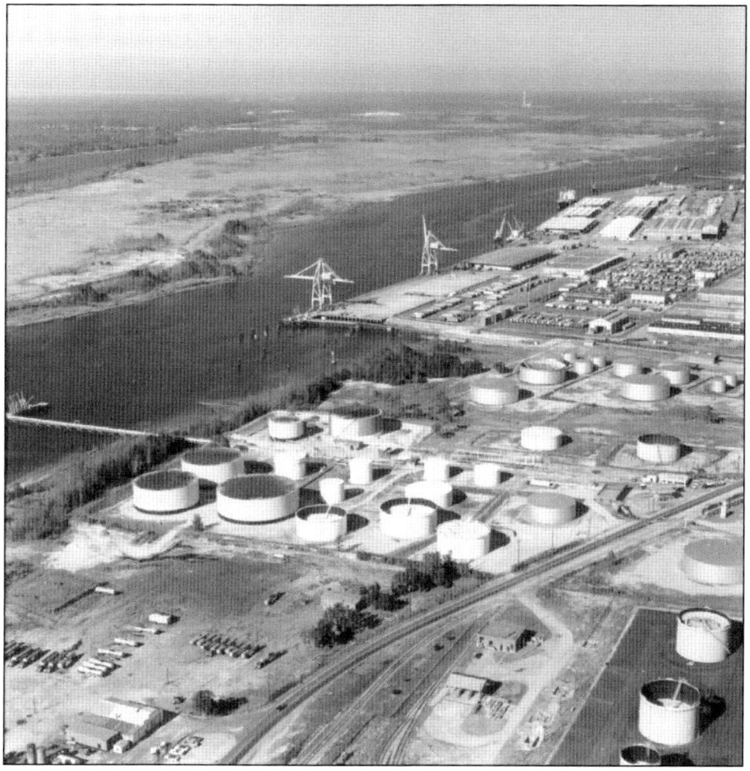

This aerial view of the state port was taken in 1979. In the foreground are privately owned oil terminals. The petroleum import business gained a foothold in the Wilmington harbor when the Standard Oil Company established an office here in 1889. After the Wilmington Terminal Company fire in 1953, most of the petroleum products business relocated in and around the North Carolina State Port. (*StarNews* Collection, NHCPL.)

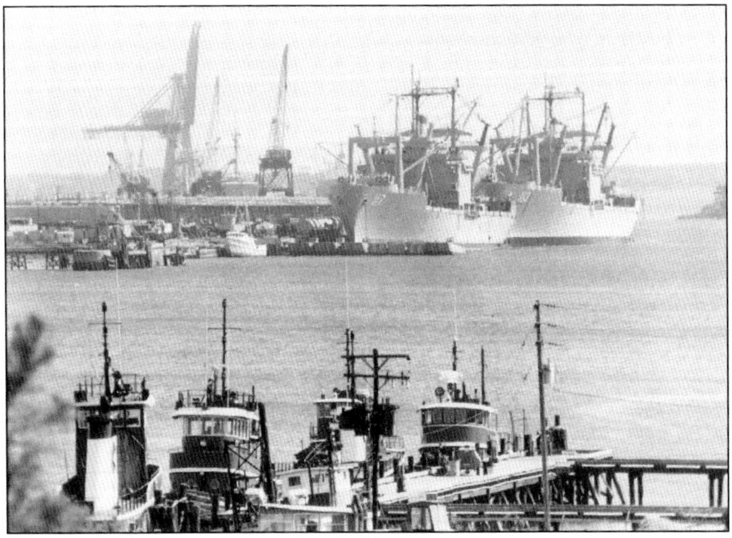

When this photograph was taken on May 2, 1981, two military ships were docked at the North Carolina State Port, while the tugboats in the foreground awaited a call for service. The tugs were docked on the west bank of the Cape Fear River, south of the Cape Fear Memorial Bridge. Both the port and the tugs operate 24 hours a day. (*StarNews* Collection, NHCPL.)

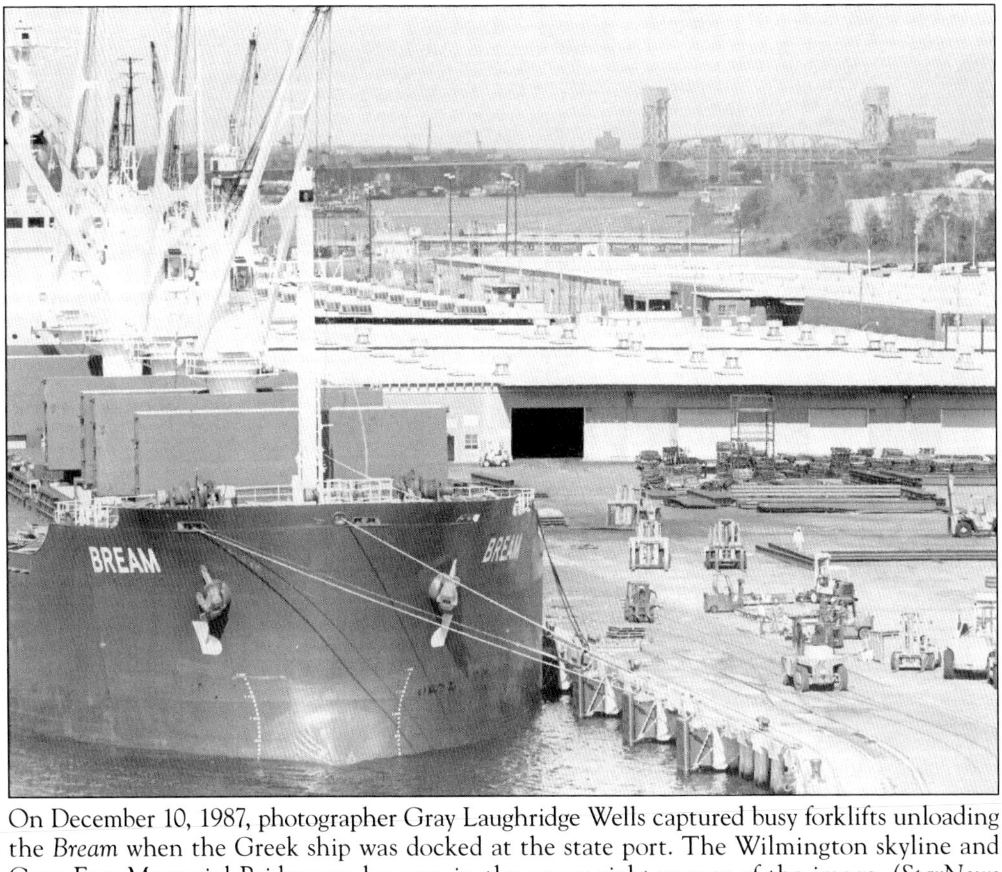

On December 10, 1987, photographer Gray Laughridge Wells captured busy forklifts unloading the *Bream* when the Greek ship was docked at the state port. The Wilmington skyline and Cape Fear Memorial Bridge can be seen in the upper right corner of the image. (*StarNews* Collection, NHCPL.)

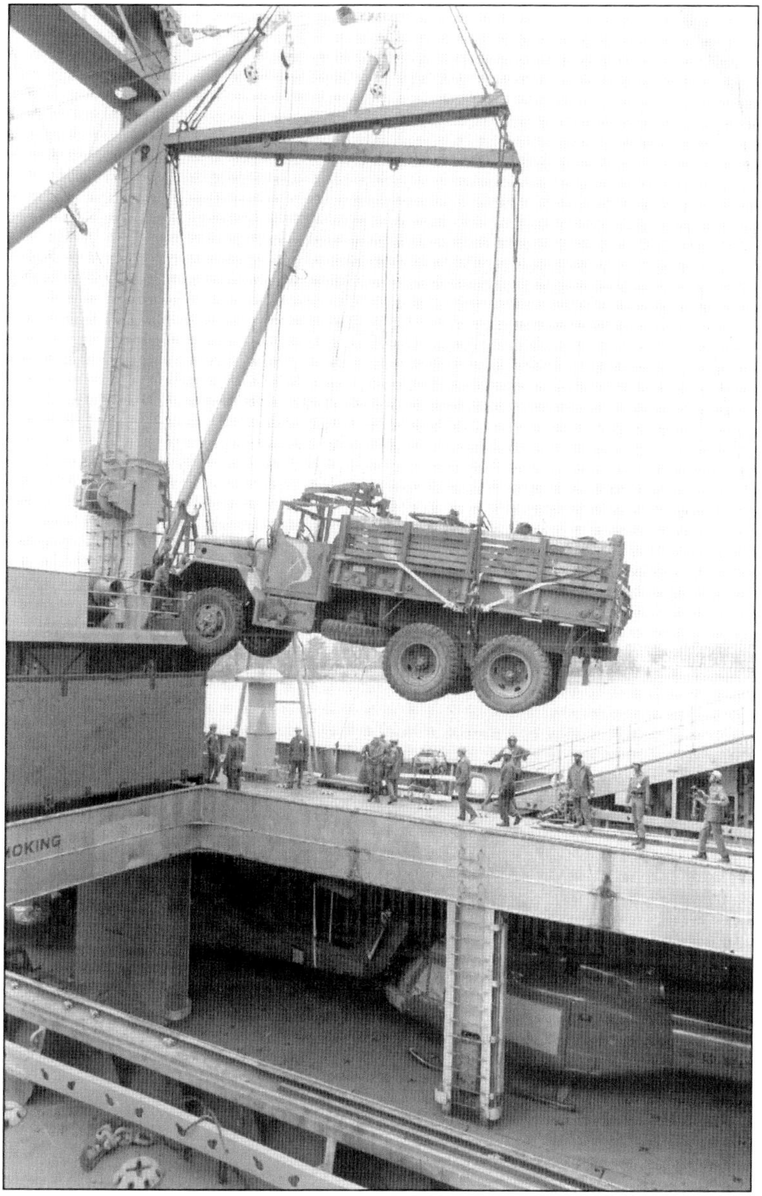

On April 28, 1982, Wayne Upchurch took this photograph of military equipment being off-loaded from the USNS *Comet*. Since its 1952 opening, the state ports authority has supported military operations, primarily for the Marines stationed at Camp Lejeune and the Army troops at Fort Bragg. Since 1981, however, military traffic has increased business at the North Carolina State Port at Wilmington. In that year alone, 40,000 tons of military goods flowed through the port. In 1987, for the first time, the army loaded a stern-ramped barge with equipment. The state docks were especially busy during the Gulf War (1990–1991). Heavy vehicles, such as helicopters, tanks, Humvees, jeeps, and personnel carriers, could be seen lined up at the state docks, ready to be loaded. Millions of tons of military cargo loaded onto 70 ships left Wilmington for the Gulf. Some military cargo has also been loaded at the state docks during the conflicts in Iraq and Afghanistan. The state docks have also supported and assisted in military training exercises since 1981. (*StarNews* Collection, NHCPL.)

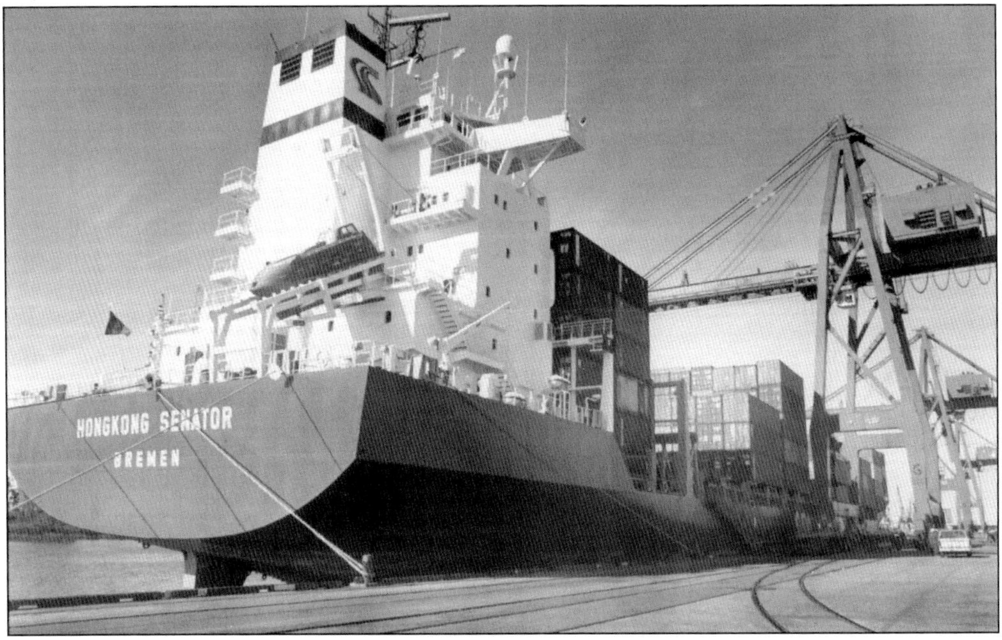

A container is a box made of aluminum, steel, or fiberglass used to transport cargo by ship, rail, truck, or barge. By 1970, the International Standards Organization established a standard size for containers—most are 8 feet wide, 8 feet tall, and 40 feet long. From 1979, the North Carolina State Port Authority's crane service has operated in Wilmington. Todd Sumlin took the photograph above on November 17, 1981, when the *Hongkong Senator* was making its inaugural voyage to the state port. The photograph below, taken about the same time, shows a container crane at work, with the crane operator suspended 150 feet above the dock. After 60 years of operation, the state port at Wilmington currently has 11 cranes. (Both, *StarNews* Collection, NHCPL.)

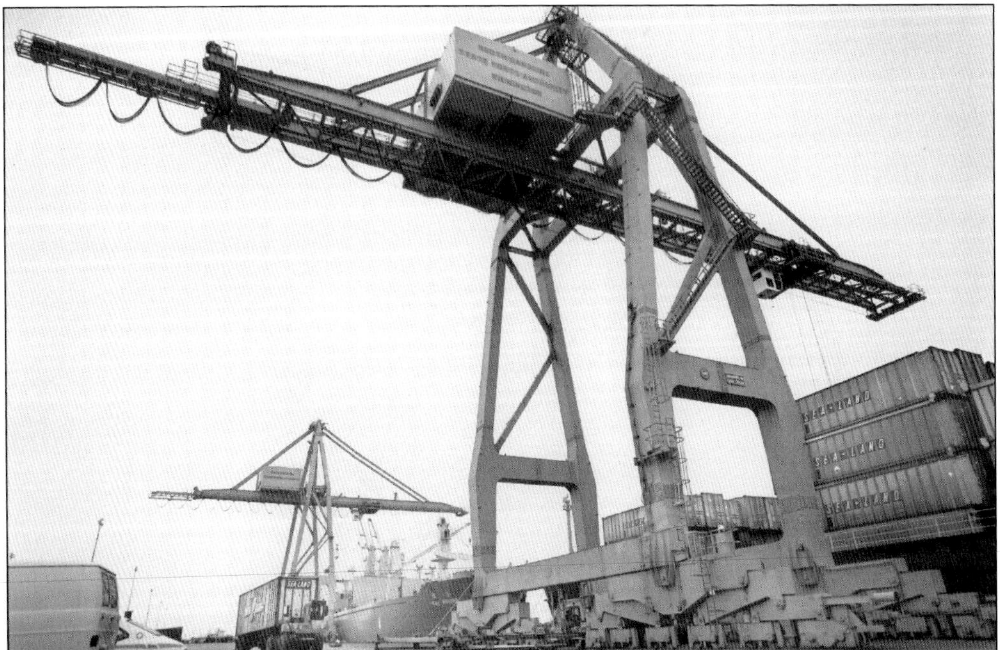

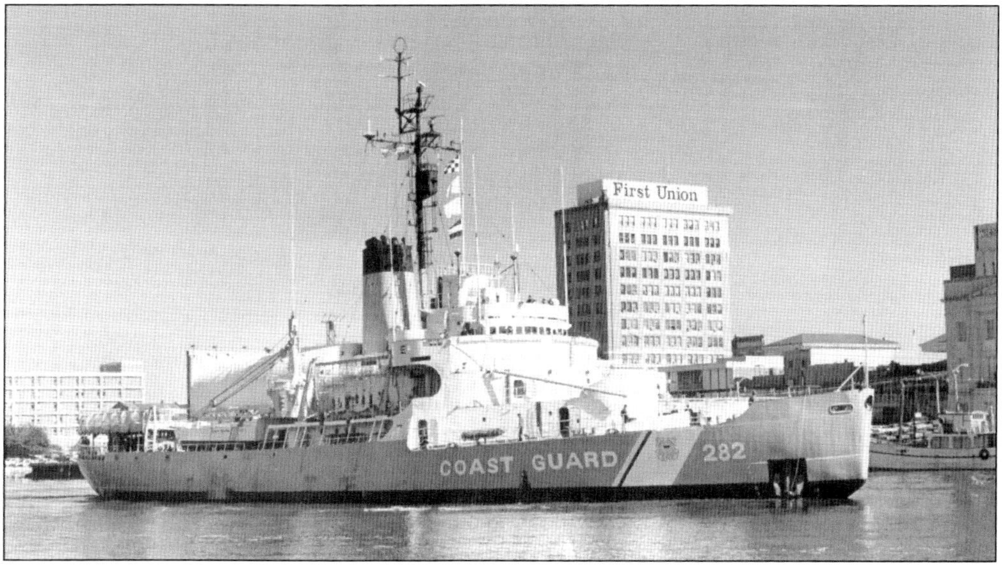

The USCGC *Northwind* was stationed in Wilmington from 1978 to 1989. As a Wind-class icebreaker, she conducted oceanography, hydrography, and cartography studies, in addition to search-and-rescue operations. She became the first icebreaker to seize illegal drugs when, on November 4, 1984, she confiscated 20 tons of marijuana southwest of Jamaica. However, most of her duty was performed as an icebreaker in the Arctic. She was decommissioned in Wilmington on January 28, 1989, then removed to the James River Reserve Fleet, and then scrapped in 1999. Some *Northwind* crewmen spent enough time in Wilmington to raise families, and some even retired here. The photograph above was taken on October 27, 1979, and the photograph below was taken on June 11, 1980. It shows the *Northwind* gliding under the Cape Fear Memorial Bridge. (Both, *StarNews* Collection, NHPCL.)

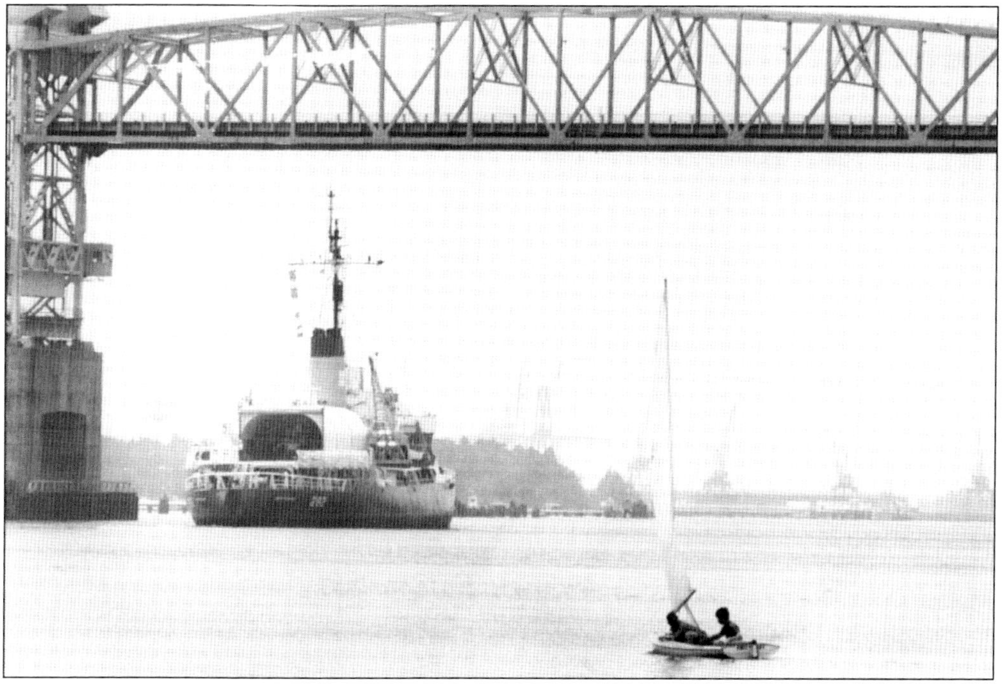

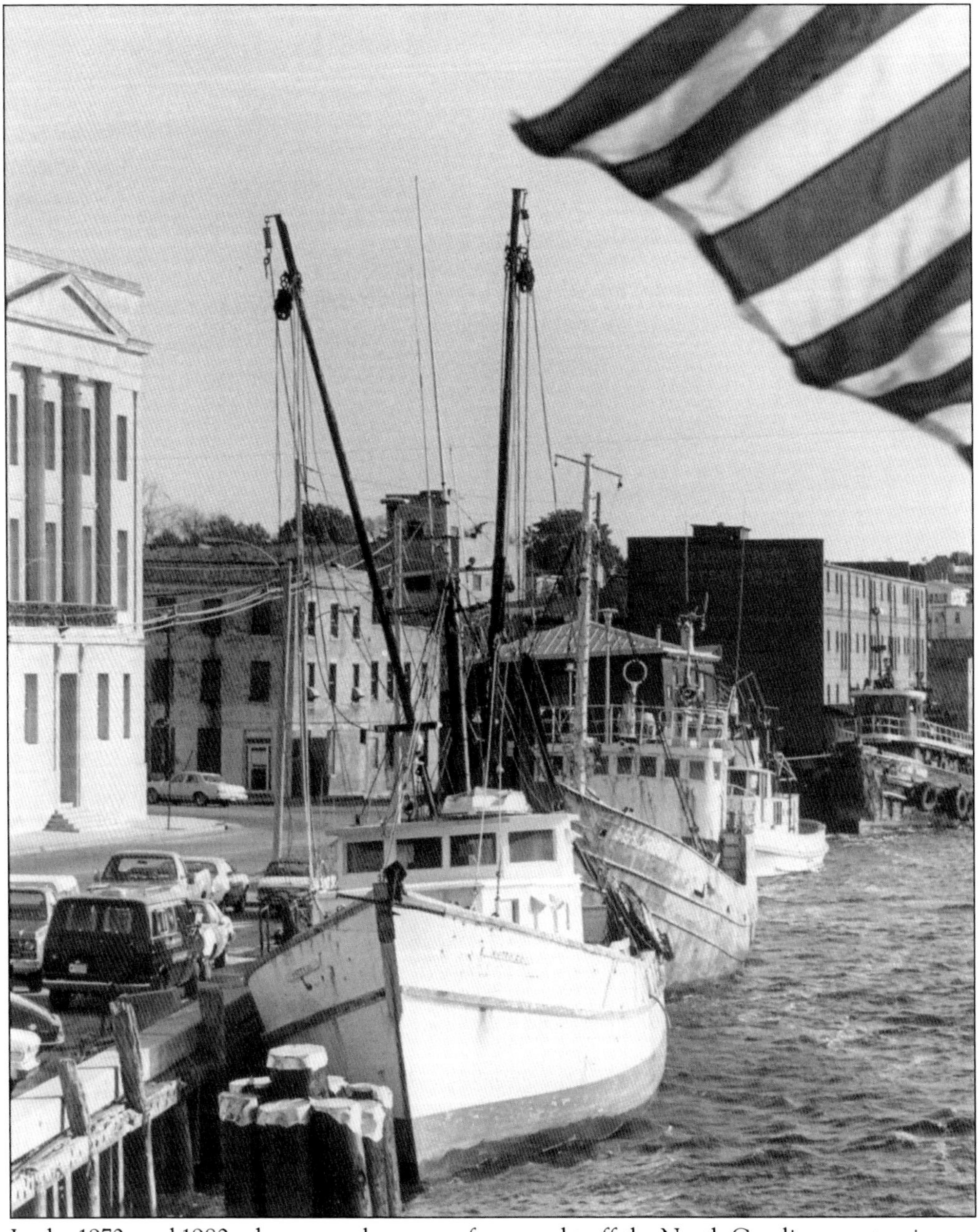

In the 1970s and 1980s, drug smugglers were often caught off the North Carolina coast or in one of the many sounds, rivers, inlets, and streams nearby. They were brought into Wilmington and tried by the federal court at the Alton A. Lennon Federal Building, seen at left. The US Custom House was renamed in honor of Lennon, a US congressman and senator, in 1978. The confiscated boats were sold at auction at the government dock. Wayne Upchurch took this photograph on January 25, 1979. It shows two drug smugglers' boats: in the foreground is the *Patty Joe*, and in the background is the *Seacrust*. The photograph also shows the foot of Market Street before it was redesigned as a tourist destination. Next to the federal courthouse is the building that became the Riverboat Landing Restaurant. The tugboat is moored at the Brooks Building, a former wholesale grocery business now home to shops and condominiums. (*StarNews* Collection, NHPCL.)

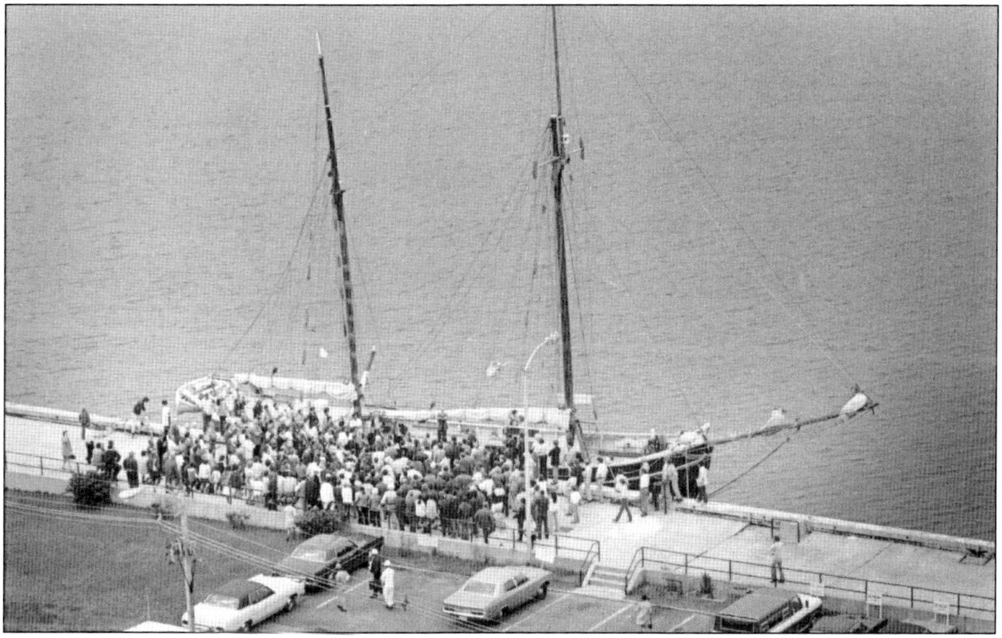

Illegal drugs were smuggled into the country on a variety of types of boats. In the photograph above, a crowd is gathered to witness the auction of the sailboat *Ingerfriendship*, which was seized in a drug investigation on January 10, 1974. The auction was held at the government wharf in downtown Wilmington, where she sold for $17,700 on April 12, 1974. The photograph below shows agents Dave Britt and John Register standing guard on the deck of the *Lillian B.* after she had been towed into the state port. The trawler was caught smuggling in January 1976. It contained the first boatload of hashish brought into the area. (Both, *StarNews* Collection, NHCPL.)

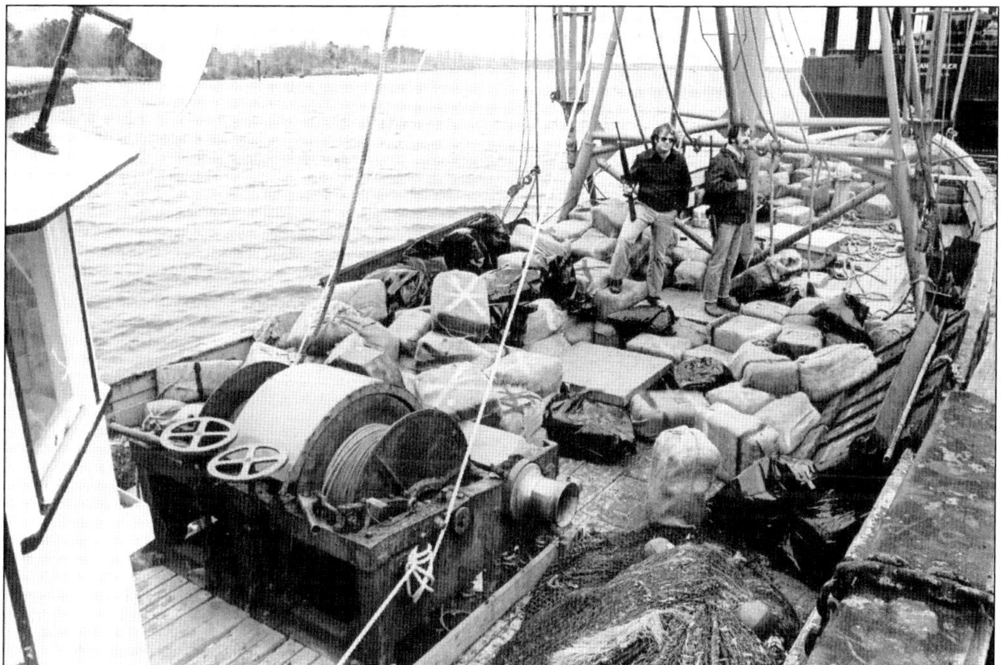

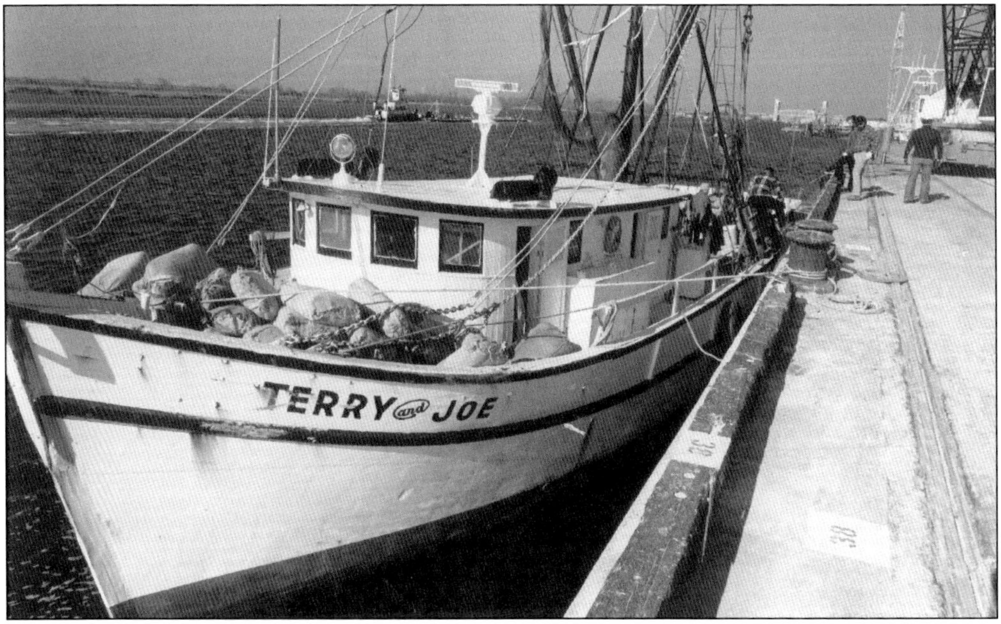

According to the caption on the back of this photograph, "Four men were arrested in federal smuggling charges on a 67 foot trawler loaded with 10 tons of marijuana. It was intercepted by the Coast Guard Cutter *Dallas* about 50 miles east of Wilmington." Joe Nesbitt took this photograph on December 17, 1980, after the drug boat had been towed to the state port. (*StarNews* Collection, NHCPL.)

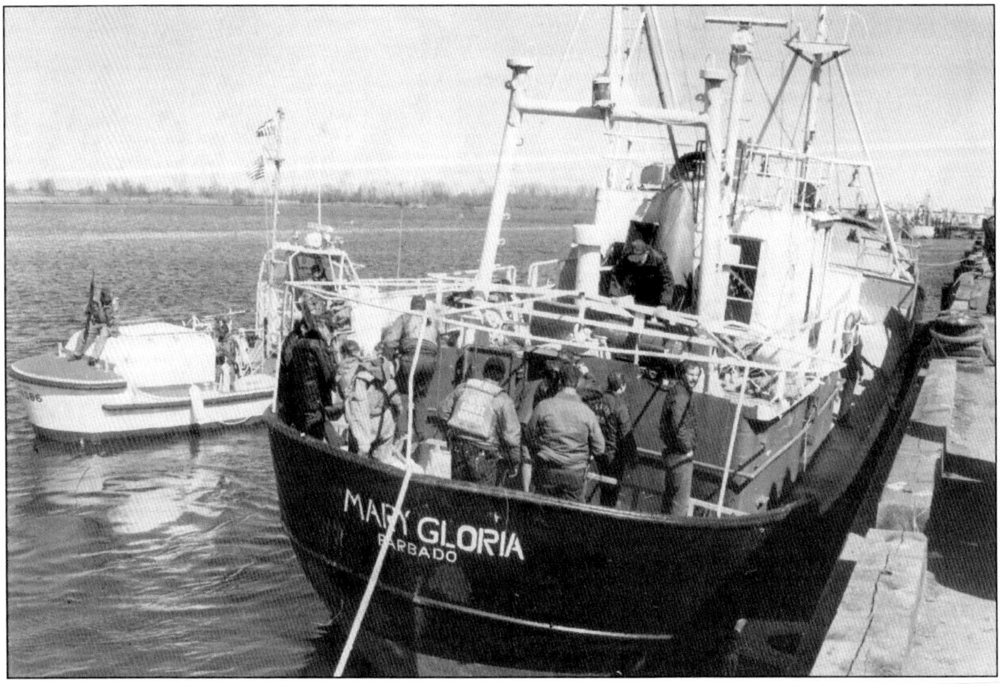

Gray Laughridge Wells snapped this photograph on October 11, 1986. The caption on the back reads, "The *Mary Gloria* was boarded by State Bureau of Investigations agents, Drug Enforcement officers and the US Coast Guard after it was moored at the State Port. At 10:00 a.m. the prisoners were taken off the boat and placed in custody." (*StarNews* Collection, NHCPL.)

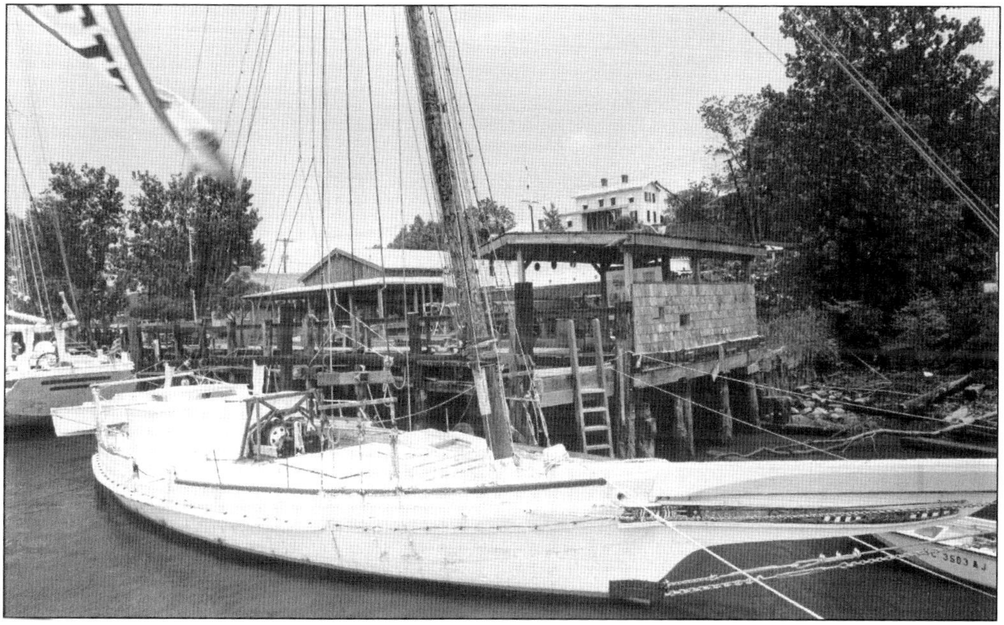

Chandler's Wharf, a replica of Wilmington's 19th-century waterfront, was the idea of Thomas H. Wright Jr. In 1978, he took an abandoned wharf between Ann and Nun Streets and moved historic houses and shops that were in danger of demolition into the area. A reproduction of a 19th-century warehouse was built to house a nautical museum, and Wright's collection of historical vessels was moored in front of the wharf. As one of the first projects to bring Wilmingtonians back downtown, it helped revitalize the waterfront. The photograph above shows the *Geneva Mae* docked at Chandler's Wharf Museum. The photograph below was taken from inside the museum, looking toward the Cape Fear Memorial Bridge (left). (Both, *StarNews* Collection, NHCPL.)

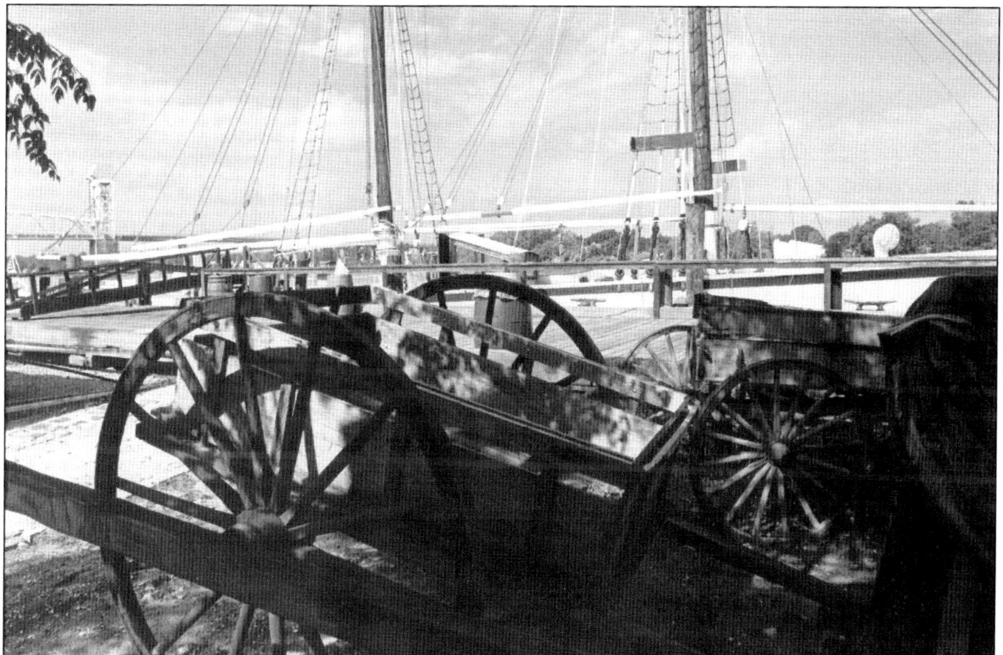

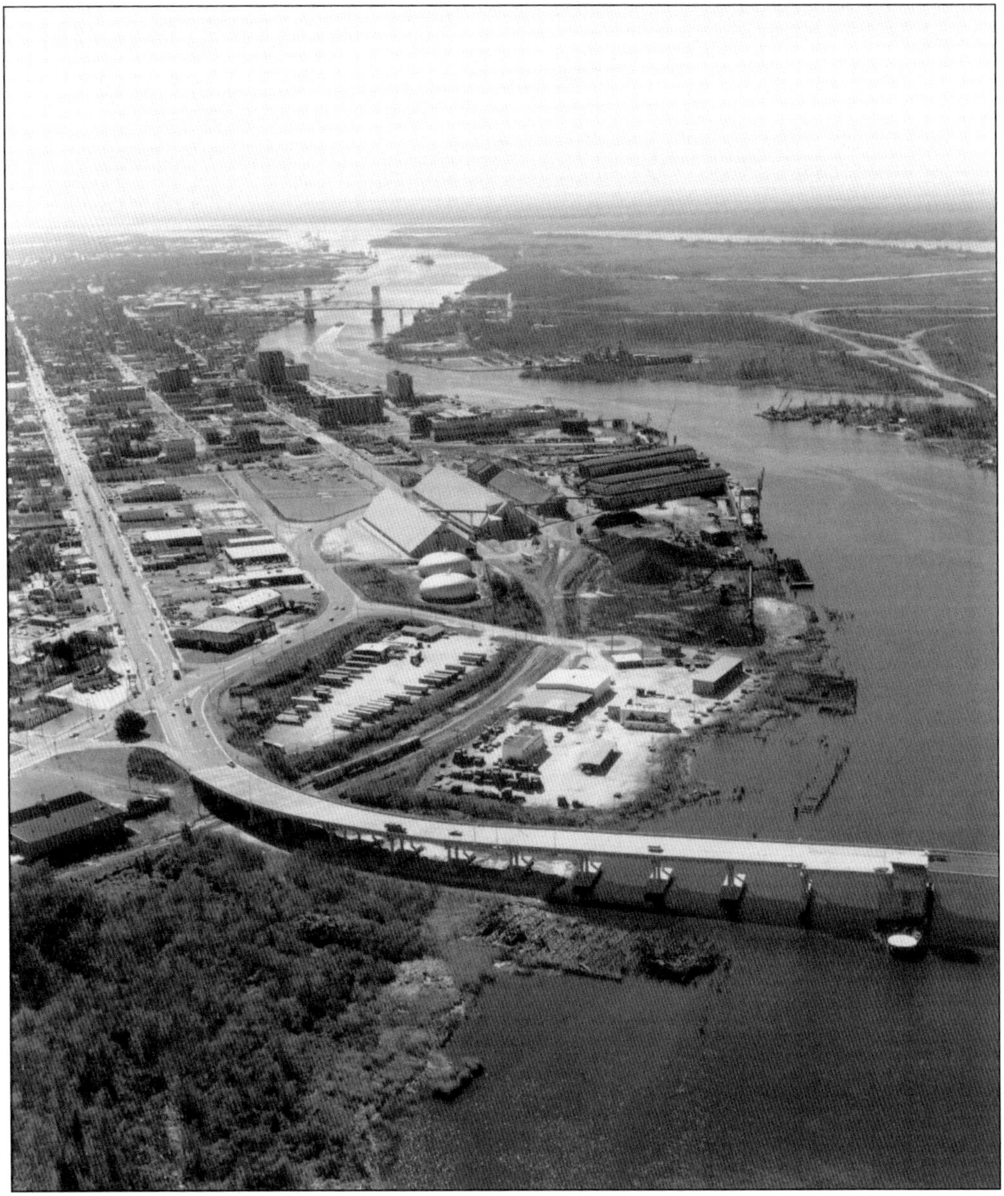

Joe Nesbitt, head photographer for the *Wilmington StarNews*, took this aerial shot of the Cape Fear River on February 5, 1981. The Isabel Holmes Bridge, seen in the foreground, had recently replaced the 1929 Northeast Cape Fear River Bridge. The new bridge was named for Holmes, who served as deputy secretary of the North Carolina Department of Transportation in the 1970s. While in office, she actively promoted the construction of the bridge for her hometown. The Almont Shipping Company owned the large warehouses seen on the Northeast Cape Fear River. At the time this photograph was taken, the company handled 1.5 million tons of dry bulk cargo annually. Estelle Carter Lee, the first female to run a large shipping company, purchased the company that same year. She networked with the unionized stevedores so successfully that she was known as "Ms. Steveadorable." In order to buy the business, she formed a profit-sharing partnership with the employees. She sold the business in 1990. Almont Shipping Company eventually moved to the North Carolina State Port. (*StarNews* Collection, NHCPL.)

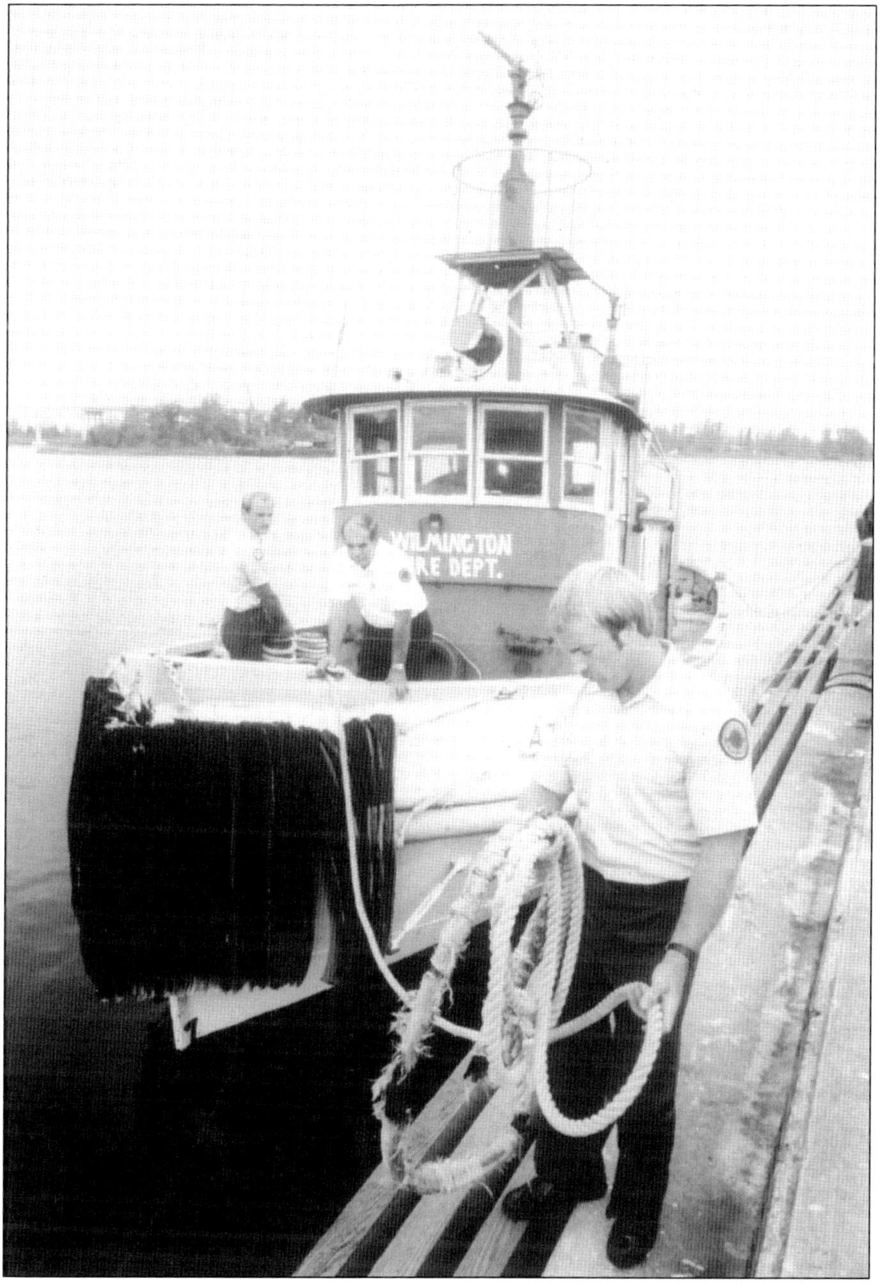

This photograph of the *Atlantic IV* fireboat was taken shortly before she was replaced. Mark Mullen of the Wilmington Fire Department is seen bringing in the towline. Capt. H.M. Gore is in the middle, and Scot Chadwick is on the left. The fireboat is on call 24 hours a day, every day. The captain operates the boat, one crew member operates the fire equipment, and at least one but usually two other crew members assist onboard during an operation. It takes an average of three to four months of additional training for interested firefighters to qualify for fireboat duty. As of 2014, there was no separate fire station on the waterfront. The crew is on call at the main fire station on Market Street. Jack Upton took this photograph, looking toward Point Peter, on September 9, 1986. (*StarNews* Collection, NHCPL.)

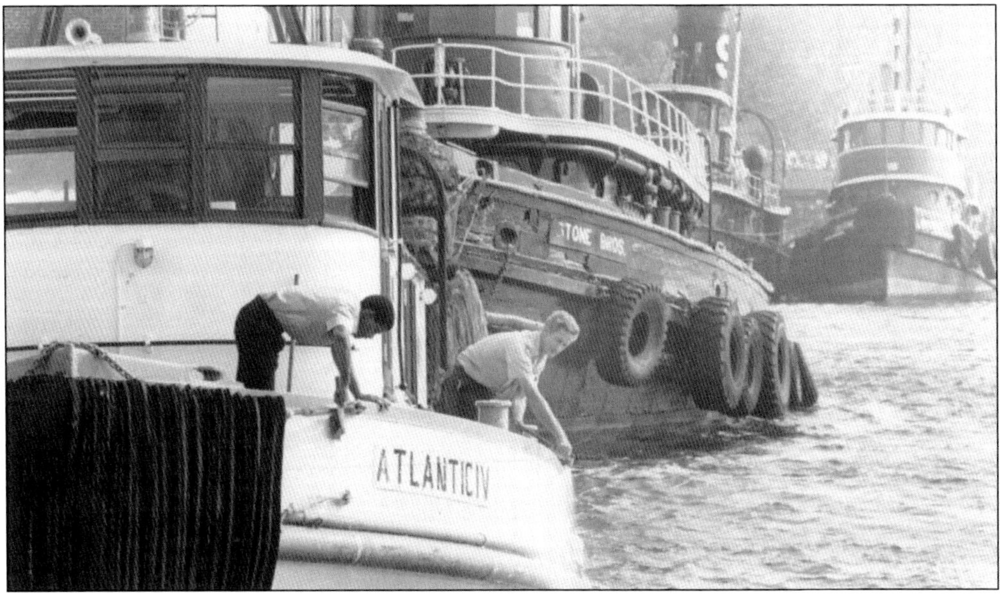

Members of the Wilmington Fire Department are pictured here on October 4, 1980, scrubbing the *Atlantic IV* in preparation for Riverfest, Wilmington's annual celebration of the Cape Fear River. Three of the Stone Towing Company tugboats can be seen behind the fireboat. The one in the front, the *Stone Bros.*, became famous for being one of the 11 tugboats that maneuvered the battleship *North Carolina* into her berth in 1961. (*StarNews* Collection, NHCPL.)

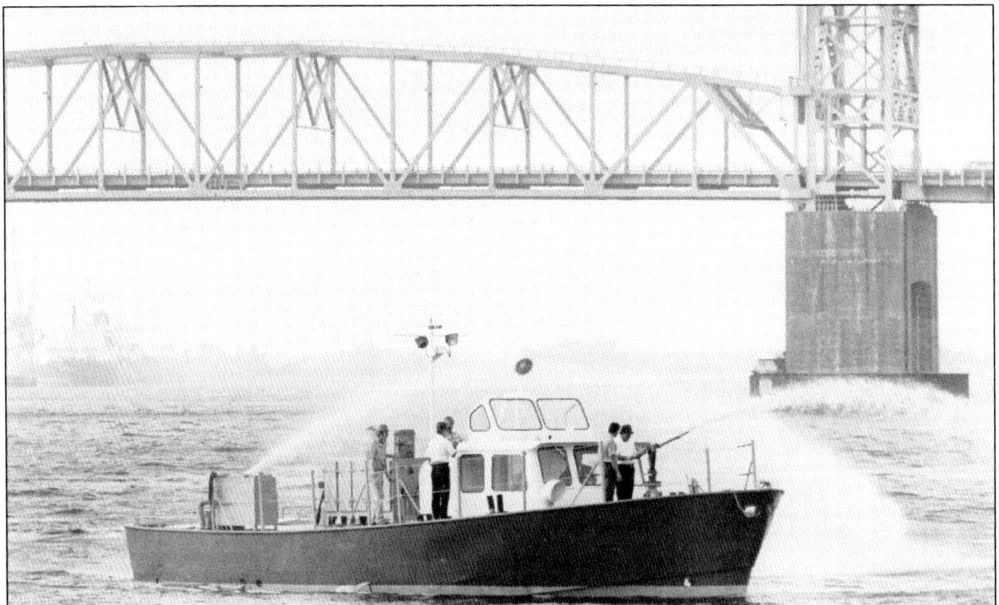

The *Atlantic V*, purchased in 1986, is shown passing under the Cape Fear Memorial Bridge during the beginning of Preservation Week, a national celebration held annually in honor of historic preservation. In Wilmington, the Historic Wilmington Foundation, founded in 1966, leads the event. They felt it appropriate to include the fireboat in the preservation celebration, since it is designed for fighting shoreline and shipboard fires. (*StarNews* Collection, NHCPL.)

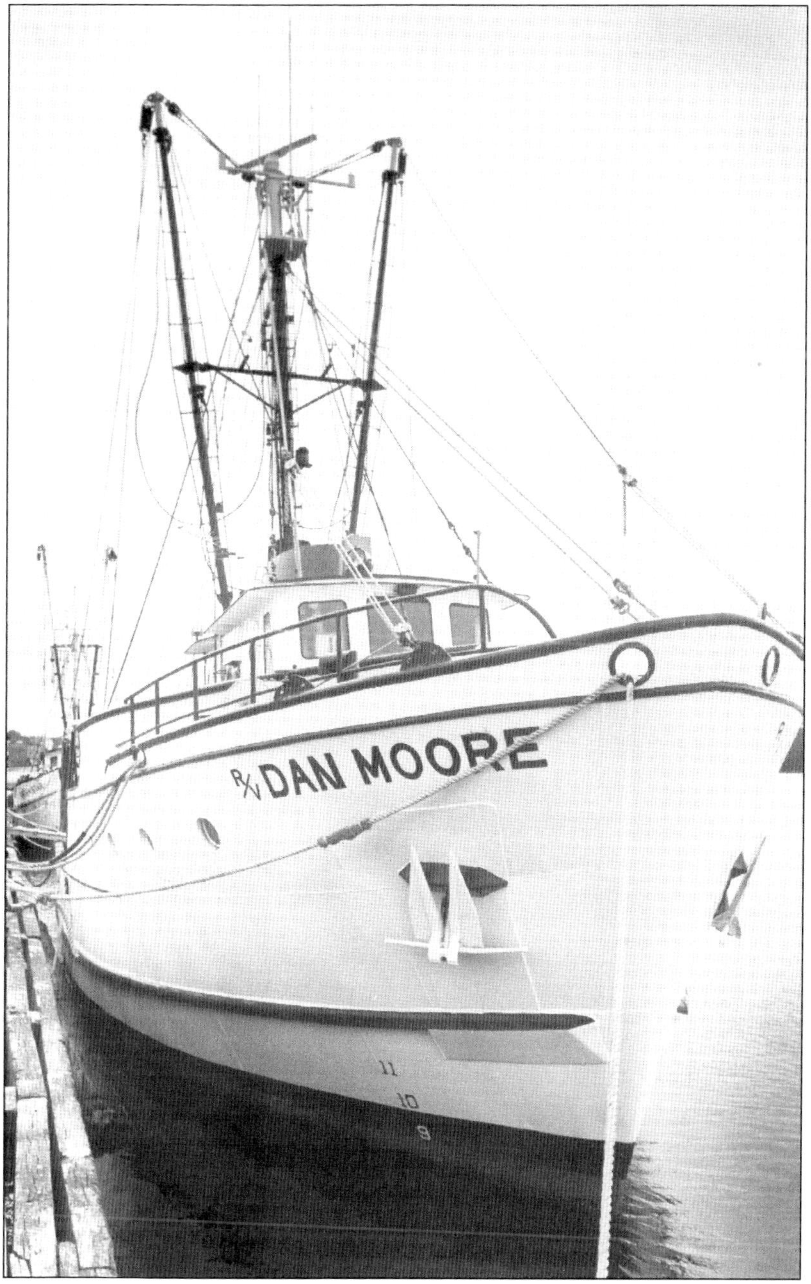

This photograph of the R/V *Dan Moore* was taken in 1982, shortly after Cape Fear Community College had purchased her for their marine technology program. An 85-foot-long fisheries research vessel, she was built in New Bern, North Carolina, in 1967, during the administration of Gov. Dan K. Moore (1965–1969). This ship served as a research vessel for the State of North Carolina Division of Fisheries until being sold to the college. With a cruising range of 5,000 miles, marine technology students undergo five different training cruises, totaling over 32 days at sea. The R/V *Dan Moore* carries a complement of 17 students, with cruise durations ranging from 4 to 11 days. Photographer Dan Sears captured this image at the college dock on December 6, 1982. (*StarNews* Collection, NHCPL.)

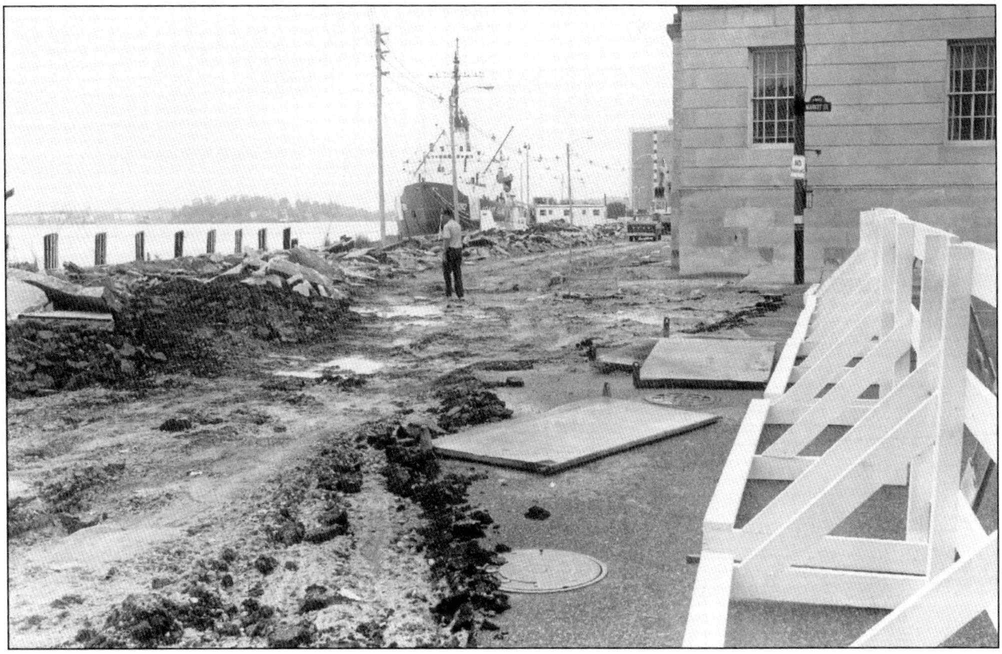

In the late 1970s and early 1980s, Wilmington joined other coastal seaports throughout the country in rediscovering the diverse potential of their urban waterfronts. After receiving a $1.1 million grant from the federal government, work began on Riverfront Park in 1979. The park was dedicated on March 20, 1982. According to the *StarNews*, "The city is here because of the river and the waterfront park will bring people down to the river, where Wilmington has its roots." City leaders declared it the "centerpiece of downtown revitalization." The photograph above, taken on June 18, 1981, shows work in progress between Princess and Market Streets. The photograph below shows Riverfront Park on opening day. The *Pride of Baltimore*, seen at right, was in town for the celebration, which included music, storytelling, and fireworks. (Both, *StarNews* Collection, NHCPL.)

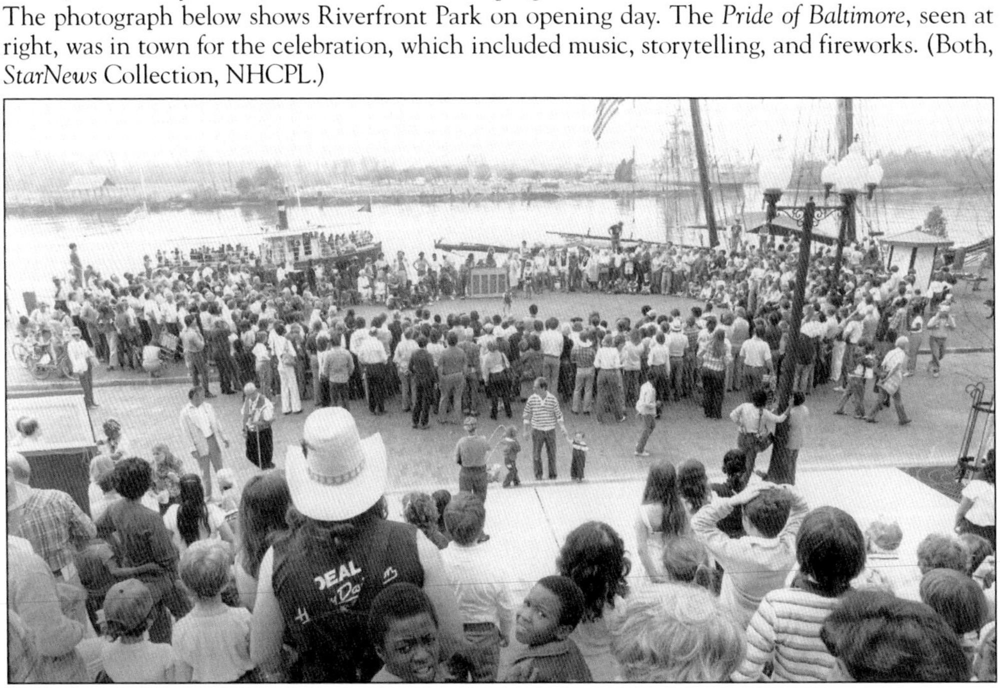

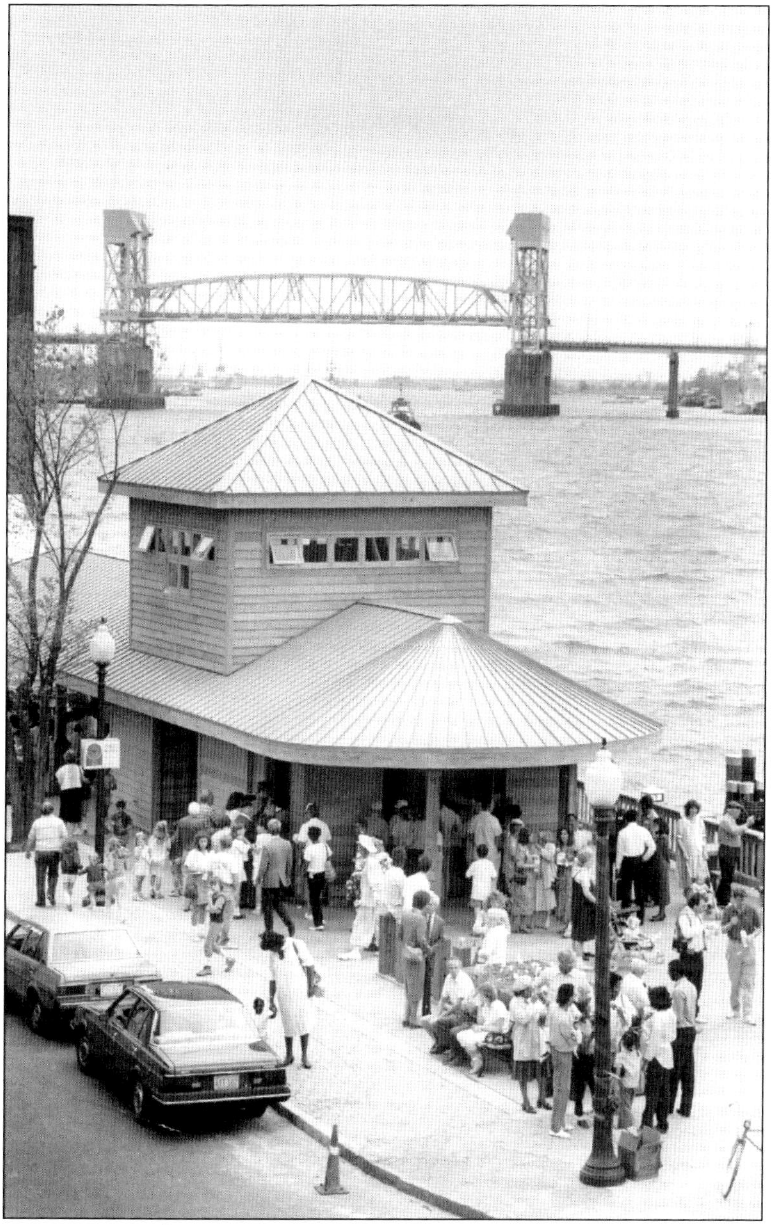

Beginning in 1987, Riverfront Park was extended an additional 280 feet to the south of the original 250-foot park. The $500,000 project included a wooden deck along the waterfront, with a 2,500-square-foot structure housing a concession area, a storage area, and restrooms. Supported by a grid of concrete beams built over pilings, the remainder of the heavy timber deck was fitted with tables, benches, a bandstand area, bicycle racks, and planters. The city fireboat began using the dock on this end of the park. The Riverfront Park extension opened on April 6, 1988, with free Dixieland jazz music, stern-wheeler riverboat cruises, and carriage rides. Shortly thereafter, the Wilmington Convention and Visitors Bureau began operating the concession stand as an information booth. The area also became a meeting place for walking tours and carriage tours. This photograph was taken during the dedication of the new section of the park. (*StarNews* Collection, NHCPL.)

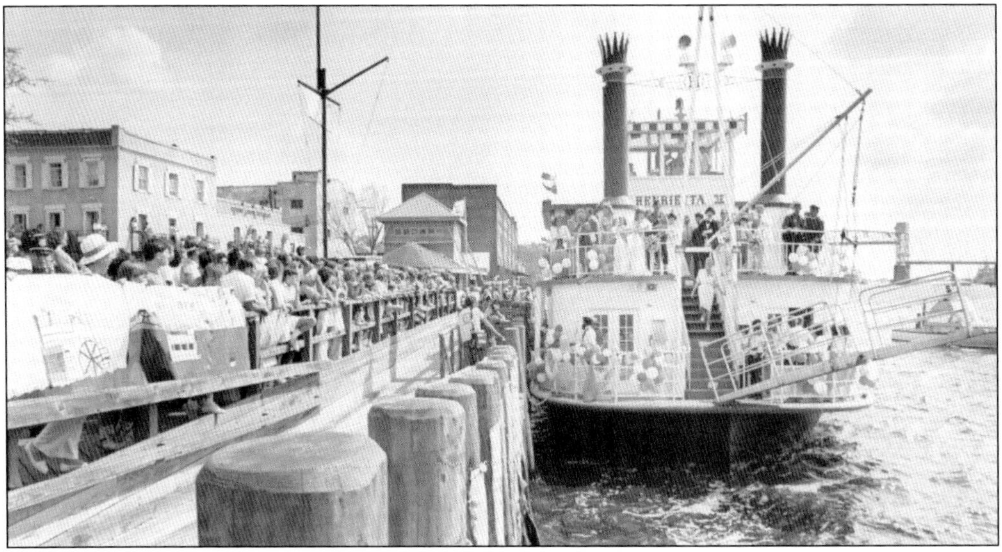

Jamie Moncrief took the photograph above of the *Henrietta II* as she pulled up alongside Riverfront Park on April 2, 1988. A crowd gathered to watch the paddleboat make its first appearance in downtown Wilmington. She was brought to Wilmington by owner and operator Capt. John Marshburn. Construction of the *Henrietta II*, North Carolina's only true stern-wheeler riverboat, began in mid-September 1987 in Greenville, Mississippi. She was named for the *Henrietta*, a steamboat that made her first run on the Cape Fear River 170 years before. The *Henrietta II* quickly became a popular sightseeing and dinner cruise ship. She was sold in 2000 when Captain Marshburn purchased the *Henrietta III*. The photograph below shows a paddleboat race held during Riverfest 1989. The visiting *Southern Star* edged out the *Henrietta II* at the finish line. (Both, *StarNews* Collection, NHCPL.)

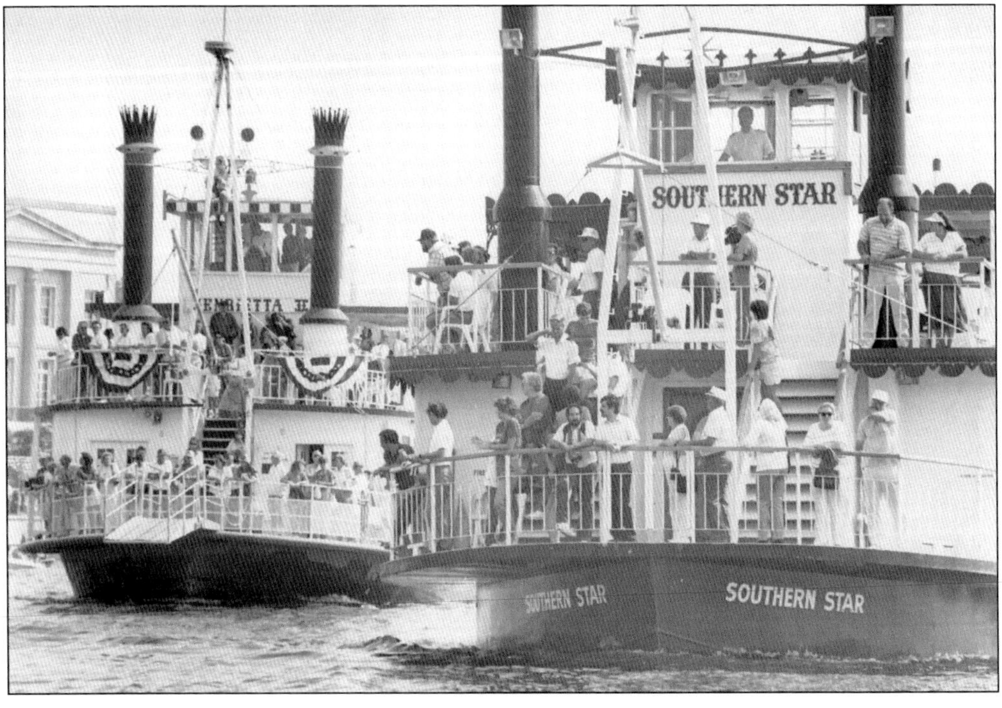

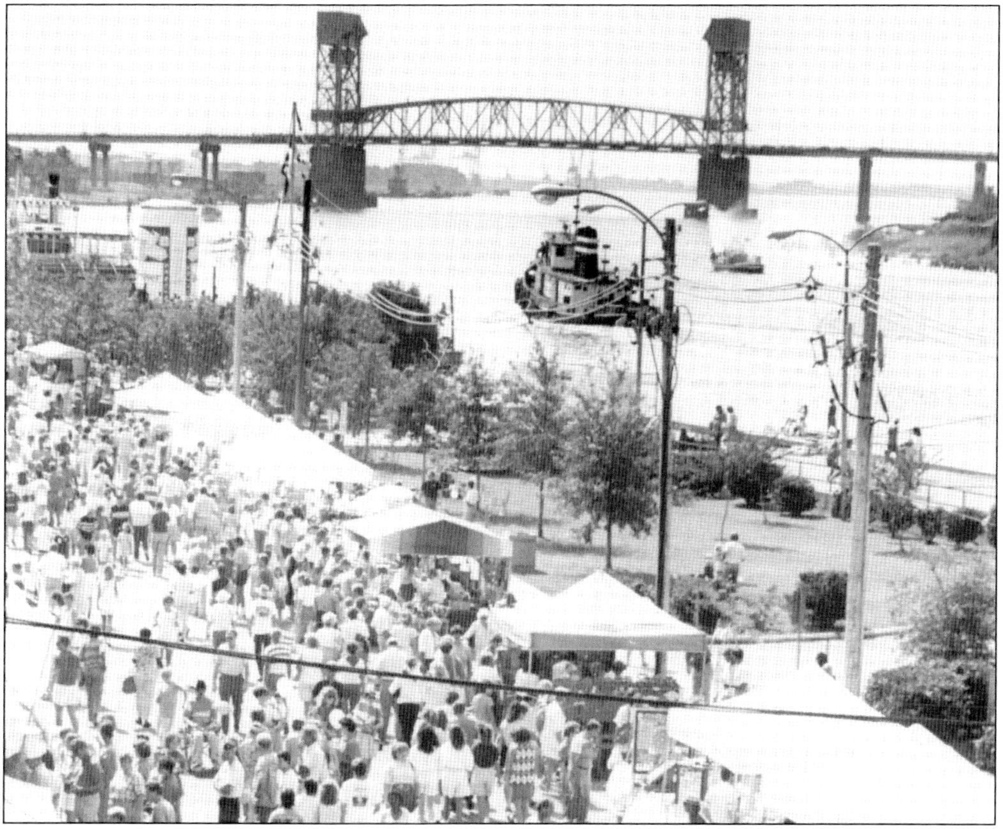

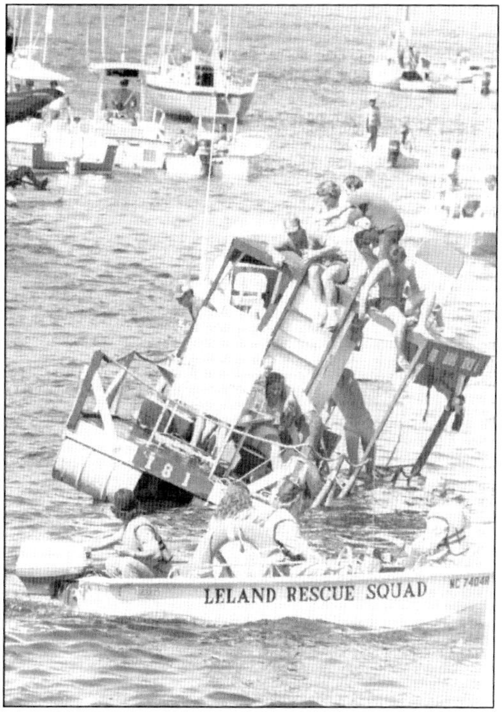

Riverfest, Wilmington's annual fall festival, was conceived in 1979 by Wilmington Downtown, Inc., a nonprofit organization whose mission is to revitalize the commercial area of the historic district. In collaboration with the Arts Council, the Residents of Old Wilmington, and the Historic Wilmington Foundation, the organization sought to promote the historic waterfront and the adjacent area with a two-day festival. The first year was an overwhelming success, with 30,000 in attendance. Included were an array of shows, contests, cultural events, bands, crafts, and concessions, along with hot air balloon rides, bicycle races, regattas, and fireworks. Visiting ships also provided tours. The highlight of Riverfest was the original homemade raft regatta. The photograph above shows Water Street during Riverfest 1989. The 1981 photograph at right features one of the homemade rafts surrounded by boats filled with spectators. (Both, *StarNews*, NHPCL.)

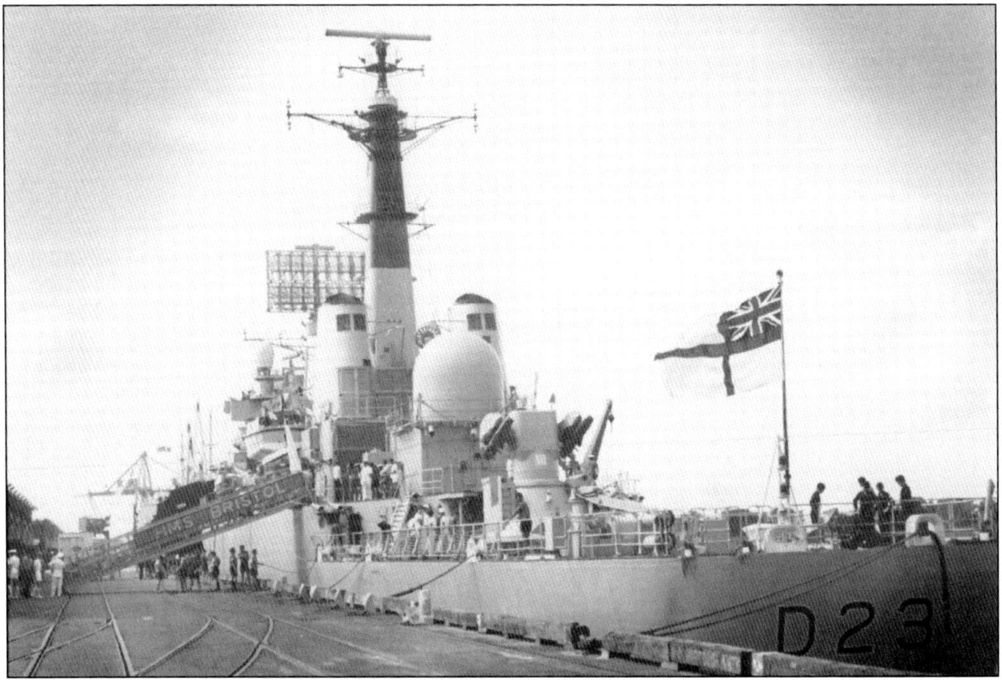

These photographs depict the HMS *Bristol* while visiting Wilmington. The photograph above shows the British Navy's fleet flagship docked at the state port on August 15, 1980. The crew was greeted with picnics and rugby games, and they hosted parties aboard the ship. The local community hosted a special hotline called Dial-A-Sailor, which allowed local families to adopt a seaman during their stay. Lasting friendships were made during this visit. The photograph below, taken on June 22, 1990, documents the second visit of the *Bristol*. By this time, Riverfront Park had been completed, and the British guided-missile destroyer could dock in downtown Wilmington. British sailors and US Coast Guard members are pulling a bowline as they dock the ship. Thousands of visitors toured the Royal Navy ship on this visit. (Both, *StarNews* Collection, NHCPL.)

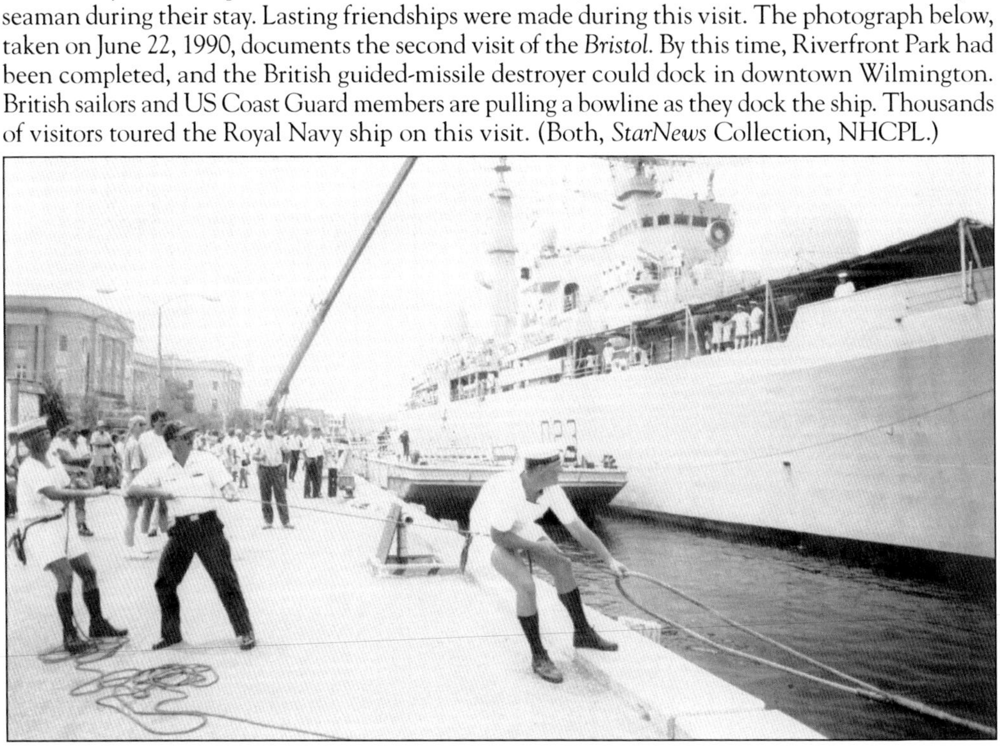

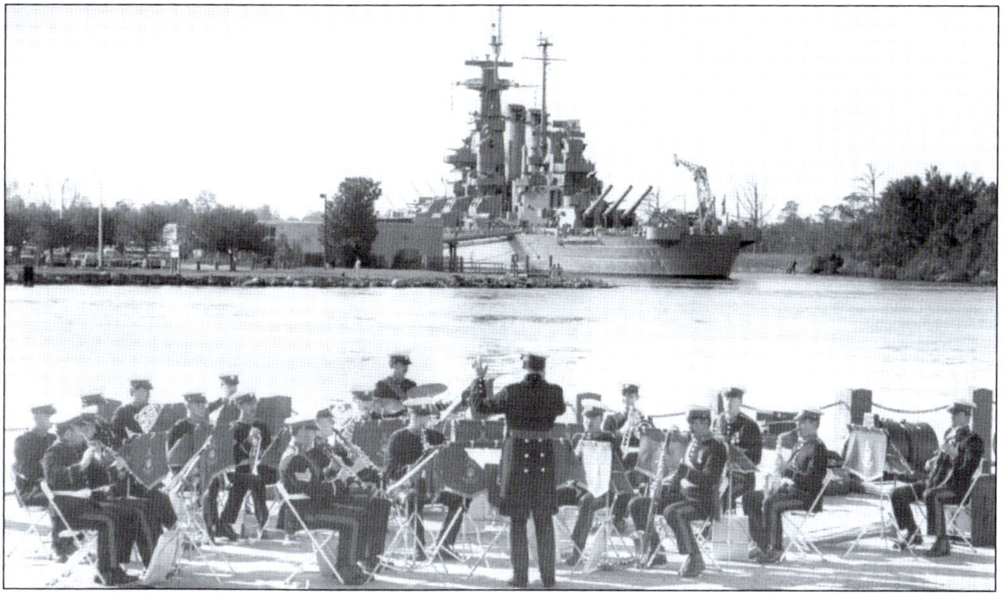

The Royal Marine Band played to hundreds of spectators at Riverfront Park during a visit from a British Navy ship in this undated photograph. Since 1767, the band has traditionally provided onboard music before and during battle. Today, they are also trained military personnel. In addition to serving as logisticians, divers, and medical technicians, they provide entertainment for troops and act as ambassadors for the Royal Marines. (*StarNews* Collection, NHPCL.)

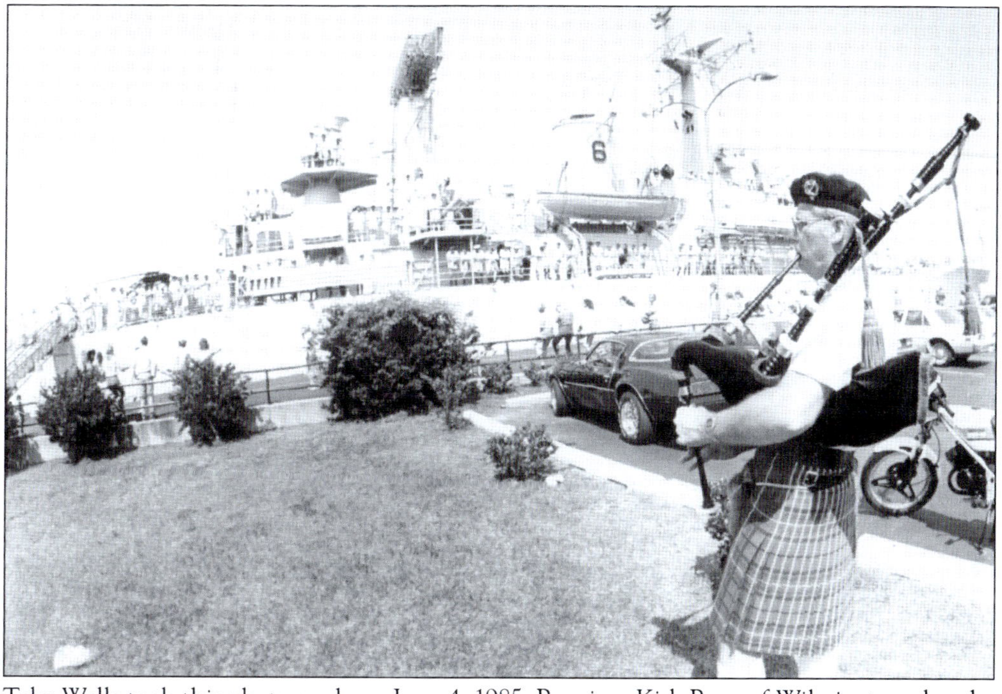

Toby Wells took this photograph on June 4, 1985. Bagpiper Kirk Rose of Wilmington played a Scottish march during the departure of the British Leander-class frigate *Diomede*. The sailors onboard affectionately nicknamed her the "Dimweed." Three years after her visit to Wilmington, she was sold to the Pakistan Navy. (*StarNews* Collection, NHCPL.)

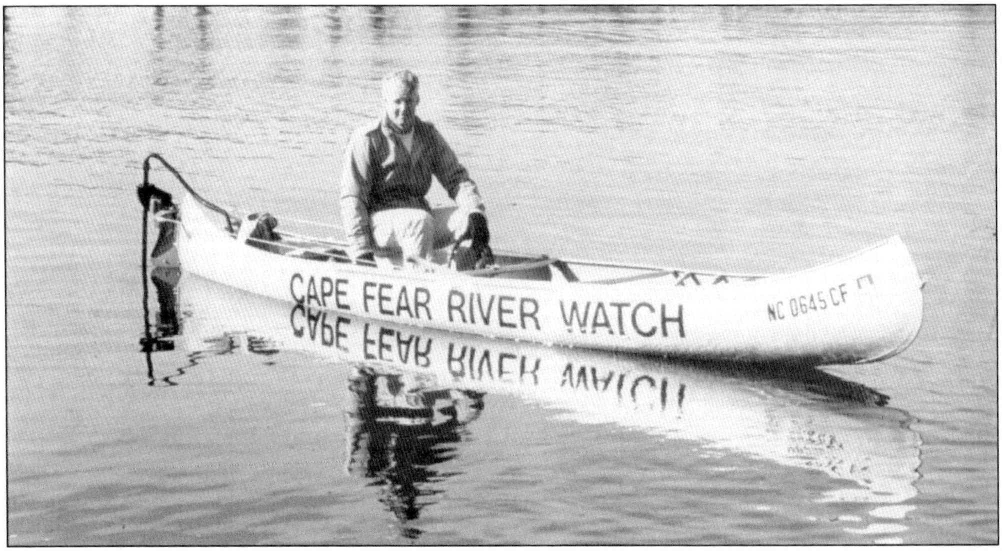

The Cape Fear River Watch was founded in 1993 to protect and improve the water quality of the Lower Cape Fear River Basin through education, advocacy, and action. Founders Bouton Baldridge and Bruce Watkins envisioned a nonprofit organization dedicated to the improvement and preservation of the health, beauty, cleanliness, and heritage of the Cape Fear River basin. The Cape Fear is North Carolina's largest intrastate river basin. Nearly one-third of the state's population lives within its watershed. The ecological diversity of the watershed is astounding, from piedmont streams to blackwater swamps and the salt marshes at the mouth of the river. The photograph above of Bouton Baldridge, the first river keeper, was taken on December 9, 1993. The photograph below, taken in 2013, shows Kemp Burdette, who has been river keeper since 2010. (Above, *StarNews* Collection, NHCPL; below, Cape Fear River Watch.)

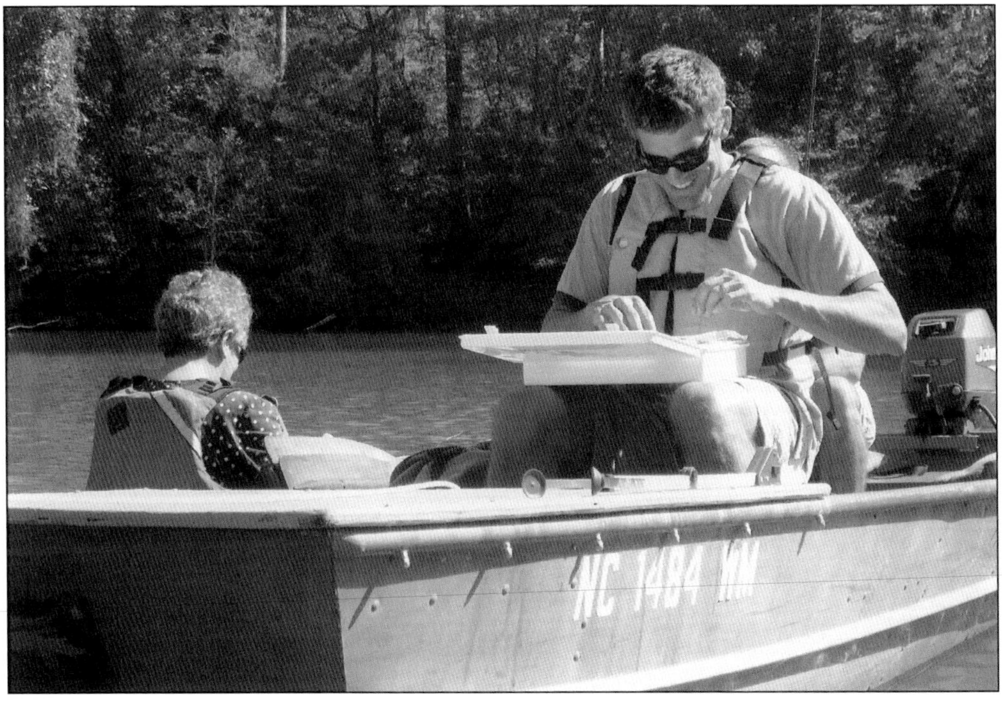

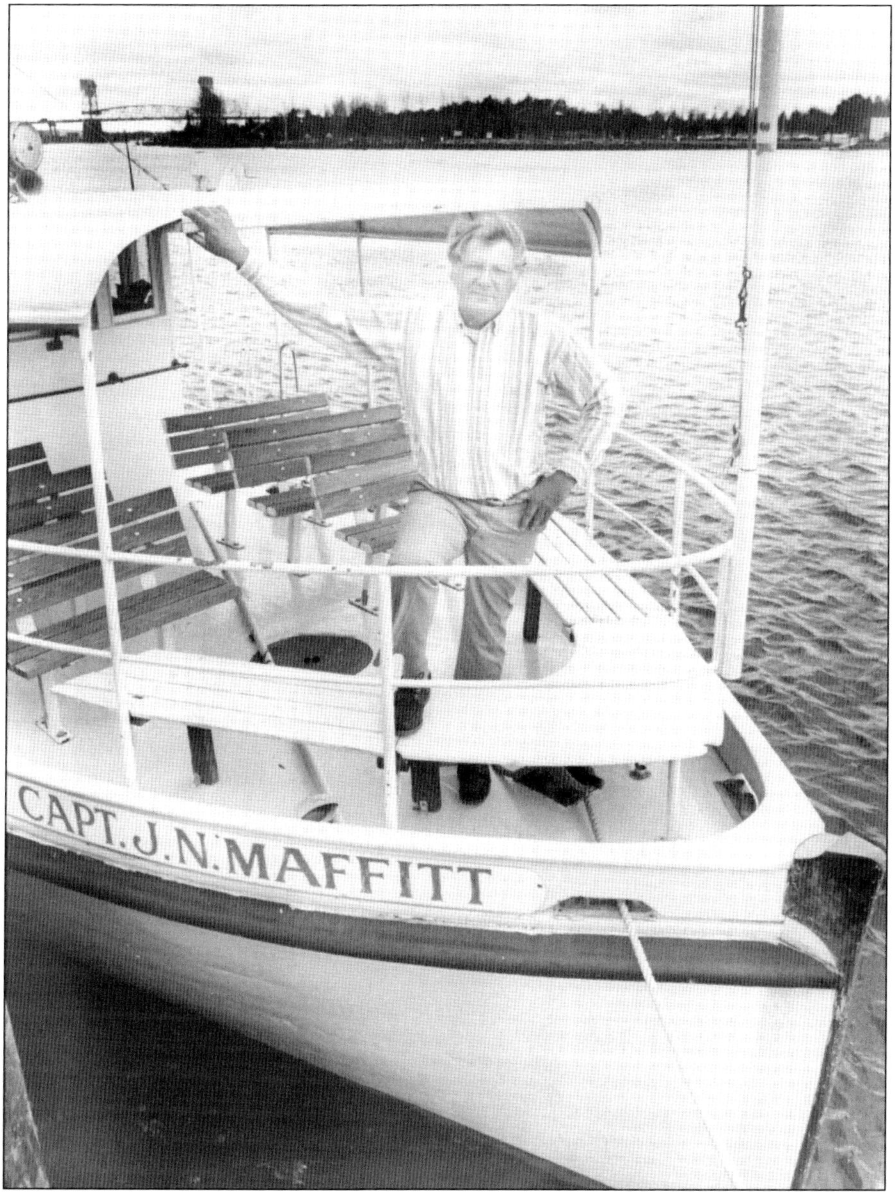

Capt. Carl Marshburn stands in the bow of the *Capt. J.N. Maffitt* in this photograph from March 27, 1992. Named for native Wilmingtonian and Confederate blockade runner John Newland Maffitt, the tour boat was constructed for the US Navy during World War II. She ferried sailors from ship to shore and back. Her hull is made from a hodgepodge of wood, including mahogany, cypress, and oak. She is 49 feet long, and, when this photograph was taken, she was certified to carry 62 people. In 1978, over 240,000 tourists visited the battleship *North Carolina*. Businesses on the east bank of the Cape Fear River wanted these visitors to see downtown as well. Thus, the *Maffitt* began operating as a river taxi, ferrying visitors from Chandler's Wharf to the battleship *North Carolina*. She also took passengers on five-mile narrated harbor tours, nature cruises on the Cape Fear and Black Rivers, and party boat excursions, including wine-and-cheese cruises. Captain Marshburn purchased the *Maffitt* in 1992 and has continued offering a variety of river tours. He also owns the *Henrietta III*. (*StarNews* Collection, NHCPL.)

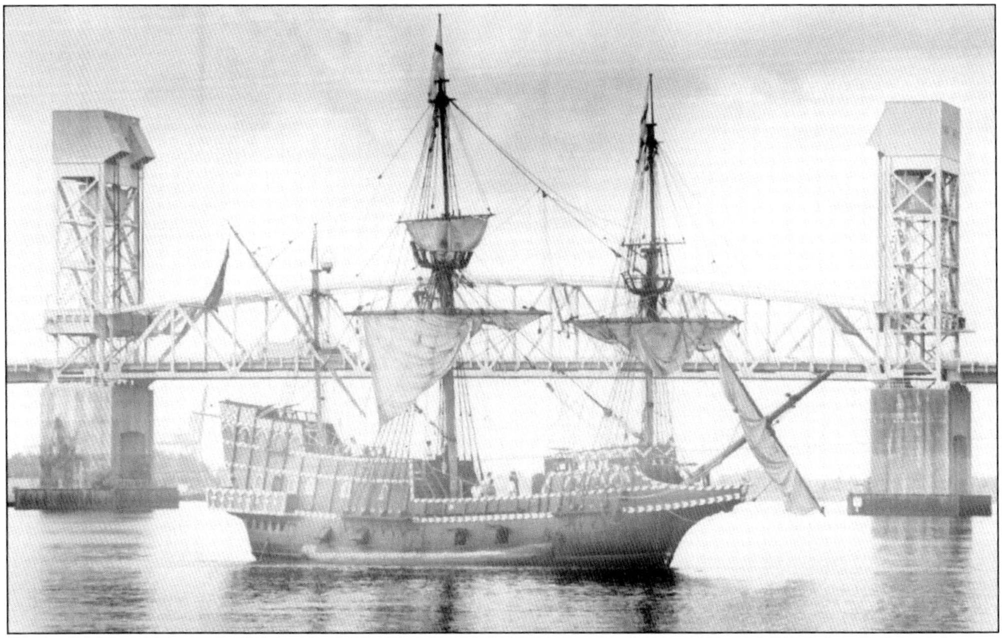

Todd Sumlin took this photograph of the *Golden Hinde*, a replica of Sir Francis Drake's ship, as it glided past the Cape Fear Memorial Bridge on July 20, 1990. Hundreds of Wilmingtonians visited the ship while she was docked at Riverfront Park for 18 days. Like the original *Golden Hinde* that Drake sailed around the world, this replica was on a world tour. (*StarNews* Collection, NHCPL.)

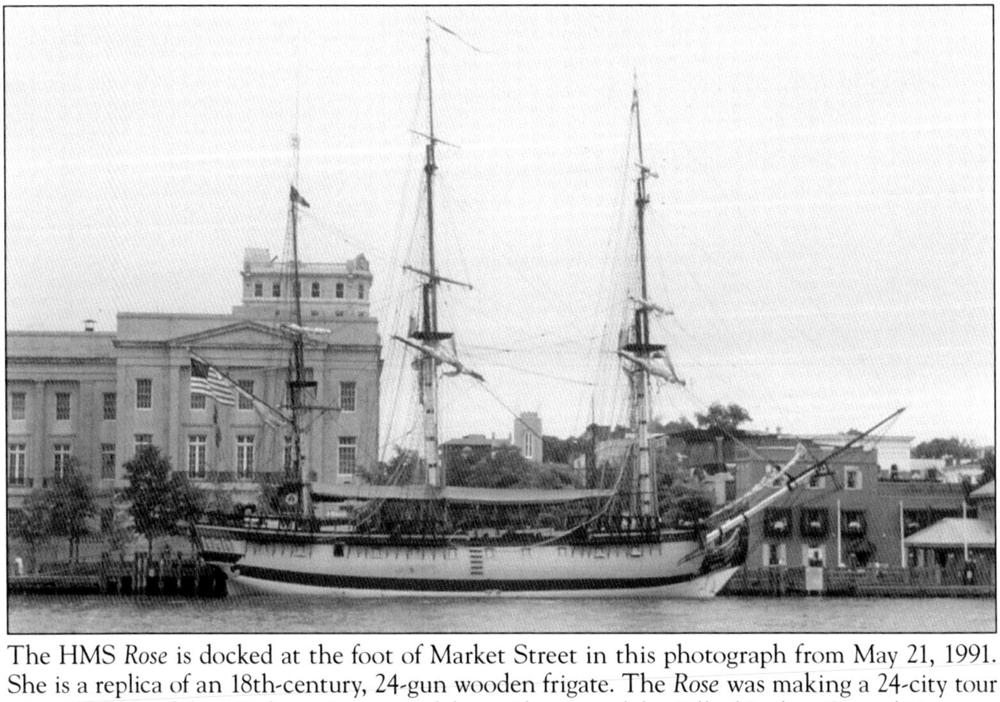

The HMS *Rose* is docked at the foot of Market Street in this photograph from May 21, 1991. She is a replica of an 18th-century, 24-gun wooden frigate. The *Rose* was making a 24-city tour in celebration of the 200th anniversary of the ratification of the Bill of Rights. One of 12 copies known to exist was displayed on the ship, along with other historic documents and artifacts. (*StarNews* Collection, NHCPL.)

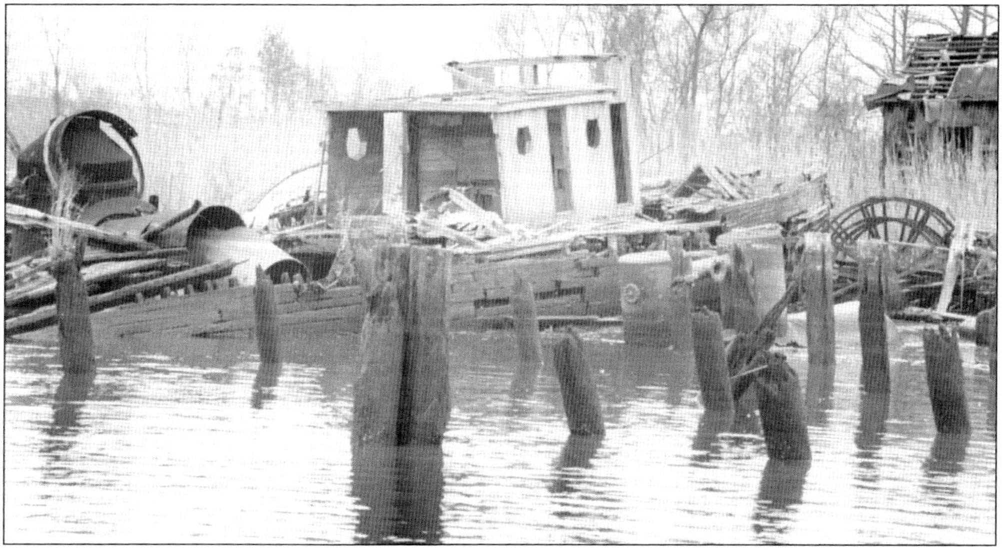

These photographs, dated March 6, 1986, show the remains of former wharves and vessels on the west bank of the Cape Fear River. This section of the river is part of the first "shipwreck" district to be listed in the National Register of Historic Places. There are 66 known ship remains located between the Cape Fear Memorial and Isabel Holmes Bridges. They are not technically "shipwrecks" but "abandoned vessels." The photograph above shows the wooden tugboat *Isco*, jokingly referred to as "the second most photographed ship in North Carolina," after the battleship *North Carolina*, moored a few hundred yards to the north. To the right of the *Isco* is what was left of the stern-wheeler steamboat *H.G. Wright*. Much of her machinery was removed and is now on display at the Cape Fear Museum. (Both, *StarNews* Collection, NHCPL.)

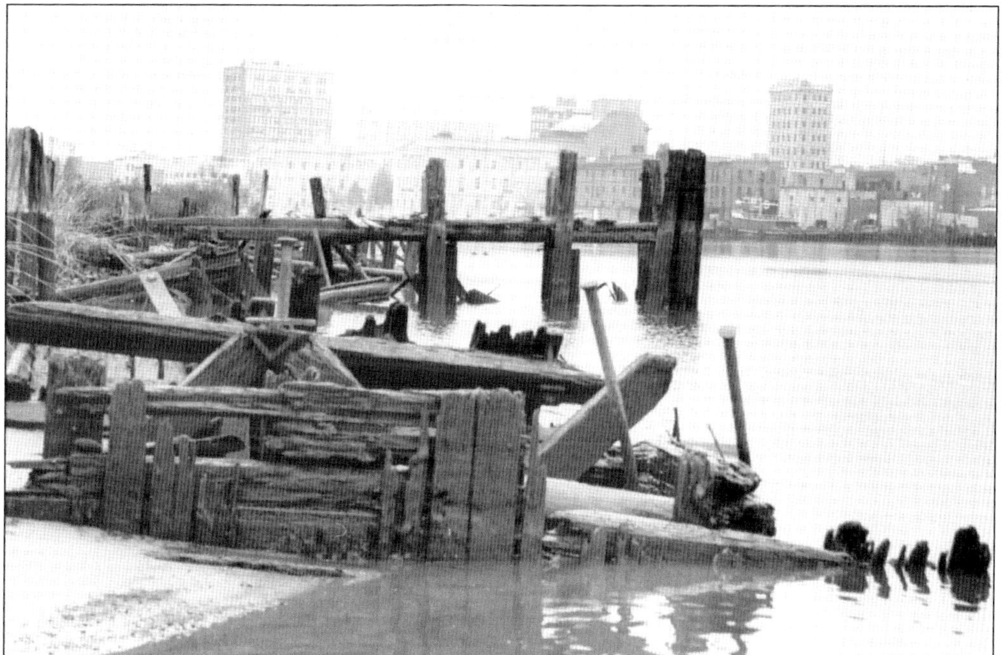

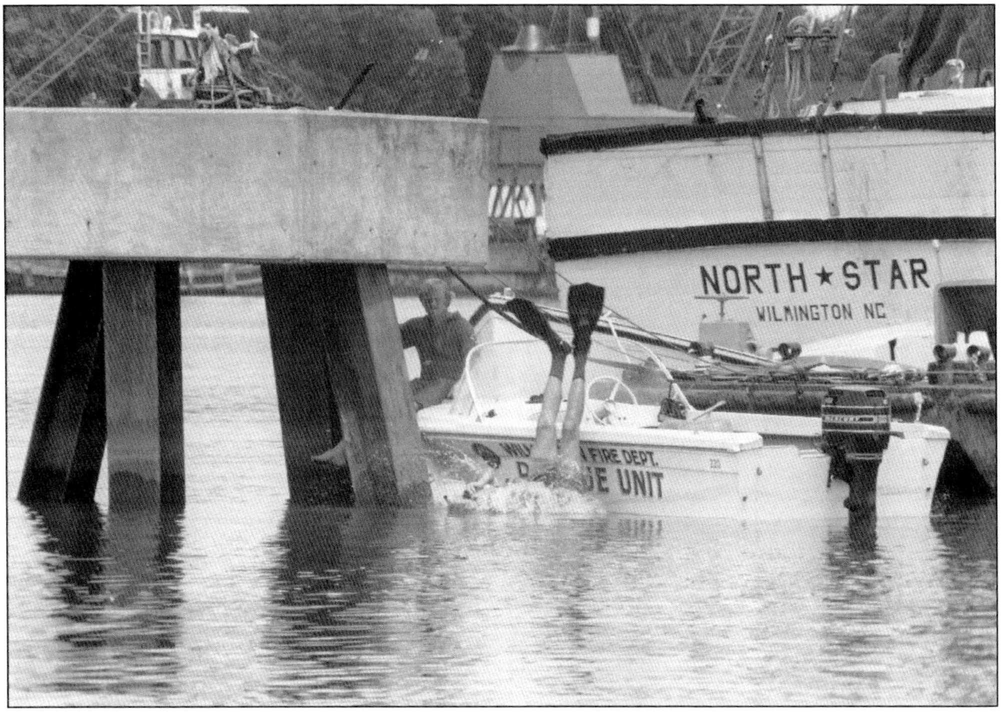

The Wilmington Fire Department operates a rescue unit that is on call 24 hours a day, seven days a week. Here, on September 12, 1980, a city fire department diver goes in one more time in search of an alleged drowning victim, last seen at the Hilton Riverside. (*StarNews* Collection, NHCPL.)

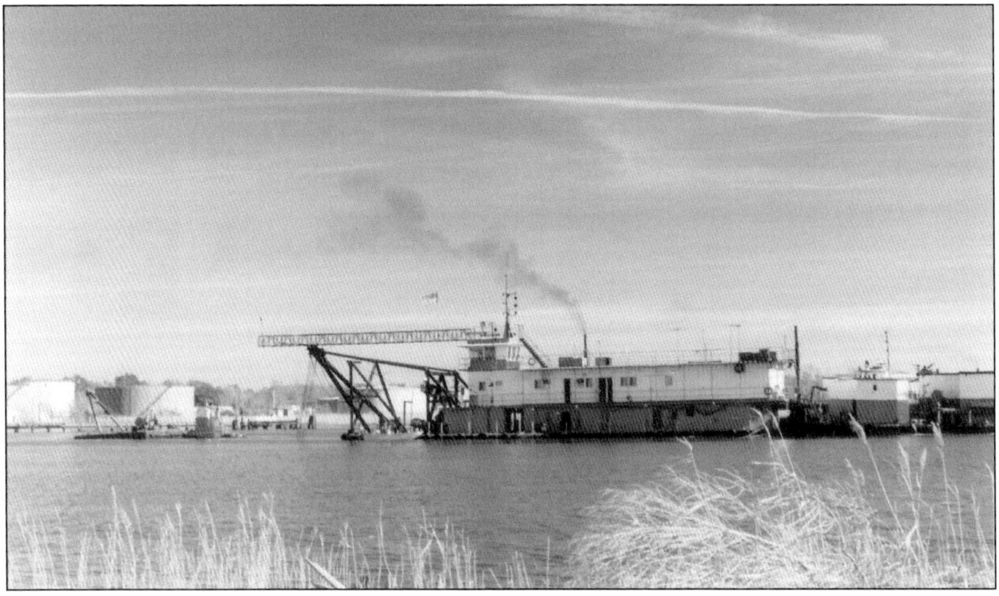

Sam Bissette took this photograph of the US Army Corps of Engineers base in 1997. The longstanding relationship between the Corps and the Wilmington harbor is inestimable, with the two working together to dredge and deepen the river channel since the 19th century. Beginning in 2002, the channel was deepened from the mouth of the river to the port, and, in 2013, the anchorage basin at the port was deepened to 42 feet.

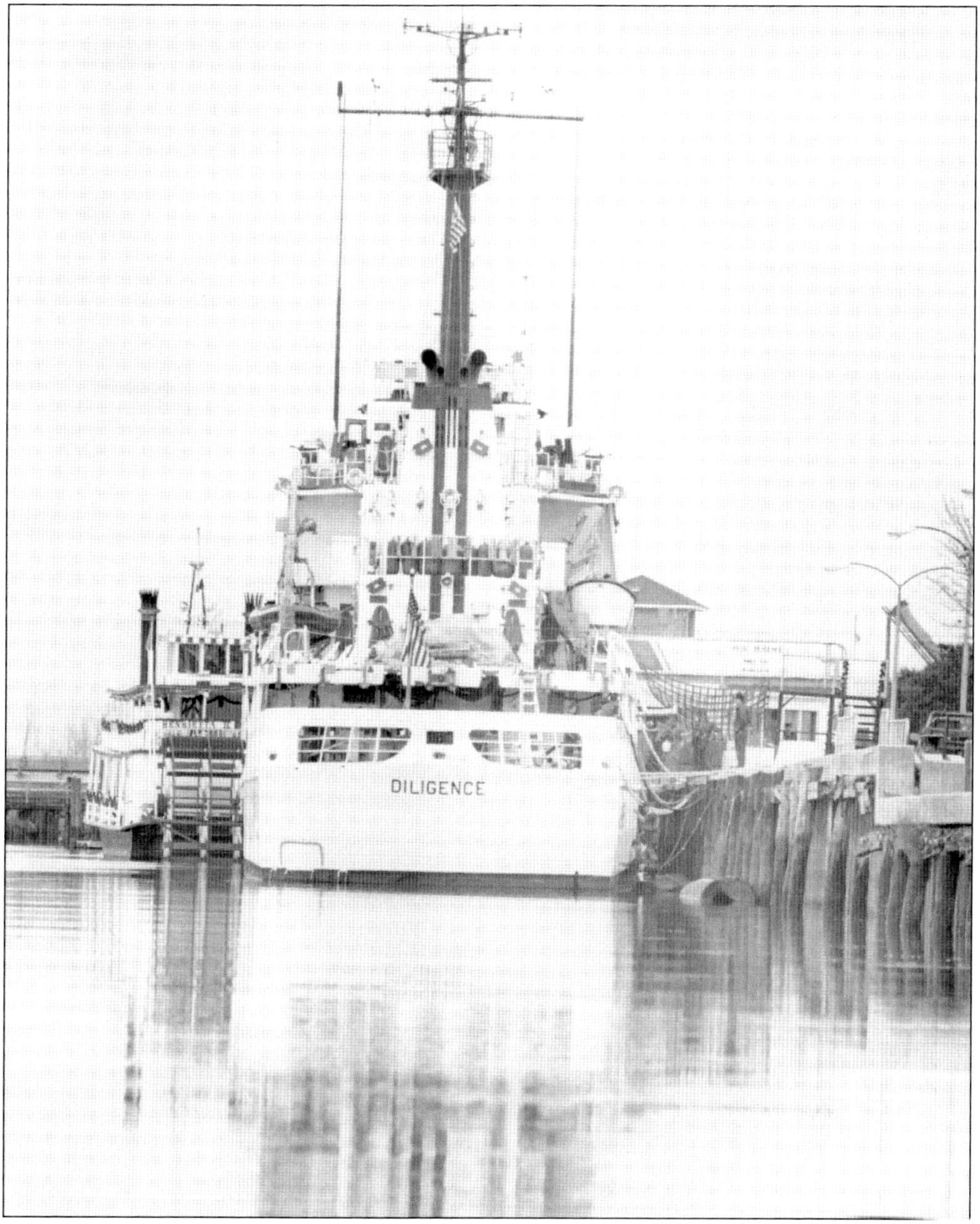

In 1992, almost 200 years after her namesake, the USCGC *Diligence VI* was assigned to Wilmington. Since 1797, there have been six Coast Guard vessels with a home port in Wilmington to bear that name. Built in 1963, the white-hulled cutter performs alien-migrant interdiction operations, drug interdiction missions in the Caribbean, and fisheries protection along the Atlantic Seaboard. She has also appeared in the news for traditional search-and-rescue missions. This photograph was taken on December 4, 1992, when the *Diligence* was a newcomer to Wilmington. The newspaper caption reads, "USCGC *Diligence* reflects in the water while at Riverfront Park." Wilmington was recognized as a "Coast Guard City" for the third time on November 26, 2013. Only 12 other cities share this distinction. Wilmington has recognized the Coast Guard's service at annual events, such as the Azalea Festival and Riverfest. (*StarNews* Collection, NHCPL.)

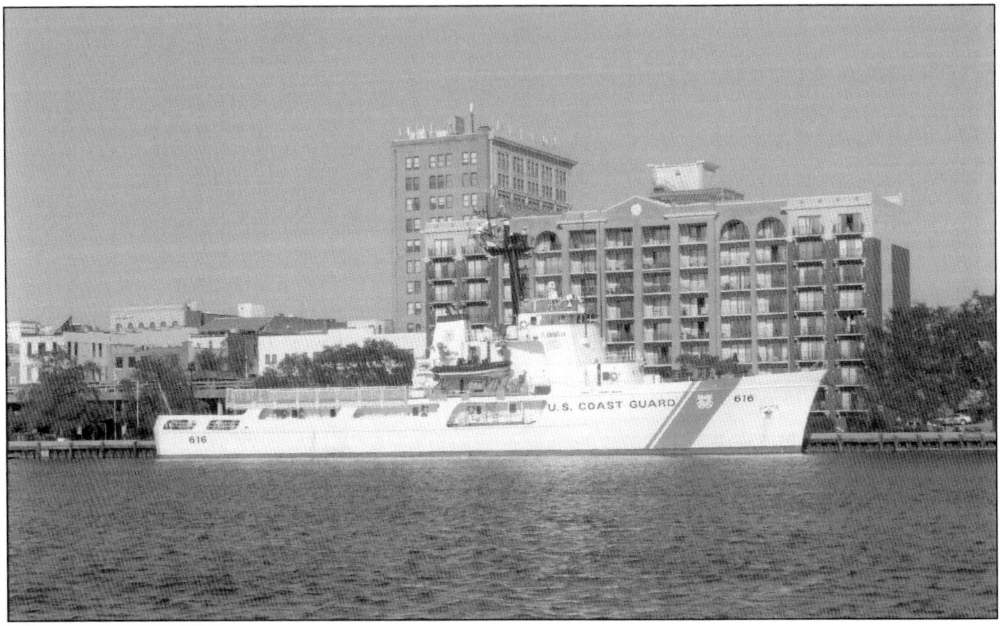

While the *Diligence VI* (above) remains the most visible US government presence on the Wilmington waterfront, most of the shoreline provides docking space for pleasure craft. The catamaran seen below is the *Wilmington*, a tour boat operated by Capt. Doug Springer and his wife, Diane Upton. In 2007, they began Wilmington Water Tours, conducting popular river cruises. Docked north of the *Wilmington* is the *Henrietta III*. Owned by Cape Fear Riverboats, the riverboat replaced a smaller vessel of the same name, the *Henrietta II*, in 2000. They take visitors on sightseeing tours and are available for private parties. Dylan Lee took these photographs in December 2013. (Both, City of Wilmington.)

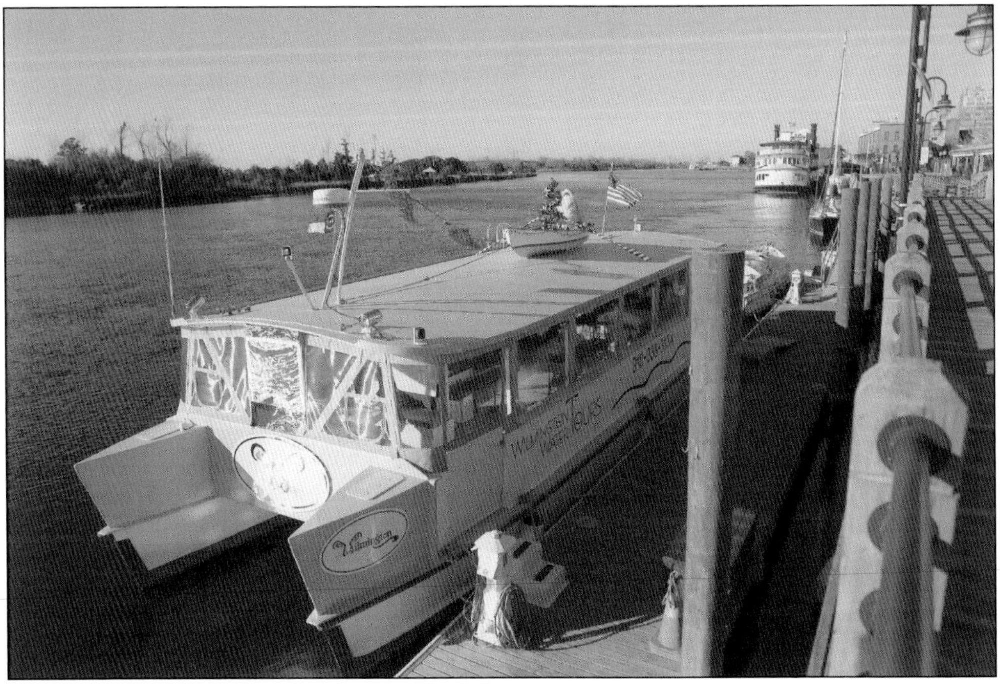

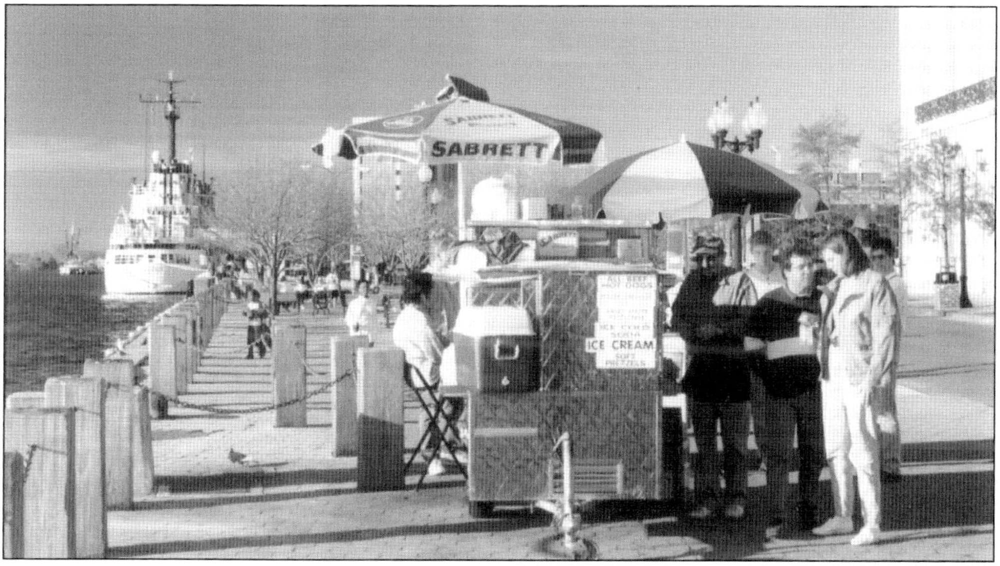

The Riverwalk was conceived in 1983, when the city secured grants from public and private organizations to study the construction of a waterfront walkway. The first phase, from Ann Street to the Coast Guard dock, was finished in 1985. The next phase, completed in 1986, continued the Riverwalk from Dock Street to the Hilton Riverside Hotel. The third phase, completed the next year, continued the walkway to Castle Street. Public improvements included lighting, paving, and landscaping. The heart of the Riverwalk is Riverfront Park, seen in the photograph above, taken by Sam Bissette in 1997. The Federal Building is shown at right, and the *Diligence VI* is at left. One component of a successful river walk included waterfront restaurants, which can be seen in the photograph below, taken by Dylan Lee in 2013. The *Henrietta III* appears on the left. (Below, City of Wilmington.)

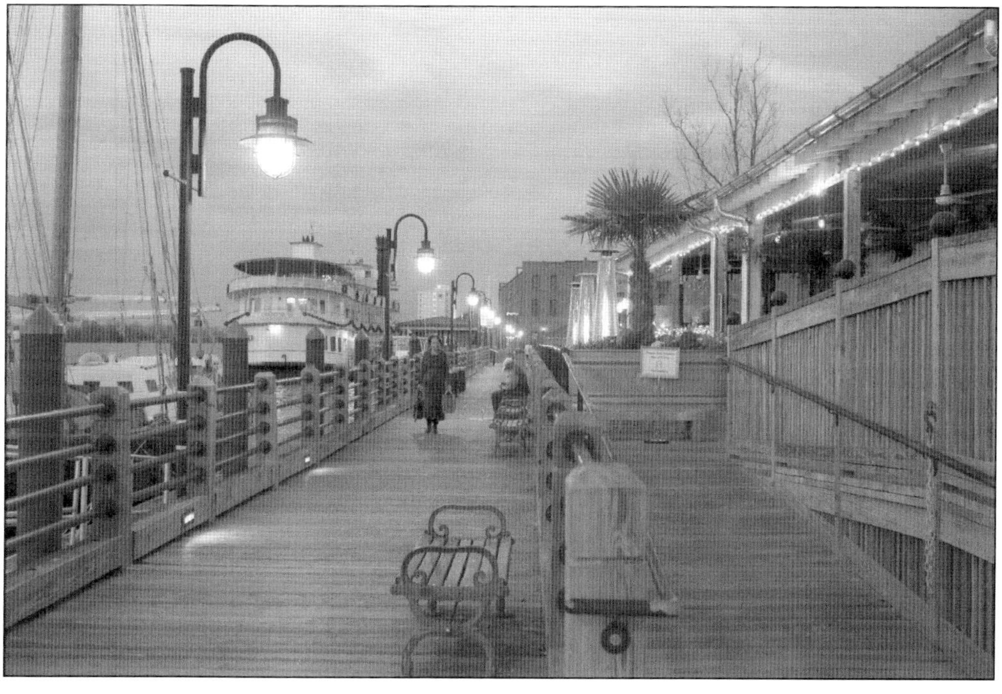

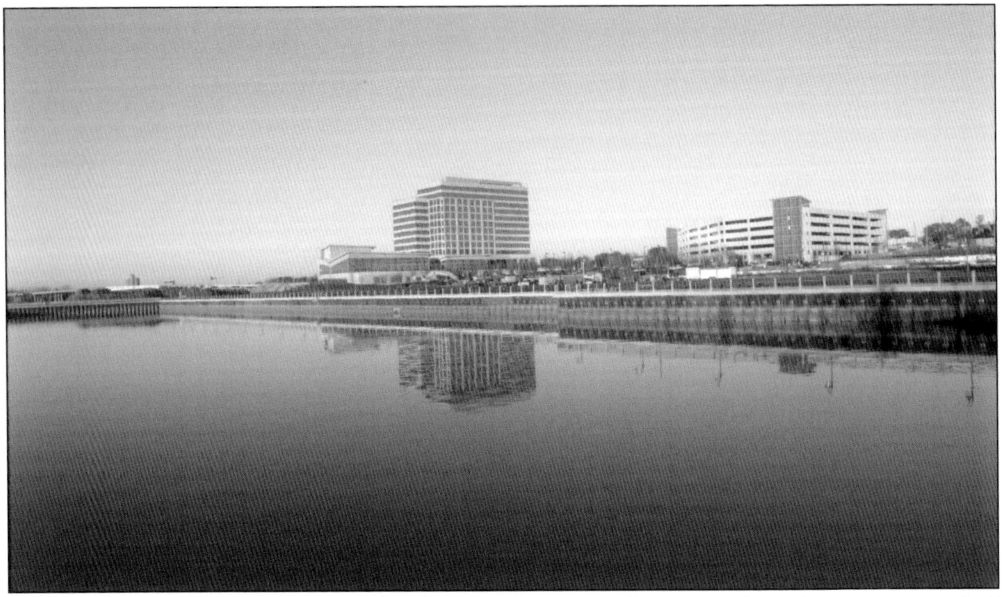

The motto for the original Riverwalk plan was "Imagine what two miles of riverfront can be." In 2013, the mission was accomplished when the City of Wilmington completed the Riverwalk around the Wilmington marina. It is now the longest river walk on the East Coast. The multistoried building in the center is the home of Pharmaceutical Product Development (PPD), a contract research firm that employs over 1,500 people, providing drug discovery, development, life-cycle management, and laboratory services. (City of Wilmington.)

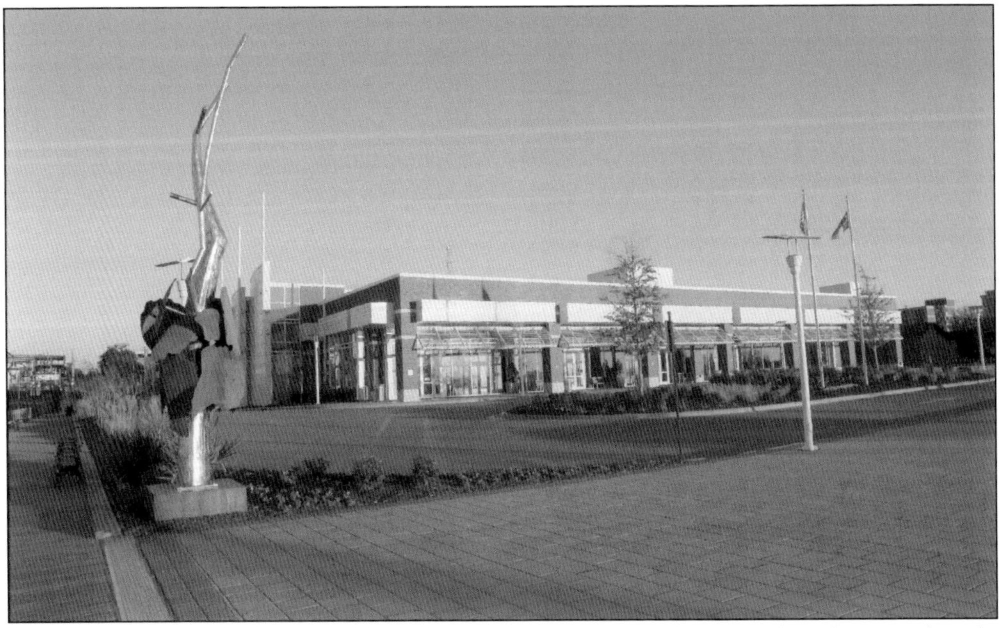

The Wilmington Convention Center was dedicated on January 13, 2011. Built on former rail yards, it is located between the Northeast Branch of the Cape Fear River and Nutt Street. After decades of planning, the 105,000-square-foot building has proved to be an anchor for the revitalization of the northern end of the Wilmington harbor. Dylan Lee took this photograph in December 2013. (City of Wilmington.)

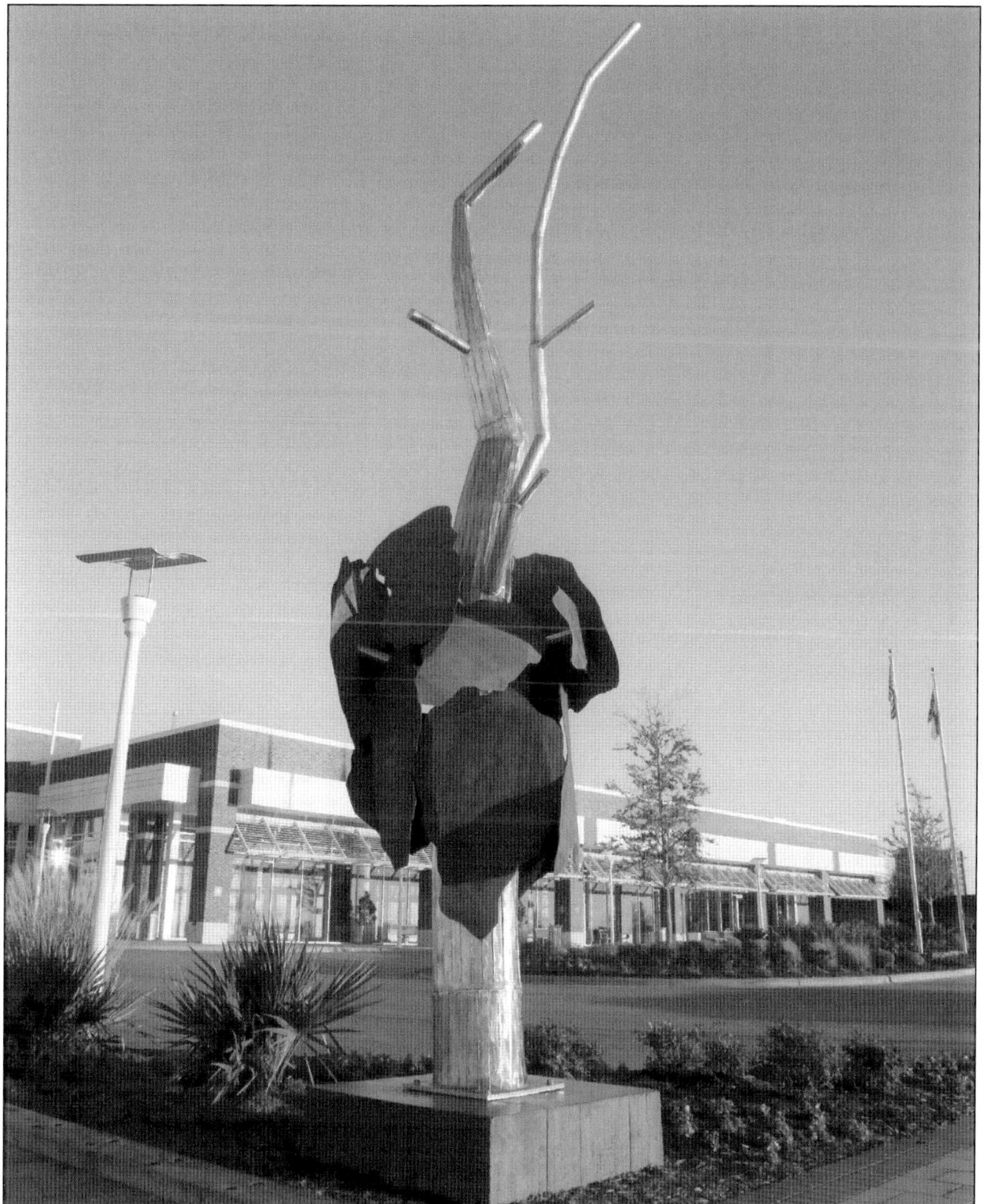

The Wilmington Convention Center artwork committee chose to decorate the interior of the building with a maritime theme by hanging historical photographs of the Wilmington Harbor. This piece of sculpture, inspired by the old Dram Tree, was also commissioned. The ancient cypress tree stood at the southern entrance to the port of Wilmington. Said to be thankful for a safe trip into the harbor, mariners celebrated by drinking a dram while passing the tree. In hopes of a safe journey, they did the same when leaving the harbor. Metal sculptor Dumay Gorham, a native of Wilmington, was chosen to create the 23-foot piece of art. The stainless steel trunk opens into branches tipped by rust-colored COR-TEN steel leaves. Gorham based his design on photographs of the original Dram Tree. Dylan Lee took this photograph in December 2013, a month after the sculpture had been dedicated. (City of Wilmington.)